RED
ADMIRAL

Epic's Voyage Around Cornwall
Clockwise from Morwellham Quay
on the River Tamar

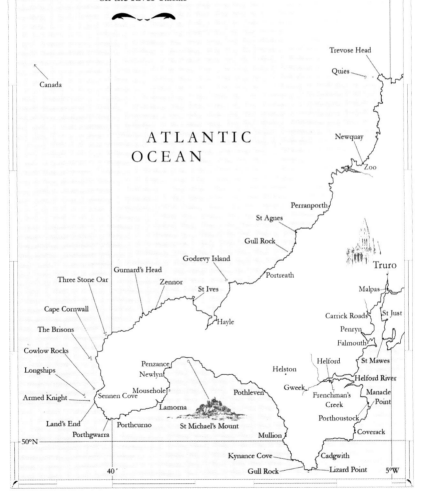

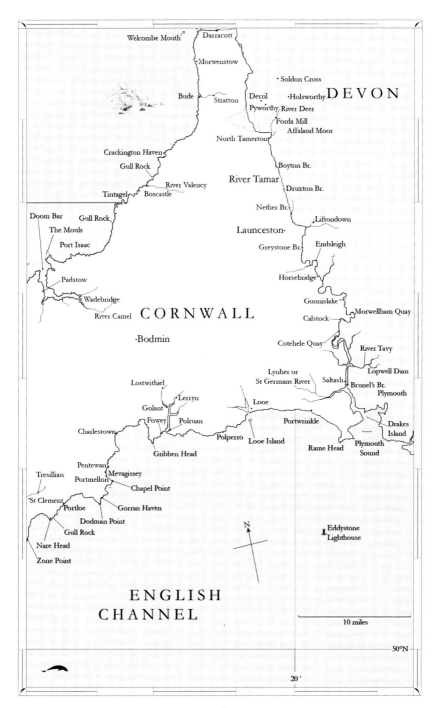

Welcombe Mouth
Darracott
Morwenstow
Soldon Cross
Bude
Derril
Holsworthy
DEVON
Stratton
Pyworthy
River Deer
Forda Mill
Affaland Moor
North Tamerton
Crackington Haven
Boyton Br.
Gull Rock
River Tamar
River Valency
Druxton Br.
Tintagel
Boscastle
Nether Br.
Doom Bar
Gull Rock
Liftondown
The Mouls
Launceston
Port Isaac
Greystone Br.
Endsleigh
Padstow
Horsebridge
Wadebridge
Gunnislake
Morwellham Quay
River Camel
CORNWALL
Calstock
·Bodmin
Cotehele Quay
River Tavy
Lostwithiel
Lynher or
St Germans River
Lopwell Dam
Lerryn
Saltash
Golant
Looe
Brunel's Br.
Fowey
Polruan
Plymouth
Charlestown
Portwrinkle
Drakes
Polperro
Island
Pentewan
Looe Island
Gribben Head
Rame Head
Plymouth
Sound
Tresillian
Mevagissey
Portmellon
Chapel Point
St Clement
Portloe
Gorran Haven
Dodman Point
Gull Rock
N
Eddystone
Nare Head
Lighthouse
Zone Point

ENGLISH
CHANNEL

10 miles

50°N

20'

To sea again; to see again.

David Weston

RED ADMIRAL

A Voyage Around Cornwall

David Weston Gallery
Mevagissey Cornwall England

Typeset and Produced by
Edward Weston

ISBN 978-0-9517290-5-2

Sunrise

Oil on canvas 30˝ x 30˝   2003

CONTENTS

Epic at Lawn House
10˝ x 10˝
'I pushed my little voyager home round the one-way system and parked
her on the lawn behind a clump of marguerites.'

(All illustrations are watercolours unless otherwise stated.)

for Julia

Preamble

For a few memorable moments the roadside hedges were alternately illuminated. The revolving Wolsey came to rest, headlamps pointing north, the direction in which I should still have been travelling. I had fallen asleep at the wheel. The solid old motor, after striking a rough stone wall, had deposited me on the tarmac. Standing in that quiet country road (not so quiet now) a few miles north of Oxford, I remember thinking 'lighthouses', though several years were to pass before the sailing bug bit. The precise forms of the searching beams held me transfixed for a while – perhaps as well; otherwise I may have worried unduly regarding my explanation for the car being on its roof.

The sixties were beginning to swing. The weary art student was returning from London having collected the Wolsey – impounded following a breach of parking regulations. A four by six feet oil painting had been carried on the roof to the capital. The Law, partly responsible for the demise of a future classic car, compensated by providing overnight accommodation, courtesy of her Majesty's 'B&B'. Sadly my leather seated, walnut dashboarded motorcar, was claimed by a Chipping Norton garage in lieu of recovery charges.

Vacating my cell early the following morning, I set off to hitch home. The final leg of lifts found me sharing the confined space in the back of a Morris Minor van with a few boxes of reeking fish-heads and a souvenir section of yellow mudguard, shed from my late car, foraged from the crash scene while waiting for a lift.

Less than a year later, with canvases and painting equipment in the back of an exceptionally heavily built 1938 Vauxhall, I arrived in Cornwall. Again I painted the motorcar with bright colours befitting a fledgling artist, or a parrot. The red, yellow and green, certainly livened up the original battleship-grey. Despite the jaunty appearance, the car was decidedly unwell on arrival in St Ives. The natty livery did not prevent the garage-man requisitioning my vehicle – payment for disposing of an automobile too sick to resuscitate. There followed a season both fruitful and enjoyable, painting and washing up, marred only by occasional glimpses of a large Vauxhall with arty, non-matching headlamps, running surprisingly healthily.

Following my extended vacation I returned to art-school. A couple of years later, as a qualified potter/painter with no idea how to function in the real world, I was kindly loaned a cow-shed at the end of a butcher's yard in the small market town of Tenbury Wells on the Worcestershire / Shropshire border. In that confined space I set up a pottery workshop. Renovation at the chemist's, a few shops down the street, enabled me to acquire, gratis, a four by four-foot piece of plate-glass and a heavy counter. The new (and only) window provided ample light to appreciate the decorative quality of the counter that exactly fitted across the narrow premises. The Victorian robustness of the 'great divide' precluded any attempt to reduce its length. Visitors wishing to do more than pop their heads into the workshop had to clamber over the counter. Occasionally the next stall would house a large, agitated beast that sensed short-term occupancy. Hoofs would rattle the dividing planks, making life precarious for pots and potter. One day an athletic bullock, seeking the desirous environs of the adjacent meadow beside the gently flowing River Teme, hurdled the gate outside my window. He exited death row pursued by white coated, navy aproned butcher and assistant. I remained with thoughts of bulls, china shops and pastures new.

For four exceedingly long nights a week I became a 'Snowman'. The Snow was a big grinding machine – one of many in the local factory where items for use in car manufacture were produced. Those ten-hour shifts, excluding time out for vacuum flask tea and cheese and chutney sandwiches, were a potent incentive to move on. It was wintertime when I visited the local surgery with 'Snow strain'. The doctor happened to be a governor of a secondary modern school, some ten miles distant, which had an idle pottery facility. Prescribed light wedging and kiln fixing, I was taken by surprise one day to find my little group of eager helpers had become my first class, and I, their 'Please sir'.

Though my ultimate aim was to be a painter (of pictures), by default I became a teacher. After a year and a bit at Ludlow Sec Mod I moved on to a half time teaching post at Shrewsbury School of Art. The other half week I taught blind children to make pots in a castle, where they boarded and I resided four nights a week. Though mock (early twentieth century), the impressive building had turrets, a courtyard, numerous flights of stone steps and several carp ponds. It was deemed necessary for a sighted person to be around – to be led to safety in case of fire, and humiliated on the football court where the visually unimpaired were savaged during night-time matches.

One weekend, while queuing to see a James Bond film with my new (and only) wife Julia, my attention was drawn to a picture of a sailing boat on the cover of a yachting magazine. 'Of all the newspaper stands in the world, I …' Hooked – just like that. Such practical beauty. That sculptural form, hull flowing into a deep cutting keel, captured my imagination. Not only a beautiful piece of engineering, but one incorporating a magical element – sailing into the wind.

With both of us working in Shrewsbury, the purchase of a property seemed a sensible move to save paying rent, and to build capital for our escape, 'hi diddly de', to the artist's life.

"Half down (£350) and £6 a week to settle."

"All right then."

In this way we acquired our first home. Twixt disused canal, prison and gasworks, it may have been humble, but it was also desirably close to the River Severn which ran down to the Bristol Channel, on into the Atlantic Ocean; cue the crashing sound of cymbals. Hang on a minute; sail into the wind, could that really be true? The evening after the encounter with the newspaper stand and 007, with Stanley knife in hand and a recently purchased Readers Digest World Atlas on my lap, I fashioned the experiment. Several six-inch nails were encapsulated within the keel of my cardboard boat which was faced with masking tape and sported a mast cut from a wire coat hanger. A half handkerchief triangle was rigged. With the hair-drier on low speed, substituting 'head' winds, the craft actually sailed down the bath, more towards than away from the prevailing drier. Magic.

That is how I became captivated. Soon I was drooling over ads for thirty, forty, eighty, ninety foot, oak framed, mahogany planked sloops, yawls, ketches and schooners, dreaming of trade winds and epic voyages. Bearing in mind that my entire sailing experience was concentrated at the non-tap end of the bath, it was with coincidence and great fortune that one evening, while taking a pottery evening class, I chanced upon my old woodwork teacher. Mr Fisher was taking a class in a workshop across the corridor. It took him a while to recall the indifferent pupil 'taught' twelve years earlier. An extract from my first report: – JUNIOR ART DEPART-MENT, SHREWSBURY TECHNICAL COLLEGE. Woodwork: C, rather useless. Everybody got a C. I was happy with the 'rather'- it could have been a 'totally'.

"Why don't you send away for some plans then?" I had casually mentioned to Mr Fisher that I would quite like to build a boat, but would need a little guidance. There are degrees of understatement, but mine, to one who penned that cutting phrase in the 'any special remarks' box, was totally misleading. It would not have helped my cause had I informed Mr Fisher of my year teaching woodwork to a class of first year Sec Mods. Knowing practically nothing of the craft, I was instructed five minutes before each lesson by Alf, head of department and true craftsman. I would lecture with authority on the importance of finding 'face edge', but be rather evasive concerning the next week's lesson.

The eagerly awaited package arrived. It contained one very large sheet showing side and top elevations of various craft. There was a vast selection – small dinghies to whacking great schooners – from rudimentary 'bookshelves' to ocean-going thoroughbreds.

Mr Fisher thought in practical terms. Not wishing to clutter up his workshop, size was a major factor. This fitted well with my ideals – finance, and storage after construction. Our house, 'two up and one and a half down', was rather compact and sparsely furnished, in need of most things including a place for books. So the six foot six Gremlin Major it was. With two inches to spare between the ceiling and its flat front end, it stood imposingly opposite the front door. We did, in fact, store within its varnished interior, among other possessions, our few books including the Stanley-slashed atlas. (The outdated publication is still with us – useful for nostalgic musings over the likes of Rhodesia and Upper Volta.) Mr Fisher, bless him, built the Gremlin entirely without my help. Even the tan sail was made professionally. My contribution was most of the work on the spars and oars – rather useful.

The multi-coated white painted hull exterior was a blemish free delight; so it was rather a shock when it rapidly filled with the River

Severn on its maiden sail. The internal centreboard housing did not fit flush against the floor of the 'Gremlin'.

Imagine a screen. Picture the Gremlin filling with river water. The image becomes wavy; harp strings tremble. The screen clears. Twenty-two years have passed. There is the dinghy; no, not the Gremlin Major; though with flat bow, white outside and varnished within, the craft is similar but seems to have grown to over ten feet (almost eleven). The location is now Morwellham Quay, beside the beautiful River Tamar on the Devon / Cornwall border.

Mission Premeditated
Morwellham to Cotehele Quay

Setting out in sunshine dreaming
no thought of nature's dark side scheming.

The oceans backed the river fifteen miles up the valley. Soon the moon would release the waters and my elemental journey would begin. Tide and wind, with a dash of rowing, would propel me and partly dictate the course. The aim was to explore at leisure, and record through watercolour the creeks and quiet backwaters. I would travel without the help of an engine, unnoticed rather than unwelcome.

Alongside the Lynher, the last Tamar barge, drying and draining ready for renovation, my dinghy looked so tiny on the slipway. The old trading vessel was in a sad state, having been excavated and salvaged from the mud of the River Lynher (sometimes called St Germans River) a tributary of the lower Tamar on the Cornwall side. That river I hoped to visit. Mud in general, I would soon find out, would make its presence felt. While we rigged and loaded, the river crept round my little boat. An hour before high water I pulled away, then quickly rowed back for I had forgotten to screw in the drainage bung, situated low down on the outside of the transom. It was not the Severn this time that flooded in, just a cautionary baptism from the Tamar. After re-launching I removed my wellies and hung my right sock on the stern to dry. A patch reminds me which is the leaky boot – it could do more. I waved a second goodbye to Toby, my nineteen year old, eldest son. Utilizing the light fitful breeze, I set the jib (small front sail) and headed upriver.

An hour or so earlier, Toby and I stood in warm sunshine on high ground by the roadside at St Ann's Chapel (a village). We tried to pinpoint the course of the Tamar and tributaries, but could only pick out a couple of vague, silvery 'lakes', close to the hazy coastline where river met sea, thirteen miles away. It was ten in the morning on 5th July when I was delivered to Morwellham Quay. The inverted plywood dinghy sat on the car like a large sun-hat. The early shipping forecast foretold the favourable change. I was eager to discover what mysteries lay hidden in the expanse of inviting wooded valley before us.

There had been a few weeks preparation with a little trepidation. I was finding it difficult to relax – empty pages tempering a rare freedom. Virgin sheets of handmade watercolour paper and a pristine spiral-bound notebook reminded me of the mission. A booklet, produced quite painlessly the previous year, 'just happened'. Text to accompany an exhibition of my paintings expanded into an illustrated story. This was different – a floating painting trip with publication in mind – a mission premeditated.

Heading up to Weirhead, a winding two miles up-river, seemed a reasonable proposition, taking me to the head of tidal waters. A spot of leisurely rowing, non-taxing and quite therapeutic, was required when the wind direction became unfavourable. I revelled in the solitude, enjoying the glorious surroundings. The river duplicated sensational subject matter, inverting reflected grassy banks and swathes of mature trees. Around one o'clock, at high water, I reached the area downstream from the weir. To my right, sandstone cliffs towered, supporting tenuous occupation of gravity defying trees. Time was on my side. As I adjusted to nature's pace, the uneasy sensation within gradually ebbed. The tide turned and my unhurried journey to the sea began.

Five hundred yards below the weir, a light breeze held me almost stationary. I rested, listening to relaxing guitar music drifting from a riverside cottage. Banks and trees were very green. The river on which the dinghy slowly revolved was brimful and coffee coloured after the rains. Cows appeared from a field above. Standing silently in the reeds, they watched as I drifted down to Morwell Wood. Tiny fish 'plimped' on the surface, forming split-second rings, barely noticeable, as if small grains of rice had been flicked into the water. 'Derangements' of ducklings – delicate dandelion clocks – fluffed about the river margins.

Nature had restored much of the landscape, tortured during the copper-mining era, but there was still evidence of the vast scale of industry. Quays and wharfs, mostly hidden by vegetation, were still in good order, testimony to the skill of those early engineers. Back at Morwellham I passed the Beatrice Maud (Thames Barge) and the Garlandstone (merchant ketch), great ore-carrying ships enjoying retirement, enhancing the Great Dock. Further on, the rattle of mine trucks sounded through the trees before conveying visitors 'back in time', underground.

Mechanical intrusion faded. Presently I arrived at a long straight stretch of river. A defunct old mine chimney stood out powerfully above the wooded hilltop horizon, adding a focal point to the 'tree-dimensional' landscape. The bright breeze-rippled river contrasted with darker green woodland – a subject for painting. I tied my boat to a few stems at the edge of a reed bed on the Cornish side of the river. For the following hour or so as I painted, the falling tide repeatedly settled the dinghy on the mud. With an oar I re-floated, occasionally lengthening the painter (bow line). After completing the watercolour, I whip-snatched the painter to extricate the dinghy. To break away from a few reeds seems quite simple, but not when afloat. The boat rushed onto the mud into which the line buried itself. My next snatch twanged out the line, showering the scene with mud splashes. Miraculously, the painting remained 'un-mudified'. I stowed it safely before re-engaging with more thrashing of painter, by muddy painter. Finally I broke free, leaving a bedraggled boat and crew fast in the mud, with the river inexorably receding. With a session of desperate mud-rowing, I escaped my glutinous captor, then set about the craft with trusty sponge. As the current hurried me on, I cleaned up and tidied away the painting equipment. A few oar strokes were required to counteract the gusty breeze and keep the dinghy away from the banks.

It remained warm, becoming hazy with the sun vaguely discernible from time to time. The mud banks being revealed were a cocoa ochry hue – a surface colour only, for mud lifted on the oar blades was a dead, graphite grey. Hidden in mini-creeks, or cradled at the fringes in mud-berths, were old wooden sailing cruisers, full of rustic charm and mud. Mothballed beneath old tattered and patched tarpaulins of faded dusty greeny-blues, they awaited their adventurer dreamer, who would not return. No doubt there were other machines of dreams, claimed by the silt, that I did not see.

At six o'clock I hitched to a mooring buoy a few hundred yards upriver from Calstock Viaduct, which I proceeded to paint. In less than half an hour the tide began to turn and I repositioned myself as the boat slowly swung round. Over the next thirty minutes or so, as I completed the picture, the atmosphere dulled and the temperature dropped, heightening anticipation of a relaxing evening at a local hostelry. While the current was fairly slack, I rowed down to Calstock. Finding access to the town car-park area protected by mud, I carried on a little further, landing on rocks at the bottom of stone steps, where I temporarily hitched. Wandering up a narrow side street I chanced upon two men engaged in conversation. Seeking information regarding the dinghy's wellbeing, I was extremely fortunate to be offered by Douglas, one of the two, the use of a running mooring close to where my boat was rock-bound. Thanking the kind elderly gentleman, I returned to the steps and tied the dinghy onto a long loop of heavy rope fixed between two pulley-wheels, one beside the steps, the other way out on the riverbed. Remaining ashore, I 'pullied' the boat twenty yards out, out of harm's way. Pointing poignantly seaward, she strained against the increasing current.

What a wonderful day, I must have thought, as I wandered down to the riverside car-park area passing several cowboys and the sheriff. Casually propping up the bar in the saloon of the Tamar Inn were more docile 'Wild Westerners' – though the night was young. I drank beer and 'chilli concarnied', but still felt out of time and place. I 'mosied' on up to the Boot Inn. The pleasant pub was peaceful, 'beamful' of character, and free from cowboys. Before finishing my drink, lights flashed before my eyes. Had those benign looking, 'heel-wheeled pokes' laced my previous pint? No: the cosy gloom was shattered by a grand lightning 'son et lumière' display. The rain laden sky brought a premature dusk followed by a few spots of heavy rain. Perhaps I should be talking size of

Tamar Green
11" x 13"

raindrops, for all rain is the same weight, isn't it? Anyway, after hastily downing my pint, I raced to the running mooring, 'pullied' in, boarded, and as the sky emptied, cast off, obviously carried away by the dramatic turn of events. On reflection, after 'polythening' my gear, I should have left the boat on the mooring and returned to the Boot.

Having rowed to the middle of the fast flowing river, I tied to a buoy and spent an interesting half hour under plastic – a technique already perfected, as I will explain shortly. From my low vantage point on the rising river, I beheld cow-persons, inelegantly cantering on high boot-heels to the shelter of Calstock Social Club. From there, cacophonous country music erupted. The rain stopped and darkness descended. I decided to call it a day, and with polythene at the ready, lay down to sleep. The music became 'megatonic'. As the tide began to slacken I cast off from Douglas' loop and rowed down to a more peaceful floating mooring, a few hundred yards down-river, beyond the huge viaduct. After dozing to the sound of distant drums for an hour or so, peace eventually reigned, and the tide turned. Then with the wind increasing I was treated to a series of showers. By dawn I was quite alarmed, for the outgoing stream was at its maximum and a strong wind howled under the viaduct (no doubt over it too). It was impossible to reach a landing place back up at the village, so I waited anxiously for the early shipping forecast at five to six. Unpleasantness was predicted. I let go of the buoy, knowing it would soon be necessary to temporarily abort the mission before arriving at exposed reaches.

I passed a boat-yard to my right, immediately hoping I would not regret doing so. It all happened so quickly. Cotehele Quay, just a mile away, seemed an appropriate objective. Forgetting the mud factor, the 'Quay' word triggered my assumption that there would be a place to land. The river of seawater, reflecting grey/green sky, was replaced with 'fresh' muddy brown by the time I reached Cotehele. It was seven o'clock, exactly low tide. The Shamrock, the last surviving coastal barge, a powerful workhorse similar to the rugged Thames barges, rested between quay walls in its mud berth, gracing the picturesque setting. An imposing group of ivy clad stone buildings with archways and crenulations stood in harmony against a backdrop of dense wooded hillside. I ran the dinghy into the expanse of exposed mud that concealed all but the very top of a stone slipway. Squelching up to the quay wall, I secured a long line (the other end being attached to the boat of course). Being too early to seek permission for extended parking, I took advantage of a spell of rare sunshine. Seated upon the wall I bared my frozen feet, restoring feeling with a spot of massage.

Whiling away an hour or so before Toby collected me, I produced a watercolour detail of one of the buildings. As we left Cotehele Quay, a sailing sloop of approximately twenty-two feet, the only craft I saw under way on the river, was receiving quite a buffeting as she was taken down-river. I would follow when the weather settled.

In The Beginning

Although I have described the chance delve into the magazine that led to my flirtation with small sailing boats, I have jumped the gun somewhat – set off half cock, wing and leg, without even mentioning the new dinghy's name. Come with me while I lightly sketch in details of my journey into a world of art and small-time boating – the eggs from which the voyage hatched. For argument's sake, let my boating trip be the egg, and my art training to professional painter, the 'chick to chicken phase' that spawned (or should that be laid?) the double-yolker. Back now, if you will, pre-chicken, to begin at the beginning.

Sex: 'It's a boy'. Location: Stoke on Trent, or The Potteries as the 'Six Towns' in Staffordshire is / are called. So it was destiny; one day I would become a potter. My first recollection – frogs under corrugated iron in a bomb crater. A big war had just finished. We played with gas masks and used ration books for real. My family, including me, the middle one of three boys, moved to Birmingham. Being three or four years old, I obviously had no say in the matter; my preference would have been the seaside. Our holidays, I remember were wonderful weeks, pioneering in rudimentary caravans – parquet-patterned linoleum and hissing gas mantles. Sites were Spartan – the long uphill trek through wet grass to the lonely tap. The rough and the smooth – sunburn and coarse army-blankets – sunshine and sand dunes near Talybont, close to heaven in merry Merioneth. Father used to be a Scout leader. I have vague recollections of us infiltrating campfire singsongs; ging-gang goolieing with roasted faces and knees, and frozen backs.

A carefree time: swinging on lampposts (gas lit), marbles, hopscotch and kicking a fluff-less tennis-ball about. On one occasion, a man said he would hold my ankles and lower me into a drain to retrieve a ball. I refused the offer. The street was our playground: almost car-free. Our half-timbered shooting brake, with fold down seats and 'pretend wood' lino, was one of the first vehicles to invade the territory. Horse and carts delivered bread, milk, coal, rag-and-bone men, goldfish and a scattering of manure.

Travelling by tram I arrived at a catholic school. Big church – Latin sung, incense swung. The fear of men in flowing sinister black, forcing you to go to confession on a Saturday and get up early on days of obligation to go to mass without having breakfast, was all too real. Worse was the fear of burning in hell. How cruel was that? To be saved, we confessed sins that we had not committed. There must have been many more like me, confused and frightened. Suffer little children … Fortunately, not all was doom and gloom. Maypole dancing (or was it tangling) provided much entertainment. We wove chaos with bright ribbons, delighting in feigning lack of direction and coordination. Art lessons were also a pleasant escape, having a 'not real work' feeling. (Painting for me is still the same). My chalked trees with tapering branches, brown with black outlines drawn on grey fluffy paper, seemed in advance of most kids' straight stick creations (very wooden). At the age of eight or nine, with less chance of a career in 'Maypoling', I decided to be an artist when I grew up.

My dad cut out cardboard shields to decorate the house for Coronation celebrations. I helped, hardly at all, to paint them with British flags and the odd lion that could have been mistaken for a rampant caterpillar. With Q E II came TV – a part-time distraction in fuzzy black and white. Some folks still found time to paint their houses, brick by brick, red, white and blue. We tore ourselves away from the 'nine-inch screen' celebrations. Harmonizing with brother John (thirteen months my senior) we won the three-legged race. Little brother Michael (three years my junior) came third in the egg-n-spoon. Sadly, he fell on his tin plate double-decker when rushing home to show off his prize. There followed a deal of placating and panel beating.

About that time we waved goodbye to the last tram, bedecked in flags, as it headed for termination. Our next move, when I was ten, was to Highley in the beautiful Shropshire countryside, a mile or so from the River Severn. A timely move, for our old house is now in the lee of Spaghetti Junction (thank you, Mummy and Daddy). Had plans for emigration to Canada been a little more advanced, we boys would not have become Shropshire lads. Father may have become a lumberjack (which would have been alright) instead of a haberdasher in the spanking brand new row of shops, with accommodation above, overlooking the green in Woodhill Garden Village. The development had something of Bath's Royal Crescent about it – it was curved! Our shop was number two of six fledgling enterprises serving a relatively small community. It was not an area of 'passing trade', so father continued 'doing' the markets. Mr Fox, the butcher (his trade) from number one, made ends meet by doing daily deliveries. On some Saturdays I would go with Mr Fox on his round. Arriving home late in the dark, cold and tired, put me off the idea of ever leaving school.

We boys thought the move great: winding brooks in tangled woodland; stick fishing rods; the tingling, trembling thrill, half felt, half seen – sensitive fingers detecting the tiny tug from minnow or millers thumb; musty leaf-mould and the sharp smell of wild garlic flowers. I did not want long trousers. I did not want to grow up. I suppose I never will.

School was a seven-mile bus-ride away in the castle-walled town of Bridgnorth, beside the River Severn. Five to fifteen year olds were housed in two classrooms. The infants were behind a folding wooden wall, while the rest of us were in a high beamed, single-storey area divided by a row of four-foot high wooden screens separating two groups of desks. Seated the other side of the partition was brother Michael. Miss Flexman's tall desk, which housed a fearsomely thin bamboo cane, dominated the open space in front, flanked by a pair of large cast-iron, coke-burning stoves. Those welcome monsters (not including the headmistress) resided behind bars, supporting a rail on which dozens of coats steamed on rainy days.

The 'campus' was somewhat cramped. Playing 'footy' on the boys miniscule playground was one sided in the extreme – for it sloped excessively. The downside, covered shed end, had two wooden uprights supporting the corrugated tin roof. The natural goalposts ruled out a fair cross-gradient game. We developed the ground-level 'bending ball shot' before the Brazilians perfected their aerial banana kicks. The outdoor urinal was sited off a narrow alley running up to the playground. Except in dire circumstances, the regime did not encourage "Please miss, may I leave the room?" pleas for solo hikes up the alleyway. We were led in single file by Miss Flexman, waited in line until we had all 'been', then marched back to class.

"Would you like to go to the Grammar School?"

"I think my father would like me to", I remember mumbling. It was not the expected and possibly most sensible, 'Yes please sir.' My heart was set on going to the 'Junior Art' in Shrewsbury. My Mum and Dad would have been thrilled had I gone to the Grammar, but Dad said I must do 'what a boy's gotta do'. I stayed at St John's for another two years, enjoying 'short trouser' life. With the aid of bamboo pipes, carved by the versatile Miss Flexman, there was musical instruction. I seem to remember a few triangles, and just two or three tambourines (thank God). How and why could so much effort be invested in creating such a terrible din? Once a year we marched off to a field to do athletics. For me there was a third place (twice) in the 'Bridgnorth And District Branch, under thirteens, two hundred and twenty yards flat race' (I peaked early). There was English, which I did not enjoy because of the 'spellin'. There were sums, which I loved and was good at. Then there was art, which I loved even more than sums.

The day of reckoning arrived. A great deal was made of the Technical College entrance exam. There were three candidates going in for art. We each had a large table, and an overwhelmingly large piece of grey paper – big time. My picture of a country scene featured a river winding into the distance. John's (not my brother) painting I remember more clearly. Not troubling himself with perspective, he positioned on his painted strip of green (river bank), a deformed rubber boy sprawling in an attempt to capture a very large, very green, black-eyed frog. The next quarter depicted a grey/blue river standing on its edge. Then came a section of grey/green with curvy tops (hills), and to finish off, naturally, grey/blue sky. The picture was striking in spite of the wishy-washy, muted grey that all three pieces exuded – courtesy of the cheap, fluffy grey paper. The primitive style of the frog painting is now in vogue. John was ahead of his time.

That September, after a long steam-train journey, two thirteen year olds wearing new bottle-green blazers walked along the towpath beside the River Severn. The shorter boy wore long grey trousers, concertinaed over his shoes. The taller, sported short grey trousers. Lambs to the slaughter, they crossed the English Bridge, entered the Technical College and climbed the stairs to the Art Department on the third floor. Naked legs were few among the boys, but as most attention was directed towards the girls, it did not matter.

Grown-up Gremlim

Before continuing the story, onwards from Cotehele Quay, I will backtrack a few months to the conception of the venture. While waiting in a travel agency to book a flight to Spain, my attention was drawn to a large poster depicting the mosque and minaret skyline of Istanbul, simmering in a smouldering sunset. The exotic scene exuded romantic mystery, and possibly hypnotic power too, for I came away with a ticket to Izmir instead of Malaga. My new destination was only two hundred miles from that depicted on the magical poster. The exceptionally low fare was quite magical too.

The account of the Turkey painting trip, my first foray into publishing, did a little more than break-even. If I could successfully sell Istanbul in Cornwall, where we now live, a book featuring local locations should be a sure winner. But what angle? Why not a sailing / painting trip? An illustrated story of a mini voyage appealed to me. The tidal Tamar and tributaries between Devon and Cornwall would be an ideal area in which to paint and indulge in a spot of boating.

On a sunny day in early May I drove with Julia to Weirhead, near Gunnislake, where the tidal section of the river ends (or in my case, begins). A large wire-meshed, locked gate prevented access to the weir pool. Had the gate been open, or had I paid more attention to the barricaded scene, I would have spared myself a future unpleasant surprise. Not having a definite time or date for starting the trip, I sought a more accessible and less intimidating launch site. Just two miles down-river lies Morwellham Quay, a thousand year old copper port, reclaimed from nature's advance and opened to the public. That was my next port of call a few days later.

A gentleman member of staff dressed in period costume (early Victorian) ushered me into the Ship Inn Restaurant, where I was soon to be joined by the Director. It could have been Isambard Kingdom Brunel (whose famous local bridge I was soon to know intimately) who ducked into the room wearing an exceptionally tall top hat. Gary was most civil, though not an engineer. When not dressing up he painted The Tamar Valley in watercolour. I lunched with the erstwhile Isambard, and in due course, launched at Morwellham.

If the trip was to be undertaken when the hours of darkness were least, to make full use of the tides, I had to acquire and equip a vessel without delay. A few days later I spied a beautiful ten-foot traditional clinker dinghy (overlapping planks) lying on the mud in Mevagissey Inner Harbour. It was a fishing-boat tender, locally known as a punt. This particular one had once sailed, for it sported a centre-board case and fittings for mast and rudder. In the harbour office the following day, Jim – the Master – said the punt, which we could see afloat in the outer harbour, was awaiting her skipper's return from a fishing trip. Later, following my request for temporary punt captaincy, Michael replied in the affirmative, "… and there's no leaks; I've glassed over the centre-board slot."

My search continued. The grapevine suggested a possible boat at Gorran Haven, two miles to the south as the seagull flies. A perfect little gem lay in a harbour-side boathouse that opened onto the sandy beach. Alas, it could not be spared. It was another clinker dinghy, but on reflection, rather too spick and span and tidily varnished. It was pretty heavy, and may not have suited later when I became an abuser of small craft. Harbourmaster Dick was able to give me another lead. J. Fuge, boatbuilder on the Fowey River at Golant might be able to help. The renovation of quite a large half decked, slender keelboat was nearing completion in the shed. The sight of the re-born greyhound (a swimming breed) gave me pleasure, but assistant boat-builder Luck was unable to help with my quest.

At the tidal limit of the Fowey River (twixt Mevagissey and the Tamar) lies the ancient town of Lostwithiel. There I visited the Boat Market. At first sight that port of call looked hopeless – nothing to stimulate eye or pocket. Then I spied, amid shiny plastic craft of all sizes, an aged plywood Mirror dinghy. It exuded neglect. Ravages of time and a much-patched hull were mostly hidden beneath a 'newish' coat of sky blue paint. Several gallons of 'occasional showers' stagnated within the hull, proving the boat was fairly watertight. The drain hole, as you know, is quite sensibly situated. Senselessly, the dinghy was tipped forward, half off its trolley. Perhaps I was too, for I bought the sad specimen. Perhaps it was nostalgia (the lines so reminiscent of my first boat) that tempted me to purchase the 'grown-up Gremlin'.

Included in the sale price were the spars, red sails, rigging, centreboard and rudder. (The dinghy is gunter-rigged – a two part mast having the top section hoisted vertically against the lower. When not sailing, the sections can be fitted inside the boat.) Launching and retrieving solo would be possible, and the comparatively flat bottom would enable it to float in a few inches of water. I had imagined being captain of a boat with character, chosen to appear in some of the Tamar paintings. The plywood Mirror was certainly not designed to enhance pictures. At first sight to many it is rather an ugly duckling. Looks are not everything though. The sale of tens of thousands of the very popular Mirror bears testament to that fact. We may have come together in desperation, but I now love my boat. Failure to find the 'model' dinghy and opt for the common lightweight had advantages – not least the low cost. There would be no possibility of expensive damage to my craft, or much to worry about if I left it unattended.

It rained every day up to the 14th June, so I was not surprised to be fitting rowlock mountings at the Boat Market in pouring rain. Between showers, three days later and a quarter of a mile away, I painted the bridge pool from where my shakedown journey to Fowey would begin.

Thursday, 20th dawned fair, preceding a hot summer's day. At half past twelve I trundled the trolley, with Mirror, over a level crossing, across the old river bridge and down to the water's edge. It was high tide and the bridge pool was full and still. The shingle from where I had painted a few days earlier was under clear water. On the grassy bank, in pleasant sunshine, Julia helped me raise the mast and dump half a carload of equipment into the dinghy. I pushed the boat a few feet down into the water and gingerly stepped in between the jumble, hurriedly sitting down to maintain stability. Afloat for the first time in the nameless boat, I clumsily rowed around the pool for a minute or so. With the river level beginning to drop, and gravel making contact with the hull, I drifted off downstream, waving to Julia while guiding the masthead between over-hanging branches.

Shakedown
Lostwithiel to Fowey

Gently rowing, I slipped away from Lostwithiel. The river gradually widened as the backs of buildings gave way to grassy meadows. The flow was sedate. I went with it, resting on the pile of gear, watching the mast turn lazy circles against a few cotton wool clouds. I was to use the tidal ride like a bus service. Though reliable, the timetable was not always convenient, and confusingly, about an hour later each day.

A mile or so downstream I tied up to a little timber jetty set at right-angles from the wooded left bank. The river speed increased to walking pace. The boat swung to a taut rope, the river chuckling past her. On a rough bench, alongside two small beached boats, I sat for a while enjoying the idyllic surroundings. Unfortunately, before I had set out my painting kit, swarming bees from a nest in a nearby tree-trunk hastened my departure. I continued my leisurely drift while setting about a sun-warmed Mars bar. The melted chocolate stuck to the wrapper, providing several minutes of enjoyable licking. I thought of Winnie The Pooh – must have been the bees.

The dinghy was unnecessarily cluttered. The stuffed sail-bag was

Lostwithiel

15˝ x 19½˝ 1980

'Painted from the launch site, the same spot that eleven years later I produced a second
watercolour a few days before setting off on the 'Shakedown' voyage.'

19

useful to lie on, but the gaff (mast extension), boom, rudder, centre-board, buckets, easel and wellingtons were a nuisance in such confined space. At that stage, with minutes of experience, my desire was for a dry ship – in the dustpan and brush sense, rather than bailer and sponge. Shipping the oars caused rivulets of Fowey River to come aboard, which was a nuisance. After a spot of trial and error I managed to position them on the gunwales so they drained overboard. By degrees I became used to watery ways. I am wholeheartedly of the school preferring all water to be outside the boat. My worry of capsizing, if I leant a little this way or that, soon abated. It was pleasant to look over the side, knowing the dinghy would not suddenly flip over.

Two miles on, I glimpsed St Winnow's sunlit church tower above the trees. With the dinghy tied to a mooring buoy fifty yards upstream, I viewed over the stern, a varied collection of small craft beached in dark recesses below tree cover. Tempted to produce a watercolour while afloat I set to, half expecting not to be able to work from such an unsta-ble platform. The oars lay across the gunwales forming a work surface, and the sail bag against the mast provided a comfortable backrest. With gentle boat motion and warming sun, I was almost too relaxed to work. (You may 'tut-tut' at the reference of work, but all that looking can be quite taxing.) My early fears were unfounded – I was happy with the result. Spending more time looking at the subject than the work in progress, my mind remained in the real world, without disorientation leading to sea (or river) sickness. The 'boating painter' was really chuffed.

At four thirty I cast off from mooring. The river, running and drop-ping fast, carved four foot high mud walls on the outside bends, con-trasting with the wide, almost flat 'beaches' on the inner. Rushed along in deeper water, close to the mini-cliffs, I looked up at a heron feeding just a few feet away. Carefully standing, with bird's-eye view, I spied more feathered feeders foraging in leafy, mud walled tunnels. All these birds ignored my head as it whizzed by.

The river widened to quarter of a mile below St Winnow, although the navigable width for boats larger than mine was just a few yards. I wished to turn left, to head up the little Lerryn River, but as expected, on reaching the mouth, there was too little water. A couple of hundred yards down the main river I picked up a mooring at a spot from where

I could produce an interesting painting incorporating the rivers' junction. Soon the dinghy was stranded on a sand bank.

At eight o'clock, after completing the picture, the slow moving incoming tide eased the dinghy, along with a squadron of ducks, into the narrow river. The evening was still. In complete silence, save for a quack or two, my journey continued in growing darkness. Travelling with and not through the water, I appeared to be stationary, watching a moving chocolate landscape of rounded mud banks and reflections slide by. Dark chocolate became pitch, and I was relieved when the lights of Lerryn loomed. 'Bewellied', I slurped up a steep bank on the outskirts of the village. I tied a line to a post and proceeded to the Ship Inn, washing my boots at convenient stepping-stones before entering. It was ten o'clock.

Ninety minutes later, a contented captain re-crossed the fairy-tale arched bridge that spanned a narrow creek close to my landing point. The little boat had been elevated several feet above the mud that had made climbing out so awkward. I was then able to step back aboard from the grass in a most civilised manner. The air stirred ominously. A trace of rain prompted me to don an all-in-one, olive green oilskin suit loaned to me by Mevagissey fisherman Mike, (not to be confused with Michael 'of the watertight punt'). Prior to landing I noticed a vacant buoy a few yards down-river, dimly lit by distant village lights. In darkness, I aimed the dinghy in the remembered direction, running into the little beauty a few seconds later.

I expected to be sleeping on riverbanks next to the boat, but as the night was exceptionally dark, I felt I would be more at ease on board my mini floating home. There was little problem making the bed. The space between the centreboard case and the starboard buoyancy chamber, I filled with sail-bag and buckets, topping them with the centreboard to form a 'flattish' surface. ('If you can remember, 'there's a little red port left', you will know that the portside is the left [red] side, and starboard the right [green], when looking towards the bow of a boat.) I lay down diagonally, head on the foredeck beside the mast, and attempted to sleep.

To avoid becoming mud-bound, I had to be on the move within two hours. In fact, movement was much sooner. Within half an hour, light from cottage windows appeared to be circling the boat. I naturally assumed the tide was turning, but it was the result of freshening wind. Along with the rain, the tempo of my trip round the buoy increased. A few heavy raindrops were followed by a far from light monsoon. Soon I was under a polythene sheet with my accoutrements. Unfortunately, my covering was un-tucked repeatedly. How close to 'a perfect day' it had been, I must have thought whilst holding the plastic down with my face. Gripping the inadequate covering about my head, I peered into the darkness as the spinning lights, one by one, were extinguished. The unexpected event tested my first night nerves (and prepared me for the 'deluge at Calstock').

There were several heavy showers before the dinghy began to ground at three thirty. To avoid entrapment I pushed off into the void. Rowing blind, but cautiously, I headed to deeper water. Soon the faint blue/green light of dawn revealed vague silhouettes of dark towering tree shapes. With the wind decreasing, I made my way safely back to the Fowey River.

Fowey Harbour begins a mile and a half below the confluence where I painted the second picture. Golant lies between the two, hidden behind a riverside railway embankment. Low tide prevented access under a low rail bridge into the peaceful retreat. The Fisherman's Arms, a roadside pub, becomes a riverside pub at high-water springs, when motor vehicles are liable to become semi-submersibles, if warning signs are unheeded. (Spring tides occur roughly every fifteen days when rise and fall are greatest. Neap tides are in between and can be five feet less in the area.)

Around five o'clock in the morning I hitched to a mooring close to a group of unoccupied yachts. Two or three hundred yards downstream, a left hand bend leads to Fowey River Harbour. Barely sixteen hours had elapsed since the bridge pool launch, but it seemed odd not to have seen any craft underway. After an orange juice and chocolate breakfast, I warmed myself in the sunshine, soaking up the scenery. Further upriver a slight breeze distorted mirrored masts, smudging tree and hill reflections in the misty morning haze.

Rejuvenated, I raised the jib (small, front sail) and cast off. The sail provided steerageway as the fast flowing stream sped me past large ocean going ships, loading at the English China Clay jetties on the west (Fowey) side of the river. Vessels up to twelve thousand tons transport the clay. The scene was in extreme contrast to the upstream, dreamy riverscape. Rounding a bend I made my way to the slip at Caffa Mill car park – where Fowey begins and the car-ferry crosses to Bodinnick. I removed the rudder and centreboard and stood towards the back of the dinghy, lifting the bow. Under decreasing momentum the little blue boat glided onto the sloping concrete. Dry-shod, I stepped clear of the water.

The shakedown had gone well. The previous night was just a memory, and I sincerely hoped there would not be another like it. After all, it was the end of June.

The trip, short in time and distance (eight miles 'ish') was undertaken to work out logistics for the Tamar expedition. It was a perfect trial course – from place of purchase to a handy car park. Following a roof-rack ride home, the dinghy resumed its rain collection roll on our front lawn. While waiting for a favourable change in the weather I carried out a minor refit. Minimum equipment would be carried on the painting sortie – more room and less to worry about. The upper mast section, boom and mainsail would be dispensed with. (The mainsail was too big for the short mast.) Those items were not used on the shakedown, only serving as annoying, unnecessary deck cargo. A smaller sail area would be sufficient. Lack of wind would not be a problem – I could use the tide, or do a bit of rowing. I would be in no hurry.

A white jib, the same size as the Mirror red one was borrowed from my friend Stuart. The boom-less mast would carry the white triangle as a loose-footed mainsail. It could be wrapped round the mast to make it smaller – or reefed as we sailors say. With the boat came a spinnaker (sail), resembling a ten-foot bikini cup, used for downwind sailing. It induced thoughts of trade winds, flying fish and large mermaids. For one intending to paint and sail on the Tamar and its tributaries, I went a bit over the top with preparations. My old pair of non-matching, six foot six inch oars were rather worn where they had rubbed against rowlocks. In renovating these I used leather and copper tacks – most nautical. From a previous boat, along with the oars, I took a boathook and small compass (you never know). With the Mirror came a large, extremely useful sponge, also a bailer, for which I found another use.

Forgive me listing more 'essentials'. I present: a plastic, one gallon, lidded ice-cream container – to keep dry such precious things as note-book, Ordnance Survey map 201, Walkman radio, water resistant camera and Elastoplasts (a more comprehensive first aid kit would have been in order); two, five gallon plastic lidded buckets to hold mooring lines, small screwdriver and pliers, shackles, copper nails and sail-maker's needles and thread. To the rear of the front buoyancy compartment is a small storage area in which I kept cartons of orange juice, a two-gallon, plastic water container (a quarter full, otherwise it would be unnecessarily heavy), my vintage wellingtons and a folding anchor. (I pictured my floating studio riding at anchor while I painted tranquil, watery scenes – I really did). The purchase of a survival bag – a long, tough, orange plastic bag with survival instructions printed on it – was the result of my Lerryn experience. Strong plastic bags were also used to protect my paintings and painting equipment. How on 'earth' did Drake, Magellan, etc, manage without plastic bags?

My plywood Mirror was nameless. With such circumnavigators as Sir Francis Chichester, Chay Blyth and Sir Robin Knox-Johnston, I had made epic voyages – between book covers. Ocean voyaging for me was just a dream. Unlike my mentors, I was planning to cover less than one of their three hundred and sixty degrees. For me, it seemed, the only way to make an epic voyage was to name the dinghy Epic. The blue hull colour would have to go. Though it was growing on me, I did not wish to portray it in the paintings. With roughly torn pieces of wide masking tape I hurriedly formed the name on the transom (back of the boat). After painting the hull, sides, stem and stern (back of the boat) white, I peeled away the tape to reveal sky-blue letters. Then it was just a question of waiting for the rain to stop for my 'epic' voyage to begin.

Get Out And Walk
Cotehele Quay to the River Tavy

It rained and blew. I listened to many shipping and weather forecasts. July was half over before I returned to Cotehele Quay to be reunited with damp little Epic. Upturned in the boat compound, my angular vessel looked more like a picnic table pining for the sun than a sailing boat. Toby chauffeured me through the showers and helped rig and re-clutter the dinghy. We sheltered in the car during a particularly heavy downpour wondering when the 'later', in the weatherman's 'clearing up later', would begin.

At ten thirty as the river began to fall, I drifted away from Cotehele under rather depressing cloud cover. It was not long before the sky lightened and patches of blue appeared. Two miles down-river I met Dave, a salmon fisherman. He was sitting on a wall at Halton Quay. It is not exactly a shipping port; in fact, Dave and the wall was all there was; oh, and his boat of course. I stepped ashore on the shingle and chatted for a while. He explained the purpose of the rowing boats with large numbers painted on their sides which I had passed earlier. Worked by a crew of one or two, the boats around fifteen feet long are found on all the rivers which empty into Plymouth Sound. At high and low water, when tides are slack, long nets are stretched across the river, snaring the game fish that suffer the misfortune of being very tasty. Fishing had steadily worsened due to excessive sea fishing, according to Dave, who had caught nothing that morning. Wishing him better luck for the evening session, I unfurled the red jib and continued on my way.

Half a mile downstream, below Pentillie Castle, hidden behind trees high up on the Cornish bank, stands a grand boathouse of stone and two-tone tile construction. This enhancement to the riverside has a gabled, open sided porch, and roof resting on four stone columns. It is very pretty and, though tempted to paint the structure that blended so well with its surroundings, I gave it a miss, respecting the 'No landing' sign. (I bet it had no stairs either.)

Down from the boathouse the river forms a giant S. The first three-mile loop almost encircles a portion of Devon. At low tide, Cornwall's sector reveals a half-mile wide mud plateau that, unfortunately, became more than a passing interest. On reaching what appeared to be a large lake, there was no indication that the average depth was a rapidly decreasing six inches. It did not occur to me to keep to the outside of the bend and my corner cutting cost me dear. Within a minute, what was a floating flotilla of seagulls became a pedestrian flock. Mud flats emerged as shallow winding channels rapidly drained into the main stream. After a vain attempt to escape down a rivulet, I stood up and commenced an over optimistic escape strategy. To take the weight of the boat while I pushed the oars against the mud I half jumped. (You may have thought that impossible). The net result of the repeated action, besides progressing an insignificant twenty yards, was to leave tracks that could have led to speculation that a huge turtle had arrived. In forcing the dinghy along in that strength-sapping fashion, I had unknowingly pumped a gallon or so of glutinous grey up the centre-case. On reaching total exhaustion, I accidentally sat down in the goo. Had the weather been against me, I fear my tether would have been nigh. Happily, the secretive sun relented, and shining warmly, it filled me with as good a cheer as I could have reasonably expected. After removing muddy jeans and shirt, and donning denim shorts, I stepped over the side. Folk from Hooe and Hole's Hole on the Devon side of the river, had they been following my progress round the bend, may have wondered what entertainment lay ahead.

From the moment I settled in mud up to my knees, I think I acquitted myself with distinction. The sensation of cool fine silt oozing between my toes was rather pleasant. Foolishly, I gave no thought to hidden sharp shells or discarded scythes, as I pushed Epic the hundred yards or so to the edge of the deep river. The flat-bottomed boat slipped surprisingly easily over the wet mud, providing a firm platform to push down against, saving me from sinking. On reaching the main channel, I was washing my left leg when my standing foot settled on a smooth object. Tune in next week … No; it was nothing like a World War Two, unexploded bomb. Happily, it was a non-aggressive object. Holding firmly to the back of the dinghy I reached down through the mud, up to my armpit, and carefully extricated an undamaged, stemmed wineglass.

Storm Force Ten – Mevagissey

13½" x 19"

'It rained and blew. (Not like this though.) I listened to many shipping and weather forecasts.'

Hitched to a large round red mooring buoy in the fast flowing stream, I set about a major cleanup of boat, clothes and myself. The only lasting evidence of the previous hour's caper is the souvenir foraged from the Tamar mud. The mundane glass, possibly a pub glass, now resides in a place of pride in our glass cabinet.

During the two-mile waft down from 'mud corner' to Cargreen, on the Cornish bank, I entertained the thought of a prolonged, restful repast, for I had to wait for tide-turning, to ride up the River Tavy into Devon. The river at that point had widened to half a mile. I tied up. Easy to say, but in situations at either side of high water, it is always a story of mud. Steps and slipways (quite apt) are usually deep in the stuff – often completely hidden. Some form of ladder leading from the water is the best scenario, and in this I was lucky. I wandered up the deserted main street seeking sustenance. The sign that would have advertised the Spaniard's Inn was being replaced, or else removed for re-painting. My 'innstincts' sadly let me down. Heading back to the boat, I was fortunate to notice the Supply Store. I entered the little shop, stepping back half a century. Many layers of paint coated the sparsely stacked shelves, and the floor was cosily covered with carpets. From a pleasant little old lady I purchased a few tomatoes, a piece of cheese wired from a small block and a packet of Ryvita – as they were quite out of bread, rolls or other savoury biscuits. Time may have passed the Store by, but I was more than happy not to have done so. I returned to the river, happily 'victualed'.

With over an hour to go before low water, I carefully descended into Epic with my treasure and drifted down-river, enjoying the simple fare. Though still over two miles distant, I glimpsed for the first time while afloat, the new Tamar Bridge in front of Brunel's earlier masterpiece. Presently, the multi-spanned rail bridge that crosses the mouth of the Tavy hove into view on my left. Whilst enjoying the bridge-enriched surroundings, I heard a telltale swishing sound of disturbed gravel against hull – the sound I knew from previous groundings. A vast mud spit clearly defined on my map should have been sufficient warning to prevent the recurrence. My frantic rowing, towards what I assumed to be deeper water, failed to save me running aground, again. The river receded, leaving Epic on a slight ridge. Content to remain beached till after low water, I lay down in the bottom of the boat to shelter from the cool breeze and rest for an hour or so. Around five o'clock I stepped onto firm, gritty mud, pushed Epic a few yards to the water, and under full sail (how grand that sounds) headed up the River Tavy into Devonshire.

Devon Interlude
River Tavy to Plymouth

To starboard, half a mile on from the Tavy Bridge, I glimpsed a small portion of a building peeping through the trees at the high-tide line. Downing sail I pulled in to the rocky, kelp festooned foreshore. The lumpy barrier was extremely slippery, and soon to be submerged. Having clambered over the 'assault course' terrain, I carried out a tethering manoeuvre, looping a long line over a rock, high up the bank.

The building detail that had interested me turned out to be part of a somewhat neglected old boathouse, built from stone and red brick. The overgrown and much weathered structure, standing in the grounds of Warleigh House, was an ideal subject for a painting. I should really have made a watercolour sketch, for that's what I was supposedly there for, but adventure was in the air. Before returning to cast off, I did take time to add to my memory-bank (camera), the intimate boathouse scene and stunning panorama which it faced. Epic, seeming so vulnerable and tiny at the edge of the wide waterway, was dwarfed by the Tavy Bridge, its numerous spans silhouetted against a dramatic, 'duskening' sky. The sun, behind clouds from my perspective, flashed the estuary with slashes of silvery light. To capture such glowing luminosity, the landscape would have to be painted on a transparent surface lit from behind.

To port, a further mile upstream, I passed the church tower-dominated village of Bere Ferrers, which was protected by a mud barrier, two to three hundred yards wide. With access prevented for a couple of hours, I carried on (not in complaining mode, mind you). The river narrowed to fifty yards, then wound a further mile between wooded banks up to Lopwell Dam.

I tied Epic to railings above a slipway close to the dam, leaving her there on the rising tide. Three young men were fishing nearby. With Liverpudlian accents, they said they would keep an eye on the dinghy while I went to eat. Shortly after setting off I was pleasantly surprised when a gentleman stopped his car, shuffled his family passengers to make room, and transported me post haste to the sixteenth century 'Who'd Have Thought It' inn at Milton Coombe. In a welcoming 'old worldly' atmosphere, my supper was enhanced by a couple of delectable pints.

After walking back a couple of miles through peaceful pine forests, I rejoined the angling trio. They had enjoyed good sport and at the time were wrestling with a slippery, writhing eel in an attempt to remove the hook. I thanked them for boat-sitting, and on the risen river rowed off towards Bere Ferrers. Speeding away on the smooth surface I sensed the faintest of sounds above the noisy rattling rowlocks. Stopping rowing for a moment, I tried to pinpoint the source, but heard nothing. A few minutes later, there it was again; or was it? Yes, and broad Liverpool to boot. In the gloom I picked out a figure running awkwardly over rough terrain towards the river. Recognizing one of my Mirror minders waving to attract my attention, I glided in through the reeds to the grassy bank. The poor chap, in a state of near collapse, presented me with my painting bag. The prized possession left behind on the slip, not only contained my camera and radio, but the most precious item of all – a collection of squirrel hair brushes in an old cardboard tube. Some of the brushes I had taken on my first painting trip to Spain, ten years earlier. The Scouse Samaritan soon revived and set off back to his mates with my fervent thanks, plus a small token for a round of drinks. Within the half hour, still recovering from exceptionally good fortune, I joined the 'fishermen three' in spirit from a Bere Ferrers hostelry. A little after eleven, before the river sank below the mud banks, I stepped back into the boat. In darkness, under oar power, I headed out from the quay wall into calm water. My rhythmic rowing induced sleepy mind wandering.

There were stars at first as I made my way with the tide to the Tamar.
They faded as I entered a vast endless cave
where sounds of oar-blade splashes echoed against night walls.
Floating dark on black, the giant rail-bridge stole over me.

Decorated with flickering car headlights, it was the Tamar Road Bridge that guided me out of the Tavy. The bridge was a mile and a half away. Among the array of random lights ahead, the car-deck was the sole structured feature. Rowing to a buoy on the Saltash side, a little upriver from the Tamar bridges, seemed to take hours. In fact, between leaving the pub and taking up swinging night-time residency in the quick flowing stream, just two hours had elapsed, including an energetic ten minutes locating and catching the vacant mooring. In near darkness, the swift flowing Tamar carried me past many buoys which I saw at the last second, before they were swallowed by the night. Rowing against the current, though I lost way, I gained enough time to eventually latch on to an elusive float.

Securely hitched, Epic swung from side to side in the outgoing stream. Sleeping bagged I lay down. With the sound of rushing water spasmodically 'over-ridden' by traffic noise, I attempted to sleep. A few lights were still on in Saltash homes, their close proximity emphasizing my bizarre situation. Somewhat tired, I floated in both nautical and metaphysical senses. The feeling of non-reality gave free reign to the wandering of my 'other mind'. It was around three o'clock when, from my exceptionally low vantage point, I stared at a frogman's masked head, vaguely discernible in the gloom, just a couple of yards away. The helmet moved slowly towards Epic. I kept very still. Drifting from semi-sleep, I wondered if I had been caught up in some drug smuggling activity. I realised Epic was in imminent danger of being left high, dry and mud-bound. It was the bottom of the dinghy making contact with the riverbed that released me from my reverie, not a rubber-suited assassin. There was not sufficient depth to submerge a frog, let alone a man. A mooring buoy, together with a loop of rope, had frightened the wits out of me. My heartbeats returned to normal along with my wits – which I needed about me.

Using the dregs of the outgoing tide I drifted the mile or so down to the Lynher River. As I negotiated my way between millions of pounds worth of tall-masted pleasure craft, strung out away from the river's edge, the eerie stillness was shattered by the 'three-thirty', rattling over-head on Isambard's mega Meccano. A little later, a powerful pilot-boat throbbed up-channel. I rode the resulting swells to the sound of halyards (sail hoisting ropes or wires) slapping against aluminium spars. As silence returned, I ghosted to the river mouth. With Epic tied to a 'frogman's head', I dozed away the hour or so till dawn.

Low tide was just after five. As I was preparing for a tidal ride up to St Germans, a bank of fog began seeping down the Tamar, engulfing the bridges, save for the concrete tower tops of the road bridge. Gently rowing in bright stillness I enjoyed the warmth of the newly risen sun for ten minutes or so before being enveloped in cold, thickening cloud. To starboard, Anthony Passage was just visible. I rowed into the mouth to allow the tide to float me into yet another world of mud. From the creek entrance I could see the ghostly mass of a railway viaduct about four hundred yards away. The fog was closing in by the time I reached the archways, which remained barely discernible. The creek was flooding rapidly. Not wishing to be trapped, I undertook a hard pull back to the river, where I was immediately peasouped.

Though knowing the current was favourable for my purpose, I had to imagine progress as my little patch of water drifted upstream. A small fog-grey naval ship, tethered between two large mooring drums, materialized. (It was quite large from my point of view.) Having drifted a further ten yards, I lost sight of the spectral vessel, along with the rest of the universe. I continued peering at 'nothing' more intently than I would have at the beautiful landscape it concealed. A leaping salmon, perhaps a five-pounder, came close to joining me in the boat. I wondered how Dave was faring. Silence was interspersed by loud shrieks from birds whose decibel levels seemed greater in the fog. I'm sure if I were flying blind up a river valley, I too would increase the volume.

Visibility slightly improved around nine o'clock when I was about three miles up-river, though I still had to use the compass to sort out a heading. In foggy confusion I had strayed from the main channel, entering a creek near Anthony (not to be confused with 'he with Passage').

Fog became low cloud, and fine sunny periods ensued. To utilise a faint following wind I set the sails goose-winged (one each side of the mast) and breezed up to St Germans. Ahead, parked on the bank, were a couple of large sailing boats and one or two dinghies. It was a little before high water when I landed at Tom Cradick's Yard. As I realized that casual sailors were not catered for, the boss arrived in a big lorry. He could have sent me off to check out the sailing club round the corner (I did not know it was there). However, before informing me of the club's location, he said I was welcome to leave Epic at his yard for a day or two. A fresh wind was forecast, making me reluctant to head onward. Plymouth Sound could wait a while.

With an hour to spare before mud would make landing difficult, I stepped back on board to sail a further exploratory mile up the Lynher. After passing under a grand multi-spanned viaduct, I wafted by the well-tended grounds of Port Elliot. The high river level allowed a leisurely return and a visit to the yacht club. I landed on a fine concrete slipway, the use of which would not limit departure time, I must have thought. A pleasant chap pointed out a gentleman who may have been able to help. In a few minutes the skipper came alongside the jetty, in his sailing boat, to pick up guests. I asked him if it were possible to pay for short-term parking. Standing on his large boat, the 'high ranker' informed me that the correct procedure was to phone first. After explaining my situation, the correct procedure was still to phone first. Mentally clicking my heels, I seethed back round to Tom's.

Leaving upturned Epic in good hands, I returned to Mevagissey. Adventure had been primed. I had the notion, after visiting Plymouth, to venture out to sea. Eager to resume voyaging, I could not wait for the weather to settle down.

A few days later, at high tide in the early afternoon, Robin, our middle son, notched up another hour of driving practise as he ferried Julia and myself to St Germans. After helping me return Epic to the water, the learner driver went for a row, during which he demonstrated his particular technique for running aground. (The 'L' plates on the car were magnetic and would not have stuck to the dinghy.) At a quarter past four, after re-stowing and thanking Tom and his son, I waved goodbye to Julia and Robin, raised both jibs and headed for Plymouth.

Sailing back down the Lynher was most enjoyable. At times, Epic cut through the water in exhilarating fashion. The river surface was comparatively flat and I kidded myself that the dinghy was actually heading into the wind. (I rather think the river flow fooled me.) Visibility was perfect, allowing appreciation of the parts that were 'mist ' on my way up. Cloud cover began to break up, heralding a mostly sunny evening.

A moderate breeze was blowing up the Hamoaze (lower Tamar – Lynher to Plymouth Sound), roughening the surface, hindering progress and necessitating tacking (zigzagging to progress into the wind.) My cut-down rig was responsible for the abysmal performance. Criss-crossing the half-mile wide waterway before passing Devil's Point, three miles on, I must have travelled ten miles, thanks to the outgoing stream. It was an interesting area in which to be delayed. Warships lined the Devon side (Devonport), a sombre contrast to a three-masted barquentine moored mid channel. Sleek, ocean-going sailing cruisers, beating powerfully, pointing close into the wind, were set more direct courses than mine. Epic ambled on.

In the area off the Torpoint ferry crossing, I assisted the sails with a spot of rowing. Had I not done so, a rendezvous with the Devon-bound ferry would have been touch and go, and perhaps more touch from the Cornwall-bound twin that completed the pincer movement.

The wind gradually increased on the nose (as we sailors say) creating small choppy waves. The tide had turned. To counteract the increasingly adverse stream I added oar-power. With great relief I rounded Devil's Point and entered the Sound. Shipping oars, I was soon speeding along the west-end tip of Devon's coastline and on past Mill Bay Docks. This was more like it, cutting through historic waters towards a haven laden with taverns – what bliss. What tragedy. With Drake's Island just visible to starboard, the wind died. With great urgency I hurriedly rowed a further mile past The Hoe, The Citadel and round to the Barbican where I tied up alongside the Mayflower Steps, twenty minutes before closing time.

From over the cobbles, The Admiral MacBride beckoned. To there I retired to refresh my inner self. I popped out from time to time to check that Epic was safe. With a length of new, excessively thick, white rope, I secured the dinghy to a large steel ring situated at the top of a flight of stone steps. The fixing was higher than Epic's mast – the general effect being that of a toy boat on the end of a piece of string. It seemed to me the steps were most unlikely to be used again that night, for they were in darkness, and it was very quiet.

While nipping out from the Admiral, Epic checking, a nose alert 'pointed' to Captain Jasper's 'foodery'. A short while later, with thoughts of grilled bacon rolls uppermost in my mind, I happened to glance out of the window. Sustenance became secondary. A multi-decked, extravagantly lit vessel was disgorging partying passengers from where Epic should have been. With barely time to think 'matchwood' and 'didn't see it guv' type thoughts, I was at the top of the steps. What joy. My midget sailer was perfectly well, happily riding to her piece of string having been safely shunted aside.

Leaving the pub, I wandered down to the Captain's stall of gastronomic delight. Situated outside the fish-market, graced with a mechanical flapping seagull, stood an overgrown, tastefully decorated shed-stall. To accompany my p.m. elevenses, thick rashers loaded into half a French loaf, I ordered a large mug of tea. For creating such an oasis, Jasper (John) should be promoted to at least the rank of MacBride. The Cap'n told me later how the business started. As a regatta attraction in 1978, he designed a handcart. Planning was required; dimensions were generous; opportunity was seized and the cart became an immovable stall. The original idea, selling grilled mini dabs (small, cheap flatfish) in a bun, floundered – three hands being required to cope with a bony dab, napkin and plate. The bacon bap saved the day. Later it was joined by dozens of other delectable savouries.

Back at the steps I rejoined Epic and rowed out to find a mooring for the night. Tied to a buoy in the mouth of the River Plym, I gave no thought to the Pilgrim Fathers who sailed from there to America, for I felt slightly uneasy regarding my imminent, English Channel confrontation.

A Little Port To Starboard
Plymouth to Portwrinkle

It seemed I had slept but a short while when I peered into the soft light of a new day. Several minutes later, while clearing the decks in preparation for departure, I looked out across the Sound and was amazed to find, that apart from a few winking red and green navigation lights, it was pitch black. The cause of my aberration 'dawned' – I had woken facing the glow of Plymouth's night-lights. After returning to my bag for an hour or so, I re-emerged at half past four, hoisted the jib and dawdled over to the lee of Drake's Island to await the shipping forecast. Epic was hitched to a giant 'Gouda' – a sure sign I was in an area of serious shipping. Most of the smaller round red 'Edams', to which I had become accustomed, were behind me on the rivers. A fine rain washed in a bona fide dawn, revealing, just thirty yards away, a twenty four foot gaff cutter moored to an identical cheese as mine. The 'difficult to spot in the dark' black painted Black Velvet was ideally suited for the forthcoming part of my trip, and Epic could have been its tender.

Three miles away to the southwest, the direction from which the wind was unfortunately blowing, stood Penlee Point where the sea proper begins. It was just visible through the gloom, between a low part of the western end of Drake's Island and Picklecombe Point. At six o'clock I sailed out into the drizzly Sound towards the breakwater. I was unable to blank out the irritating melody, 'Err lee won moor-or-ning juh staz the sun was rhy-hi-zing ...' that repeated in the back of my mind. The orchestral version of the song, part of a lively medley preceding the shipping forecast, was broadcast I presume, to perk up early risers. The front of my mind was evaluating '... southwesterly, three to four, increasing five later. Showers; moderate; fog patches ...' My desire was not to be 'perked' but to expel the curse of that repetitive jingle. The 'force four' I hoped to manage, so optimistically decided to carry on for a while, knowing I could always run back to the Barbican if conditions worsened.

A deep rumbling sound caused me to glance over my shoulder. I beheld a jingle dispelling, huge Brittany Ferry which had crept up on me from behind Drake's Island. Fifteen minutes earlier, the leviathan had been out at sea. It would take me a lot longer to break out of the Sound. Intermittent showers marred an interesting sail out to sea. Tacking caused me to pass close to Picklecombe Fort – a five-storey, semicircular, former fortress on the Cornish side of the Sound. Though housing luxury apartments, it looked somewhat forbidding at that early, grey hour. After a tack out towards the mile long breakwater I continued into Cawsand Bay, from where I inspected Kingsand and Cawsand. The villages looked as one from the sea, dominated by Cawsand Fort – receiving the Picklecombe treatment. (I'm not anti apartments – give me architecture for habitation rather than war any day, though old castles do make wonderful painting subjects.) Had I not an urgent appointment with Rame Head, I would have looked in at the 'King and Caw-sands'.

After four or five more tacks through the choppy sea, I reached Penlee Point and turned westward. In unprotected Channel waters the motion changed, allowing Epic to rise elegantly over rounded swells. Rame Head, the more southerly tip of the promontory, was still a mile and a half away. My course from The Barbican to Rame, measured in straight lines, was over six miles. By the time I added another series of tacks, the distance travelled was over twice that. The high ground behind Rame was veiled in mist. As I struggled over a depressing grey sea to reach Whitsand Bay, and hopefully a favourable wind, I wondered if the perfectly sighted coastguard lookout was manned, for cutbacks were being made. As I neared the headland the skies cleared, the wind eased and the sun broke through. My spirits immediately lifted.

Thoughts of retreating ceased and I was able to relax. Turning the corner put the wind abeam – providing the most efficient and easiest wind direction for sailing. I slackened the sheets (sail control lines), leant against the mast and controlled the tiller (rudder steering handle) with my feet. Considering my 'out at sea, small boat experience' was limited, my behaviour was rather blasé. Drinking orange juice, I surveyed the scene. Long Sands, a four mile long beach was a mile and a half away, and as the wind reduced to a waft, I angled in to take a closer look. Sedately cruising along, facing the way I had come, I was alarmed to see a mere six feet to port, a large black dorsal fin rise out of the water. Fear rapidly turned to excitement. The fin was about two feet high, narrower than the classic shark shape and curved slightly backwards towards the tip. It protruded from the hefty pale grey back of a dolphin. It submerged after a few seconds, reappeared twice at ten-yard intervals, then disappeared completely, heading in the direction of Plymouth. I thought they were wont to play around boats for a while, communing (or humouring) with mankind, and possibly being patted. I felt slightly slighted.

After an enjoyable hour sailing past many wooden holiday homes that clung to the steep, brackened cliffs, I sensed a slight acceleration. Sitting up, I paid attention. Freathy village was abeam. Out to sea, cloud cover was returning. On reaching a position about six hundred yards from the shoreline, I tightened the sheets, enabling me to sail parallel to the beach with the wind meeting Epic a little forward of the port beam. She began to run into waves that gradually increased in size to form small breaking crests. I rapidly became adept at turning into the larger waves at the last second, preventing the dinghy from being pushed towards the beach and taking extra water over the side. By degrees the wind strength increased. From enjoying an exhilarating sail a few minutes earlier, I feared an overwhelming fear of being overwhelmed. I sat in the bottom of the boat, hard against the windward gunwale which I gripped tightly with my left hand. My weight helped counteract the considerable wind pressure on the sails, but unfortunately, an unhealthy amount of English Channel came aboard. Rame Head was three miles astern when I looked back, but I saw only a mile of foam-edged beach and a bank of sinister black cloud. It was too late to run for shelter behind the hidden headland. Visibility decreased further as heavy slanting rain added to the rattle of flapping sails. Awful slabs of water formed brief horizons as Epic sank into troughs. Occasionally she fell off a wave top, shuddering and crashing down on her flat bottom. I imagined imminent break up of the thin plywood hull. At times cross waves met, throwing up pyramids of confused sea – more than enough to fill the dinghy. Four miles on from Rame Head I reached crisis point. Despite my efforts to maintain sea room, I had been driven relentlessly to within two hundred yards of the beach. Long Stone, a mile away, was just visible through the mist. The sixty feet tall, ghostly giant 'tombstone', with angry white around its base, stood two hundred yards offshore. A short distance before the monolith, the rocky shore steps seaward. My course would have taken me onto the base of that rugged cliff, close to the handy monument.

It was too late to make a crash landing on the beach, for Long Sands was astern, replaced by ragged rocks. A small white boat appeared for a second or so, just a hundred yards ahead. I saw it again, punching through the waves. Rescue, I thought, though I could hardly believe it; which was just as well, for it headed straight out to sea. A minute later, through the spray, I glimpsed a patch of beach protected by rocky teeth. Surges receded and more black pointy bits appeared, designed it seemed for plywood piercing. In those few seconds I decided to head for almost certain boat-wreck – the lesser of two evils. The alternative was certainly some degree of crew-wreck. I checked my life jacket was fully inflated, and painting equipment and other important possessions were polythene bagged and to hand. My intention was to jump overboard with my salvage when Epic made contact.

I pulled the tiller over and headed towards the incisors. The stern lifted, and as Epic was rushed in on a wave, the wind, then on the port quarter, tried to overturn her. Those few seconds taken to run the gauntlet seemed to pass in slow motion. Just a foot to starboard, a large area of rock appeared in the relatively clear passage. As other sinister shapes passed inches below Epic's hull, I yanked the centreboard out, cast off both sheets and bundled the mainsail/jib out of the wind, having let the halyard fly. Passing a large projection on my right, prior to entering the surf, I glimpsed a static patch of white – the bow of a boat. I caught the flailing jib sheet, passed it across the front of the mast and hauled it in tight on the port side. I pulled the tiller towards me, the jib caught the wind and Epic spun round, surging towards the gap. Without the centreboard there was excessive leeway (sideways drift). Releasing the sheet, I grabbed the oars from the gunwales, made a few desperate strokes and entered the mouth of the smallest harbour I had ever seen. A fisherman stood by his white boat having just returned from a dash through the surf to haul his nets.

"Hello," I croaked.

Epic grounded a few yards inside the harbour mouth. I stepped shakily out, and seizing the bow, hauled the dinghy onto the shingle.

Though my legs felt week, I was not tired. Perhaps it was euphoria, following the fortuitous escape, which caused me to take a few deep breaths. With heartbeats and breathing returning to normal, I spoke to the fisherman again.

"Where am I?"

"Portwrinkle," he replied matter-of-factly.

I had never heard of it.

Five or ten minutes had elapsed when the boat, the one I had seen leaving earlier, returned. On board were a fisherman and son, with a fair load of flatfish. When noticing that first small white boat (at sixteen feet, it was quite big compared to Epic) it did not occur to me that it must have come from somewhere. Though at rock bottom (almost), I still should have twigged.

"What strength do you think the wind is?" I asked the new arrival.

"Six." He was also matter-of-fact.

An hour or so later I removed the mast from the little 'miracle', having decided to leave her above the high-water line ready for continuation – how soon one forgets. Relatively little time had elapsed since that frightening ride, but there I was, already preparing for the next leg of the voyage. I could hardly believe we were both undamaged; but this time it was true. Twenty hours earlier, and less than two miles away on the other side of the hill, I was enjoying a pleasant sail on the Lynher. It would have been so much easier and quicker to walk to Portwrinkle; but where's the fun in that?

'I must pay attention and take great care when at sea.'

'I must pay attention …'

What an earth did I think I was doing? It seemed such a small risk at the onset. When the wind increased off Long Sands, while the waves were still small, I should have beached Epic. At worst I would have got a little wet.

When Julia arrived two hours later I was chatting to a local couple. They had witnessed from their sitting room (they must have a great view) the final mile of my journey. They were expecting to call the coastguard. What are the odds against blundering into a harbour, a harbour unknown to you, after an eight-hour trip? The outer harbour wall at

Portwrinkle is little more than a natural formation and difficult to spot, even if one knew it was there. Uncanny.

'I must pay attention …'

After tying mast and oars on top of the car, Julia helped me turn Epic over and carry her out of reach of the changeable channel. Before leaving, we looked out over the bay. Under a clear sky the sea had turned a rich turquoise blue. It did not appear at all aggressive, though the wind was still strong, flecking the surface with white horses. Julia wondered what all the fuss had been about. It was high tide and the off-lying rocks were submerged. Looking carefully though, just off the harbour entrance you could detect an area of disturbed water simmering. 'I will pay attention.'

Junior Art

My two years at 'Junior Art' strengthened my resolve to be a painter. Our class was quite small – about fifteen in total. The girls were outnumbered by something like two to one. I should remember by halving the number of heavenly bulges that developed under their green jumpers. My education developed on other fronts too, with even an upgrade in woodwork, to 'Rather slow'.

A new boy arrived one day during the first year. He showed us a tiny silver cube with three, inch long wires sticking out one side.

"My dad says transistors will be one of the most important inventions ever."

"Oh yeh." We carried on playing football.

We 'Junior Arts' spent half the week 'doing art'. There was still half a morning for games – football in winter and cricket, 'yuk', in summer. Gymnastics and athletics almost went by the board. However I did manage to infiltrate and do a bit of unsupervised pole-vaulting when the engineering and agricultural lot were not hogging the sand pit. Flexible poles as far as I can remember had not been invented, so we are not talking of plummeting down from ridiculous heights. All the same it was a risky business. There was no huge inflatable cushion allowing frivolous variations in technique. We stood the high-jump stands on chairs, raising the crossbar to heights from which it was rather foolish to descend onto a tiny square of impacted sand. That would have been bad enough, but the pit was framed with boards held in position with off-putting pegs. We thudded our poles into a plank (or not), performed arm wrenching hauls until combinations of injury, fear or prohibition ceased the ritual. Unlike cricket, it was not a skiver's pastime, for after almost every attempted leap there followed delicate repositioning of chairs, stands and bent bar. There was something to be said for fielding on the boundary.

At the end of the second term our family moved to Tenbury Wells on the Shropshire / Worcestershire border – the Town in the Orchard (and leaping bullock). It was not long before I gave up the forty-mile train journey and boarded at the technical College hostel during the week. Incarceration made my weekend 'paroles' very precious, and I willed the speedy advancement of the Friday steam-train. Big brother John and I would go for grayling in fast water below the long deep pool beside the churchyard. A small black fly would trick the silver flanked, flashing little beauties that smelled of cucumber. It was a thrilling contest, a flick of spray being the clue to the grayling take. Close to the churchyard in the Council works' tip was a rich source of succulent red and stripy worms. A specimen would be threaded on a large hook and be tumbled along the riverbed on a leadless line, hopefully tempting majestic brown trout. You would feel toying interest, followed by a definite bite, then strike and play the surging rushes. Such a difference in performance between the thumping tug of the golden-sided, ruby spotted trout, and the frenetic attempt at freedom by the wriggling grayling.

The hostel was close to the Tech's playing field where we could play football until late, often continuing when we could barely see the ball (without the worry of being flattened by fearless, pointy-elbowed, blind kids). In the second year, a liberal minded hostel warden arrived. In a pioneering 'get to know us' get-together, we inmates were actually asked if we had suggestions for changes in regime. After much discussion, lobbying and voting, the force of democratic desire delivered – chips, once a week. (We had food on the other days as well.) The new governor cemented his popularity by taking us for a spin in his brand new, little

Ford with the latest 'no mudguards' design.

A free 'man', now quite happy in long trousers, I walked along the tow-path away from the Technical College for the last time having completed my two year course in 'General Education and Art'. The certification was inside a large buff envelope, which was inside my large green bag, which, at the time, was exceedingly heavy. The bag, called a grip, I disliked intensely, principally because it was much too big. Were I moving house it would have been acceptable, but I never had reason to carry more than a few items. It drooped in a sad unfulfilled manner, grazing the ground as I walked. Today it would be considered un-cool by young people. Being excessively huge and decidedly 'square', it most certainly was not an accessory befitting, as near as damn it, a proper art student.

Along with another fisher-boy I had 'collected', from the engineering department's scrap metal bay, a quantity of lead off-cuts. My friend, more a course fisher than I, required his bait to remain static after casting. With the thought of never buying split lead shot again (though I never used more than a speck) I became over zealous, and consequently over burdened. (This was before swan poisoning became an issue.) Eventually, with dragged bag and lengthened arms, I reached the gradient leading to the station, having passed under a wide, dripping railway-bridge. (Little did I know then, that a dozen years later I would become a rate-paying grownup just a few minutes 'unleaded' walk from that very spot.)

I mention the episode, for although many 'heavy green bags of lead' situations followed, I really thought that life was to be all honey and chips. My exam results were better than expected, so never, never ever again would I have to confront such taxing and weighty problems. Alas, life's roundabout would not always herald herds of happy horses. Every now and then one saddled with a heavy green bag would come round. Sadly, relocation to Tenbury meant no enrolment at Shrewsbury School of Art. My fairground mount trotted off to Stourbridge College of Art on the edge of the Black Country, where I would become intoxicated by subjects both two and three dimensional – in-house and après-art.

Meanwhile there was another long summer to enjoy – communing with nature at large, and labouring for several weeks in the cut-throat, piece-work environs of the blackcurrant 'plantations'. Gangs, mostly wellie-wearing women, head-scarved, with or without babes or youngsters in tow and shrill of voice, would be conveyed to the picking fields in dillies (mini-busses). Early morning, before the invasion, birds would sing from neat ranks of bushes that glinted shiny black jewelled fruit. By evening, particularly when the rains came, the 'purpled to the elbows' hoard with their prams and outdoor catering paraphernalia had thrashed the field into a third day Glastonbury Festival landscape. Jimmy Young passed our time with his man from Laramie, and Mrs Dale worried about her Jim. Had it not been for the tiny silver cube, no doubt we would have created our own entertainment, singing about those mean old currant fields. 'Hey momma, hey, hey, hey – did that lady put mud in her tray?' Concealed clods of red clay equalled many minutes of sticky picking. To have the prized, heavy, dangly clusters of fruit stolen from bushes further down the row was a severe test of character. The weighty stems of currants that clicked satisfyingly from the branch were located low down towards the centre of the bush. When the naked inner boughs, stripped of their bountiful bunches of super currants were discovered, one was sorely tempted to substitute clods for currants – though I never did.

Towards the end of my currant-picking time, I produced my earliest sur-viving painting – 'Cottage Loaf'. When Jim, the young baker set up on his own, up the entry by the side of the Chemists in Teme Street (a couple of doors down from the butcher's), I was pleased to emblazon his Morris Minor van, and paint the 'Loaf'. The bread portrait was pro-duced with enamel paints, on location, high up on the premises. There it reigned proudly for a few years even after Jim moved on. It then lan-guished for decades, out of reach, but on an ever more grimy back-ground. Having mentioned to my brothers that I would quite like to claim my 'first commission' if any renovation or demolition of the site was afoot, I was well chuffed to be presented with the salvaged painting as a birthday present.

My Earliest Surviving Painting
12″ x 14″   1958
'The bread portrait was produced with enamel paints, on location, high up on the premises.'

Flushed

Portwrinkle to Fowey

Strong winds delayed my restart from Portwrinkle. At half past ten on the last day in July, with both sails raised in hope, for there was not a breath of wind, I rowed away from the mini harbour under an overcast sky over a smooth grey sea. A swell, resulting from the previous spell of rough weather, rose and fell against the cliffs. There was still an area of breaking waves fifty yards out, which I calmly rowed round. After lowering the white sail which kept obstructing my vision and getting in the way, I pulled on the oars for an hour. It would have been more comfortable rowing while leaning against my painting stool, but regrettably, it was on its way back to Mevagissey – overlooked when unpacking the car. With the stool legs wedged against the foredeck, the canvas seat naturally supported my back, making rowing a delight. Two miles on, just before reaching Downderry, a faint breeze materialised from the direction of Looe, my destination. With the white sail re-hoisted, sailing commenced at a leisurely pace. The sun came out. I sat in the bottom of the boat, listening to the lap of little waves against the hull. It was idyllic, a complete contrast to the conclusion of the preceding leg. Had I not been heading almost straight out to sea it would have been perfect.

It was noon when my return inshore tack took me close to Seaton beach, halving the original six-mile straight-line distance to Looe. I continued by row/sailing (one hand rowing, assisting the sails to make a better heading, the other working the tiller). Towards one o'clock, black sky developed ahead as a fresh breeze blew off the land. The resulting flat sea enabled me to stow the oar, and with a few tacks reach Looe Island at three thirty. Leaden clouds, replaced by bright 'overcastness', induced me to sail round to the lee of a shingle spit (just the one) that projected towards the mainland.

Daydreaming of distant uninhabited islands, where one might stumble upon caches of doubloons, ceased abruptly. A well-dressed middle-aged chap wearing shorts stepped out from the trees and asked for a landing fee. I paid in fifty-pence pieces rather than pieces of eight. The spell was broken. The beach parking attendant was as different from Long John Silver as Hispaniola was from Epic.

During my two hour relaxing visit to Looe Island, I had the pleasure to meet the elderly sisters, Evelyne and Roselyn. They purchased the Island in 1964 to live a unique dream. Between them they wrote and made pots. Along with landing fees, visitors contributed by buying their wares and refreshments. It would be rather nice to have your own little island. After wandering about the peaceful islet for a while, I slipped away, heading for the Looe Rivers.

High water that evening was at nine-thirty, necessitating a speedy one-mile row round to Looe, in order to use the rising river for exploration purposes. When one hundred yards off the circular, white-topped river/harbour wall-end, Epic was overtaken by a converted lugger. The Erin worked out of Mevagissey until the mid-seventies, and it was there in the late sixties that I first saw her (without the pleasure-boat superstructure). 'Spectating', at the landing of the Erin's catch at the inner harbour jetty, was one of my first memories after moving to Cornwall. The thirty-eight foot, straight-stemmed old boat, planked with hefty scarred tarred timbers, was a hive of activity on that misty, ill-lit night. Many large baskets of slippery ling (cod-like, but longer) were offloaded. Though the masts no longer carried heavy canvas sails, the boat's silent engine kept the secret. It could have been a re-enactment from the nineteen hundreds.

I entered Looe River/Harbour at half tide with the river flowing upstream at its swiftest (six miles per hour). In welcome sunshine, on a perfect summer's evening, I was rapidly carried through the harbour using the oars to avoid contact with fishing boats berthing against the east quay. Looe town can be over hectic in summertime, but on the river it was relatively peaceful. The road bridge seemed to offer too little headroom at first glance; then as I approached, it seemed I might just make it. It was spring tides time, and that day the rise was fifteen and a half feet (close to an inch a minute mid-tide). I shouted to a lad attending warps on the boat nearest the bridge, asking him what he thought my chances were. He gave the 'palms up, shrugged shoulders gesture' – touch and go. Rowing strongly downstream, still losing way, I edged Epic's masthead an inch or two below the keystones of one of the middle arches.

Above the bridge the river divides. The East River shares its course with a railway line. With just a little coaxing I steered Epic into the West River. The two-mile drift in sunny calm was reminiscent of my slow boat ride to Lerryn. Initially, the river was wide and mud-bounded, flowing between wooded banks till it narrowed to meadow-lapping stretches. Finally, as the tide neared its maximum, I squeezed beneath overhanging trees in the upper reaches. Before being forced to retreat by foliage, I was barked down at by a large Alsatian which could have easily bounded on board. Thankfully, the dog seemed unsure of strategy for repelling waterborne intruders. Grateful to be in a sub eleven-foot boat, I executed a hasty pivot and retreated. Apart from confronting 'another man's best friend', the two-mile excursion had been perfectly uneventful.

Back down at the river's junction, I tied Epic between other smallish craft alongside a large car park. After clambering onto terra concrete, I wandered along to the Harbour Moon in West Looe, where I refuelled. For 'afters', while overlooking boating activity on the river, I imbibed a quenching quart. As darkness fell I made my way back to the dinghy, moved her to a buoy midstream, and was soon 'lulled' awake by slamming car doors and revving engines. Before the incoming tide made leaving difficult, I would have to be on the move by five o'clock the following morning. Peace reigned and I settled down for a five or six hour sleep – forever the optimist.

Due to miscalculation, August was not two hours old when Epic started to ground – it was a Lerryn-like replay. Relocation became an urgent matter lest I became trapped and, in due course, unable to compete against a speedy return tide. With oars doubling as huge feelers, I groped my way out of the mud maze. The lights of Looe were reflected on both water and mud, making it difficult to detect a course to the main channel.

Rather than finding a deepwater mooring immediately, I decided to drift down under the bridge to save worrying about clearance later. Still half asleep, I was rushed downriver, unable to decide where or when to tie up. Intense darkness at the river's edge concealed all but vague shapes of fishing boats. I should have tied up to one, but I became an onlooker and watched instead of hitching. My interrupted sleep had obviously left me bereft of a quantity of marbles. Being on the move, I must have thought an early start in order and was swept into the night. The suicidal tendency subsided, but not until Epic was in open sea. I had failed to realize the significance of a pre-dawn start. It was much too dark to be out there, for hazards abound around Looe. As well as rocks, shoals and currents, there is an Island, just a spit away.

Unable to row upstream against the strong ebb flow, I sought the floating '5 mph' sign I had passed the previous evening. Knowing it to be approximately one hundred yards off the river-mouth, I searched for it in the darkness. A row of amber lights fronted West Looe, casting dancing ribbon reflections across the water. After rowing against the strong tide for several minutes, I noticed breaks in the ribbons, pinpointing my emergency mooring. With great relief I passed the bow line round the signpost, then wound a couple of turns about the mast to make casting off a simple matter.

For making an early start, the speed limit sign location was most suitable, but in other respects left a lot to be desired. As I settled down to sleep once more, a mechanical digger-man (not a robot) started his extremely early shift rearranging Looe beach. Low tide, in the early hours, was obviously the most convenient time for beach grooming, but I could have woken unaided to hear the shipping forecast without the caterpillar-tracked monster's clanking. A fresh and extremely chilly offshore breeze completed a night 'not' to remember. Despite being sleeping bagged and woolly-hatted, I was very cold. Hot air rises, which is a shame, for it caused cool air to flow down the valley, seeking out sea-level sleepers.

'Westerly, becoming southerly, three or four, occasional rain, good, becoming moderate to poor'. The forecast had a familiar ring, but as Polperro was less than four miles away and I expected a favourable beam wind for the first two miles, I left immediately. Slipping away from the signpost, I set full sail and was soon speeding over the relatively flat sea, heading for the misty channel between the mainland and the Island. The power created by the two small sails amazed me. Unfortunately, before I could settle down to enjoy the performance, the wind died. The 'cold rush' out of the Looe River was obviously a local affair, so it was back to rowing. In uncanny stillness I headed west.

On a syrupy sea, duplicate rows of evenly spaced concentric circles were left behind to coalesce with the misty dawn. As I pulled away, the sun broke through the cloud cover that lingered above Looe Island and within a few minutes blue sky predominated. Just before reaching the first headland, guarded by the Hore Stone (a rocky outcrop similar to the Long Stone), I observed a sign of returning wind. Groups of delicate mini-waves a few inches apart, known as 'cats' paws', ruffled the surface and were soon replaced by proper little waves. Reverting to sail-power, I tacked out to sea. My return tack took me into Talland Bay, where mist shrouded the higher ground. Similar vistas greeted me at the end of the next few inland tacks, until I rounded Downend Point and sighted Polperro. With a headwind freshening, I rowed the last half-mile in bright sunshine, entering possibly the most picturesque harbour in Cornwall.

Standing in the stern of a twenty-foot fishing boat was the archetypal Cornish fisherman. Rowing over to the navy-jumpered, denim-jeaned, stocky, weather-beaten faced seaman, I asked if he could suggest a spot where Epic could safely lie for an hour or so. The chap was friendly and amenable, advising me to tie alongside a row of giant 'ladders', just inside the harbour mouth, on the right as you enter. I stepped ashore from the top plank/rung, for the tide was well in, and strolled through the narrow walkways round to the other side of the harbour.

Before taking a seat outside a waterside café, I looked across at my diminutive dinghy. Her flat nose pointed seaward, catching the morning sun. The red jib was neatly bundled at the base of the forestay and the white sail carefully wrapped round mast. With the oars tidily stowed along the gunwales, she looked ship-shape, set for adventure. While sipping a mug of tea, I was able to appreciate the haphazard beauty of cottages that had evolved on the steep harbour-sides. The density of the habitation created fragmented facets – material for lively paintings. The same is true of the 'sunny-side' of Mevagissey. The 'money-side' of my home harbour, with its more formal dwellings, is not so interestingly higgledy-piggledy, or subject to the strong contrasts of sunshine and shadow.

While I was fitting the oars into the rowlocks, in preparation for leaving, a young couple showing interest in the venture, sportingly

Mevagissey
Oil on canvas 5' x 4'6"   2006
'... fragmented facets – material for lively paintings. The same is true of the 'Sunny-side' of Mevagissey.'

squeezed out a measure of their suntan lotion for me. I was grateful for the thoughtful donation, for by ten thirty the sun was already quite powerful and I needed protection from the reflective glare. Heading into a pleasant breeze I resumed my journey, hoping August would continue its seasonal ways, with suntan oil playing a more prominent role than plastic sheeting.

After row/sailing a little over a mile to Larrick with the wind on the port bow, I downed sail and rowed into the wind for a further mile and a half, which put me a mile off West Coombe. Cloud cover returned. I resumed sailing, hoping to tack in past Pencarro Head, close to Lantic Bay and not too far from Fowey. The 'powers that be' had other ideas. The wind strengthened, resulting in choppy seas that forced me well short of the target. Before rounding the headland I completed four tacks. When completing the first, close in to the cliffs, the linen hat, I thought wedged firmly on my head, blew off. With a fresh wind and lumpy sea to contend with, it was quite awkward coming about (as we sailors say) in an attempt to retrieve the 'sapka'. (The hat [pronounced shapka], purchased at Ephesus during my Turkey trip the previous June, was of sentimental value. It helped make possible the painting of three watercolours in one day in temperatures reaching forty degrees.) Although my lunging boathook made contact, it failed to hook the hat. I did not get a second chance for it sank surprisingly quickly. The distorting disk faded from view along with my spirits.

To counteract sideways drift, I assisted with the portside oar, working the tiller with my left hand. The developing situation became frightening. By three-thirty it was necessary to use both oars to keep away from the cliffs, for I did not wish to tack out to sea. When Washing Rocks, the point where I could bear away and enter the Fowey River, was still two miles distant, progress was barely on the right side of stationary. The fact that I could return to Polperro did not occur to me. Fear and tiredness had once again overruled my ability to assess the situation and take appropriate action. Though returning to Polperro would mean travelling twice the distance as battling on to Fowey, it would have been infinitely safer, and a lot quicker.

Further on, in sheltered Lantic Bay, the increasing sea motion was prematurely ending an afternoon on the beach for the passengers and crew of half a dozen various small craft. The proximity of the Fowey-bound, fleeing fleet, reduced my anxiety. Twice, as I struggled on for a further hour, I was asked if I needed a tow. One offer came from a duo in a dinghy, of similar length to mine, propelled by a tiny buzzing outboard motor. Progressing slightly quicker than Epic, it danced precariously over the waves.

I was experiencing a dose of the afternoon, onshore breeze phenomenon. (Sun heats the land; warmed air rises, sucking in replacement from over the sea – the opposite of the night-time Looe River effect.) It had taken me a long time to cotton on to that mystery. The wind eventually moderated, allowing me to enjoy the final half-mile row to the entrance of the Fowey River. Without wind regimentation, irregular haphazard waves were formed, providing an exciting ride. Passing between St Catherine's Castle on the west side, and the smaller fortification on Punches Cross Rocks on the Polruan side, I finally entered calm water.

Fowey Harbour and the seaward end of the river are one, making it an interesting area to explore. In that sheltered haven, ocean-going ships pass a few yards in front of steep, wooded banks. Within moments of the deep channel being vacated, swans, canoes and every other type of craft imaginable (perhaps not nuclear submarines) including very small cruising dinghies, may occupy the area. Passenger ferries cross the river passing large tugboats moored mid-channel and between yachts of all sizes heading to or from the open sea.

After threading my way between moored boats on the right hand side, off the relatively quiet backwater of Polruan, I passed Pont Pill creek. Situated opposite Fowey and containing dozens of moorings, it is the most heavenly setting. From a narrow stream it meanders to form a mile-long tributary, three hundred yards wide where it joins the main river. Having crossed to the town side, I made my leisurely way upstream, aided by the sedate beginning of the flood tide. A variety of dwellings crowd the river's rocky edge. Several have overhanging verandas or balconies, or both. Some have ladders from which, at most states of the tide, escape from the motor congested narrow streets is an option – if you have a little boat that is.

The sun was shining when I returned to Caffa Mill car park late in the afternoon. Six weeks previously an unnamed little blue boat had arrived, proving herself eminently suitable at river drifting. Now, having endured a few shake-ups, Epic had graduated to coastal survival. In so doing she had taught me to respect the unpredictable sea, particularly, when in boisterous mood, it caresses the rugged coastline of Cornwall.

So ended the second round – the English Channel ahead in both. The human element of Team Epic had suffered another bout of fear, but was far from down and out. Sporting a 'pay and display' overnight stay sticker, Epic did not look particularly out of place parked between white lines close to the slipway.

Sailing Home
Fowey to Mevagissey

The following morning, Julia delivered me to Fowey along with Edward, our youngest. Before I set off solo, our eight year old took me for a row. It being exactly high tide (still water) and progress, a splashy, very little from the novice 'oarsboy', I thought it prudent to assist in vacating the area where the car ferry docked. Away from the possible collision vicinity, Edward performed well with vigorous ins and outs. Thinking his passage booked, he thought me a bit of a spoilsport when I declined help in rowing back home to Mevagissey.

Over a ruffled but flattish sea, I sailed away from Fowey. The sun shone, warming me as I left those sheltered waters. I was comfortable in shirt and jeans. All was calm up to the fortifications. After a couple of tacks I entered an area of swells off the craggy coastline leading to Gribbin Head.

By one o'clock, after a tough hour of row/sailing and tacking, I reached a point between the Gribbin (headland) and Cannis Rock, just a mile and a half out from the harbour entrance. Cannis Rock is covered at high water but still leaves a large area of confused sea, even in moderate winds. Out of the headland's protection I entered an area of unpredictable waves and found progress in the wind-blown sea a little slow. I thought twice about continuing, but reasoned that further into St Austell Bay the motion should be easier, and if not, I could run back to Fowey. 'I must take great care …'

After donning my life jacket, which should have been donned in sheltered waters, I was thinking of putting on my waterproof coat – the exertion not being enough to keep me warm. Dithering allowed a dollop of rogue wave-top to soak me. Hoping sun and wind would dry my shirt, I left the jacket off, but in the time taken to squeeze a few pints of seawater overboard, I was frozen. Though still wet, I soon warmed up when finally putting on the waterproof; what bliss. The unsolicited practical lesson, regarding wind-chill, was short and sharp with no harm done. Grey skies returned and remained for the rest of the day.

Wind direction was unfavourable for following the coastline round St Austell Bay. There would be no popping into Polkerris, Par or Charlestown. A shame to pass by the latter, for although a small harbour, it is capable of being squeezed into by ships of up to eight thousand tons, which at the time were still being 'locked' in to take on board cargoes of china clay.

From the Gribbin, the best course I could make was towards Chapel Point, passing three miles off Charlestown and missing Mevagissey by a mile. This was satisfactory, for I could then wend my way home in the shelter of familiar coastline. With a little anxiety I set about crossing St Austell and Mevagissey Bays, aiming as tight in to the wind as I could manage. The rigging on my small boat looked so frail, and the thin ply seemed hardly sufficient protection against the endless succession of little waves that Epic pounded through.

Looking back towards Par, when halfway across the bays, the earth's curvature was apparent. From my low vantage point, a sliver of watery sphere obscured the foreshore and chimney bottoms of the china clay drying plant. Noticing the phenomenon, when so close to land, made the planet seem very small. Had I been able to head down the Channel and sail on round the world at the same speed (3mph ish) I would have returned in about a year. (That makes it seem much larger again.)

After an hour or so I became accustomed to Epic's vigorous motion, and tried to take a photograph while steering with my feet. To prevent bucking Epic and I parting company, I held on tight, snapping single-handedly.

When a mile from Chapel Point I looked towards peaceful Pentewan, two miles abeam, and recalled other happy times. The sandy beach to the left of the village was just a pale line. From there, with fellow shopkeeper John from the Pisky Cove, we launched Aquilla, a fourteen-foot sailing dinghy. Though long ago, I still recall with embarrassment our ridiculous, amateur performance. We wheeled the heavy boat round the old dock and down to the water's edge. Then, having rolled our jeans knee-high, we pushed the dinghy into the sea. A minute later I was grimly hanging on to the bow, having been lifted off the seabed by waves that passed over my head.

The wind kept up until I was off Chapel Point where I passed between a few pleasure boats mingling in the protective lee of the peninsula. Relieved to reach home waters, I followed the rocky shoreline round to Portmellon where a heavily constructed steel slipway runs down to a sandy beach. Alas, few boats are now launched down the slip, for the old sheds of Mitchell's boat-yard have given way to development. Before it became history, I took the opportunity to paint several watercolours in the dingy atmosphere splendour of the chaotic interior. The cove with its gently shelving beach has an added attraction of the handy Rising Sun Inn.

It began drizzling before I completed the final half-mile to Mevagissey. I downed sail and rowed into the outer harbour, past the lighthouse at the end of the East (Victoria) Pier. After passing between visiting yachts at anchor, I tied up temporarily alongside the middle steps on the north side. Charlie, who had been hoping for customers to take a trip with him round the bay, called it a day and motored off to his outer harbour mooring. Drizzle turned to rain as I wandered off with my lidded plastic buckets to check out the gallery. Later that evening, towards high water, I bailed out Epic and rowed to the slip in the inner harbour where my boys were waiting to lift Epic on to the trolley. I pushed the little voyager home round the one-way system and parked her on the front lawn behind a clump of marguerites.

Bringing Epic home could have been a tidy conclusion to the venture, but my heart was set on continuing the voyage – sailing into Carrick Roads, past Falmouth and on to Truro. Already I had been absent from the gallery long enough and should have put voyaging on hold. Empty spaces between the paintings caused guilt, but not quite enough to halt the mission. The sensible course of action was to complete the adventure the following summer, but …

Portmellon Boat-shed

9″ x 11½″ 1987

'Before it became history, I took the opportunity to paint several watercolours
in the dingy atmospheric splendour of the chaotic interior.'

My desire to carry on can be partly blamed on the extensive coverage of Sir Robin Knox-Johnston's triumphal return from his round-the-world voyage, televised in April '69, five months before our move down to Mevagissey. Viewing in granular black and white, I was enthralled to see the weather-beaten, cutter-rigged ketch Suhaili, rolling into Carrick Roads amid an armada of welcoming craft.

Working away those last few months, enjoying mutual learning with the blind pupils, I was thrilled at the prospect of our imminent relocation to Mevagissey. I daydreamed of the balmy South West, of palm trees and the surrounding sea, and the possibility of sailing something larger than a Gremlin Major. Notice had been given to the Blind School and School of Art of my leaving to become a painter in Cornwall. Having gained honourable employment, together with an offer of a house in the castle grounds, my mother was less than enthusiastic regarding our reckless moving to the land of beatniks, and the certainty of starving in a garret.

Impatiently I waited a few days for settled weather in which to round Dodman (Deadman) Point – the dreaded headland, four miles to the south of Mevagissey, en route to Truro.

Sleeping Ogre
Mevagissey to St Mawes

August 8th – 'North-west four …' the maximum wind strength Epic could manage with safety would be coming off the land, hopefully leaving a flat sea close inshore. Smooth water meant speedier progress and, theoretically, a better angle for sailing into the wind, though ninety degrees off was the best possible heading with the cut down rig. My intention was to be off the Dodman around eleven o'clock (slack water) but had to leave the inner harbour slip, round the corner from the gallery, three hours before, while there was sufficient water to launch.

I stowed the gear and raised the mast while Epic was still in the front garden, then guided the trolley, carrying my transport/accommodation unit, down to the slipway. The mast easily passed under overhead cables. Ten minutes later, having placed the trolley in the gallery (an incongruous exhibit, or not, considering the crazy contemporary art scene), I was rowing out of the inner harbour. A faint following breeze filled the red jib as I ghosted out past Portmellon and on towards Chapel Point. With time on my hands, there was no need to set the 'half bikini top' that I hoped would be stretched into action later, helping Epic on her way to Carrick Roads. Under a blue sky in pleasant sunshine, I enjoyed a delightful spot of leisurely sailing with barely sufficient wind to make headway (my kind of sailing). I rounded the Chapel Point peninsula on which a white painted mini hamlet stands in private splendour.

The three fine individual dwellings (1934-39) were designed and built by John Campbell with assistance from a skilled mason and carpenter. He set out to show that quality work, using traditional methods and materials, was a viable alternative to structures being produced with ever more skimpy manufactured components. The uneven terrain led to creative layouts on varying levels. Interiors and exteriors were enhanced with interesting features, including vaulting, archways and towers. Many more houses were designed to occupy the impressive site. Sadly the grand scheme envisaged by the accomplished architect was prematurely terminated. Walking home one foggy night, having visited a Mevagissey pub, he fell to his death from the cliff-top.

Had I not planned to stop a little further on, I would have whiled away an hour or so by popping onto the secluded Colona Beach, tucked in tightly on the west side of the Point. The peaceful beach is often frequented by a 'holidaying' herd of assorted cows – black, white, tan and mixtures. Two miles on, I ran Epic gently into the sandy beach, a few yards along from Gorran Haven's sturdy stone harbour wall. Inside the protective arm about twenty boats lay listing or legged (supported by removable outboard uprights), waiting for the tide to turn. At that early hour, many folk were already enjoying the luxury of perfect beach weather. Occasional token waves flipped, then swished up to Epic's sun-warmed transom. I wandered up the steep, narrow hill between tightly packed old stone cottages. To the seaward side, a small church with a tower had somehow been squeezed into the storybook village setting.

Stuart was putting a finishing touch to a cottage he had built high up on the hill. My mission was to collect from him the white jib I had used before and returned a few days earlier, when his friends wished to sail his dinghy. 'Unfortunately', the weather being idyllic, the friends had planned to sail again that day. I was not unduly troubled to be without the white sail. Optimistically, I imagined 'spinnakering' all the way to St Anthony Head. Returning to the beach with Stuart, we stood outside the open doors of one of the boathouses. Within the gloom lay the perfect 'little gem' upon which I had cast an envious eye three months earlier. Down the beach I could see Epic set against a sparkling backdrop of sun-spangled sea. I felt no desire to swap; but envied the small tan-coloured sail. The direction I wished to sail from the Dodman, was more or less the same as Chapel Point to Gorran Haven. As the red jib had performed admirably, and stronger winds forecast, I felt happy to embark on a 'fifty percent sail reduction' cruise.

At ten past ten my carefree voyage continued. Within the hour I was passing within a few yards of the Dodman's sunlit craggy cliffs. Almost becalmed, steering with my feet, I was amazed to be floating on the calmest of tranquil seas. Nothing prevented me gliding over and patting the infamous ogre, but I refrained. The Dodman is the most powerful landmark between Rame Head and The Lizard. A tiny stone cross on the top (that surprisingly becomes quite large when standing next to it) further emphasises its scale. Unexpectedly interrupting the rugged

Gorran Haven
10"x 10"

coastline, to the west of the Dodman, is the wonderfully secluded sandy beach at Hemmick. Access to that summertime retreat is restricted by intimidating, steep, narrow, winding lanes. A bit further on is Porthluney Cove, looked down upon from Caerhays Castle. In the estate grounds graze a handful of Highland cattle, enhancing the seemingly timeless landscape. In fact, the castle predates the cattle by less than two centuries. Perhaps the herd is mock also – stuffed effigies dotted around for effect and moved to new locations under the cover of darkness. They would look really imposing standing on the battlements.

Though the wind direction was fine for visiting other Veryan Bay villages such as Portholland and Portloe, they were left in my wake. I needed to get a move on. The realization that under jib alone I would miss Zone Point and be carried way out to sea, came to me half an hour after leaving the protection of the feared headland. While hoping for a favourable wind shift, I assisted the miniscule sail area with oar-power. I settled down to the task of completing the long haul, battling against the elements in perfect sailing conditions for a properly rigged boat. Encountering several yachts heading east, wafting along effortlessly enjoying down-wind sailing, compounded my frustration. How I wished to exchange muscle for wind propulsion.

The steep sided Gull Rock rises from the sea half a mile offshore to the east of Nare Head. This large pointed rock served as a progress marker. As I headed towards Zone Point, it appeared to creep eastward, taking hours to be edged back along to Portloe. By four o'clock, Pothscatho at the west end of Gerrans Bay lay two miles to the north-west. I had covered approximately two thirds of the eleven miles between Dodman and Zone Point and, not surprisingly, was shattered.

Of the dozen or so sailing cruising boats that passed close by during the crossing, the skippers of three or four altered course to see how I was faring. One fine gaff cutter heading for Fowey passed a few hundred yards to starboard (right). A minute later it sped back, close-hauled (heading well into the wind with sails hauled in tight), pressed over ten degrees by a vast mainsail and full foresail stretched from the bowsprit end to masthead. As she came about, the helmsman eased her twenty-eight feet plus ten-foot bowsprit slowly by, asking if I needed help. Little Epic, two or three miles offshore with a scrap of sail hoisted on her stumpy mast and carrying an automaton flailing away with a pair of tiny oars, certainly looked in need of help, or some kind of certification. It was a privilege for me to have witnessed, at close quarters, the performance of that symphony in white. The hull, simple cabin top and sails were all pristine white. Touches of varnished timber delicately trimmed, and neatly emphasized, the satisfying lines of the aptly named Temptress.

By six o'clock I thought I was bidding a thankful farewell to the open sea – being close in off Zone Point, with St Anthony Head, the eastern sentinel of Carrick Roads a mere six hundred yards away. Attempting to head towards Pendennis Castle that stands guard opposite St Anthony Head, I was given a hard time by the wind funnelling out of the mile wide channel. Uncomfortable waves were formed, forcing Epic further out to sea. Several offers of a tow to calmer water were offered as I laboriously tacked between the headlands. Had I accepted assistance, when only a mile from port, the hastened supping would have been tinged with regret. My intention was to salute a conquered Neptune at the conclusion of a solo encounter. Fear of the Dodman delayed me sufficiently to force a final battle with the strong adverse tide at the mouth of Carrick Roads. It was another lesson that would stand me in good stead. You must go with the flow.

After fighting my way across the wakes of pleasure craft returning to moorings in creeks, harbours and marinas – legion in the region, I tangled with rocks at the foot of St Anthony Light. By the time I entered the mouth of Percuil River and bore away to St Mawes, the wind seemed to have moderated and the sea calmed considerably – owing mostly to the sheltered location, I presume. A show of 'fiery diffused stained glass' sparkled above the castle for a few magical moments as multicoloured spinnakers 'floated' across the evening sun.

With great relief I pulled down the red jib, and in the gathering gloom, rowed to the slip where I tethered Epic. I had been rowing for virtually the whole of the previous ten hours, so with hands set in pint-pot holding mode, I made my way a few yards up to the Victory Inn. My salutation was interrupted from time to time, for I had to nip down to re-float Epic. The slightly shelving shingle harbour bottom drained rapidly, which meant several 'nippings'. When my lengthy bow line no longer reached the fixing at the slip, I tied the line to a large lump of rock that I manhandled down the beach periodically.

Rejuvenated, I sensed something in the air. Placing myself in the hands of my trusty nose, if you see what I mean, I strolled away from the harbour, homing in on a nearby take-away; and took away chicken and chips. Standing by Epic in near darkness, rapidly devouring my supper, I was really in heaven. Elated, having completed the long trip to St Mawes, I was more than happy to row a few leisurely strokes across the quiet water to an 'Edam off St Anthony'. While reflecting on the day's events, in the comforting privacy of darkness, I slipped into my sleeping bag to savour a second supper – Mars bars and orange-juice – Paradise.

Final At Phoenix Wharf
St Mawes to Truro

The morning dawned sunny, though Epic was still in shadow and very wet, having floated through a damp misty night. After sponging the dewy decks, I draped my sleeping bag around the foredeck to catch the imminent rays. The bag acted like a wick during the night, soaking up pints from the moist air.

No other craft were on the move as I tacked three-quarters of a mile over calm water to Castle Point. The cylindrical stone structure of St Mawes Castle and surrounding fortified walls were surrounded by a spectacular array of hydrangeas – pastel shades harmonizing with the sun-brightened stonework. As I approached, high cloud blocked the sun, rendering the subject mundane – any excuse. The clouds advanced further, stealing the last dazzling streaks of sunlit high vapour from above Pendennis and Falmouth. I turned into Carrick Roads.

It was no hardship counteracting the outgoing tide and light wind with a spot of rowing. An hour after leaving the overnight mooring, a carefree oarsman observed Manacle Point, out to sea beyond the Helford River, appear to move across the entrance of Carrick Roads, finally eliminating the sea horizon.

By a quarter to eight, a breeze on the port beam had generated sufficient power for sailing. Making the most of the rare opportunity I relaxed, leaning against the painting stool and working the tiller with my feet. Between salt-stained boots I watched Pendennis and Falmouth recede as I edged down the east side of the channel. Two miles on I negotiated a bunch of moored sailing yachts in St Just Pool. After passing smaller boats in the creek entrance, I headed into a narrow tree-lined waterway, hoping to glimpse the picturesque waterside church that nestles in the woodland. Rapidly receding water forced me to retreat after travelling a few hundred yards. During my hasty return to deeper water, guiding Epic between emerging mud banks, I sighted the square church tower off to my left, tucked away in a secondary creek.

Around half past nine, in strengthening wind, under darkening sky, Epic rushed towards Feock at the head of Carrick Roads – four and a half miles from the open sea. Power from the red jib alone created a long wake as the little boat hissed through the water. The wind remained strong, but seemed less aggressive after I slackened the sheet and bore away to starboard, entering the pool at the bottom of Trelissick House garden. That stretch of water constitutes the mouth of the river Fal that narrows immediately upstream to two hundred yards. On reaching the 'narrows' I was taken aback, finding myself heading towards the bows of a twenty two thousand ton tanker. The vastness of the mothballed leviathan was emphasized by the intimate surroundings and the fact that it took me several minutes to pass the towering side of the surreal phenomenon, Methane Princess.

Less than a mile into the Fal I passed the peaceful setting of the King Harry crossing. Thirty or so vehicles can be conveyed on the ferry that rumbles across the river. Twin engines drive cogs against fixed chains that are lifted from, and lowered back, to the riverbed. The crossing shortens a journey between St Mawes and Falmouth by fifteen miles, providing a restful interlude on a trip through beautiful countryside – a 'win, win' experience.

To starboard, half a mile further on, stands the Smugglers' Cottage, a thatched, multi-chimneyed restaurant commanding an imposing site on a right-hand bend. It can be reached at all states of the tide via a pontoon incorporating a large fishing boat. The enchanting, creeper festooned building was, at the time, the ultimate in tranquil seclusion –

though the garden was equipped with tables and chairs, suggesting outdoor catering. I tied Epic to the pontoon boat, proceeded up the gangway and entered a welcoming interior, tastefully bedecked with interesting nautical artefacts. Some items indicated that the scenic setting played a secretive roll in Second World War naval strategy. (Something to do with 'D day', I believe).

Fifteen minutes before opening time I confronted the bar that looked temptingly under starting orders. Before the 'off', I finely tuned my taste buds by wandering down to the foreshore. From there I looked across at the dinghy, inconspicuous alongside the fishing boat. I remembered how cramped and unstable pre-Epic had seemed when I first stumbled aboard at Lostwithiel. Over the previous weeks I had become used to spending prolonged hours ensconced and found the space available for captain and accoutrements perfectly adequate.

Having chosen luncheon from a long table laden with pies, hams, quiches and mouth-watering puddings, I sat down to dine overlooking the river. The tide was turning. In a couple of hours I could easily have reached Truro, a mere four miles away. My emotions were mixed – contentment, with a touch of melancholy due to the fact that I wished the voyage could continue. Earlier I had contemplated exploring the continuation of the Fal up to Ruan Lanihorn, three miles to the east. Recharged, I rejoined Epic for a ride to Ruan.

Somehow the River Fal eluded me, though even at low tide the junction with the Truro River is a hundred yards wide. The cause surely would be the denseness of the wooded hillsides, rather than the navigator. Perhaps I was not paying full attention – the voyage-end being nigh. Oblivious of the error I headed north for one and a half miles, reaching an alternative confluence. Sailing the final few hundred yards up to the junction involved much tacking into a strong gusty wind which blew down from Malpas. What with all the fussing with tiller and sheets, and avoiding small boats on moorings, there was little time to enjoy the visual delights of Malpas village; though I did happen to notice a group of pontoons with berths for a dozen or so craft. By this time I was aware of my navigational blunder, but still had a multiple choice. Should I, (a) go back? (b) turn left? (c) turn right? (d) tie alongside? A left turn would have taken me towards the city. If I waited till after the weekend, for high spring tides, there would be a fair chance of taking Epic right into the heart of Truro. In the meantime, there was time for more exploration – so right it was.

In more sheltered waters, with a favourable beam wind, I enjoyed a gentle tide-assisted sail. Expanding patches of blue infiltrated the grey sky. Seductive silence, together with welcoming sunshine, brightened my afternoon as I sailed up to the picturesque village of St Clement. The rising river and wooded banks were still separated by inconvenient mud margins. Mud also formed a large plateau in front of the village, seeming to preclude a visit. With the wind dropping and the river filling at its quickest, I used the oars for steerage. I drifted on a few hundred yards to a spot where a couple of small boats were afloat towards the village (port) side of the river. They were tied to running lines a little way off a rudimentary landing spit, built from rocks taken from the lumpy, mud encased foreshore. Grounding Epic, I stepped onto the precarious surface and made my way twenty tortuous yards to the riverside path, edged with timber stakes and planks. I tied an extended painter to the woodwork, then stumbled back down to the dinghy where I cunningly placed a heavy rounded rock on the line, leaving about twenty 'free' feet (precisely) between rock and boat. As the river rose, Epic would ride to the free section of mooring line. On my return, a sharp tug would theoretically free her. I had not forgotten my previous snatching debacle on the Tamar, but thought the scheme had a fair chance of saving the hull from a prolonged dragging on the rocky riverbed.

Close to the river at St Clement stands a varied assortment of dwellings, from small cottages to ample three storey houses. They are as different in design as in building materials – a pleasant mixture of stone, slate, brick and thatch. When the river had risen sufficiently to carry Epic to the tidal limit, I returned to the riverside to find three boats swinging nonchalantly midstream. I jerked the painter of the small white one, reeled her in, boarded and sailed upstream in the fading wind – just like that.

Two miles 'later', in late afternoon sunshine, I reached the road bridge at Tressillian – the end of the line. I rowed back down the river a few hundred yards to glide onto the back lawn of the Wheel Inn. With no mud in sight, stepping ashore was most satisfying. Doubly so in fact, having landed on the green, green grass of a beer garden.

While 'testing' a pint of mild, I sought and received from David, a most genial landlord, permission for Epic to remain at the bottom of his garden for a couple of days. With higher tides to come, I thought it wise to haul Epic a few yards onto a slightly raised grassy mound. Other than an occasional visit to the bar there was nothing more stressful to do, while waiting for a lift home, than to oversee the draining of the Tresillian River. The waters receded, revealing the remains of two boats. I did not dwell on the cause of their sorry state; it was too peaceful an evening for such sobering thoughts.

Toby and Robin were at a loose end the following evening, so we made haste to Tresillian. The Sunday excursion saved me from making a three and a half mile boat trip against the tide at a very early hour the next day. It was much easier to set off from the pontoons at Malpas on a rising tide, rather than to launch down the bank through the muddy boat graveyard. We arrived at the beer garden at high water (half past seven) to find calm water lapping Epic's underside. Had I not moved the dinghy to higher ground, with such precise judgment, Epic may have started without me. My sons had only seen me afloat in calm backwaters. If my craft had gone AWOL, my credibility would have been seriously jeopardized. We were soon to rendezvous at a Malpas pub, where the boys would engage in humorous discourse regarding an intrepid mariner, wont to voyage 'huge' distances between public houses.

Disturbing the reflection of the tree-lined bank opposite, Epic entered the water. Leaving the flooded paddy field-like area, I set off at great speed. (Great speed for a rowed Mirror that is.) With oar-blades leaving duplicate, double boat-length spaced trails of rings behind, I sped downstream. At St Clement I paused to drift quietly into the 'village pond' – the river having covered the 'plateau'. The scene was reminiscent of a popular English landscape painting. Had an old farm cart stood in the water, I would have beheld a Constable. There was even a dog at the pond's edge – possibly a police dog.

Rapidly completing my evening exercise, I hitched Epic to the Malpas pontoon. On seeking permission for the boat's overnight stay, I was informed that the proprietor could be located a few yards up the hill. The 'pontoon man' from whom I booked a berth for the night was

St Clement

10" x 11"

'Had an old farm cart stood in the water, I would have beheld a Constable.
There was even a dog at the pond's edge – possibly a police dog.'

seated on the veranda outside the Heron pub, in close proximity to Toby and Robin. After I had popped down to secure Epic, we enjoyed a relaxing interlude overlooking the stunning river panorama. Still water reflected pearly pink clouds, veiling the evening sun. I hoped the next day would dawn as fair for my short trip into Truro.

Peace reigned. The village and river were deserted. Mist was clearing when I cast off early the next morning. With slow, easy strokes, I rounded the point to rejoin the Truro River. Soon I glimpsed the vaguely discernible, principal pinnacle of the cathedral, rising from the misty blue. Although the symbolic finishing post was still two miles away, I felt an uneasy feeling, akin to the apprehension felt when setting off from Morwellham Quay. My trip somehow had its own time, separated from reality to a degree, requiring a period for synchronization.

The smaller twin towers of the cathedral took form. Trees to port gave way to wharfs. Nature's tide-line tangs were replaced by industrial odours. A throbbing generator drowned the restful, rhythmic sound of my lightly splashing oars. The distant hum of motor traffic impinged as I passed by a mini residential, dockland type development. I imposed on a row of sleepy old waterside factories. Vast doorways leading nowhere; no hanging hooks; no cargoes lowered into holds. The weary structures reflected their presence in forlorn contrast to the red-rimmed supermarket opposite, obscuring for a while, the triple spire reflections. (The tired buildings have been rejuvenated. Perhaps one day the waterways will be taken back into the heart of a city desecrated by a dual carriageway.)

Even with the short mast down, the extreme height of the 'spring loaded' river prevented Epic passing under the road bridges. While waiting for the water level to drop a few inches I tied alongside Phoenix Wharf, close to the Radio Cornwall building. As I was floating around nearby, I decided to call at the studios and mention my voyage. At reception, I was invited to call back later – it was rather early.

Within a minute of rejoining Epic, I had unscrewed a shackle, laid down the mast inside the boat and was heading towards the dual carriageway bridge. There seemed ample headroom (about three feet) when I entered the space beneath the highway, but by the time I reached the far side, the clearance had halved and my head was pressed against the gunwale with coarse concrete passing an inch from my cheek – a close shave. Passing from the gloom, I squeezed into bright sunshine and was soon gliding under a graceful, shallow-arched, timber footbridge; then onwards, beneath the stone arch of Bridge Street, bridge. The sun-drenched east side of the cathedral shimmered its reflections on the flooded river before me. It was all pretty perfect – a fine finishing.

Assisted by the falling tide I returned to the radio station. My story appealed, and a live interview on board Epic was arranged for the following morning.

The day dawned misty, with a promise of precipitation. The harbour people had allowed me to moor overnight against a floating pontoon, just a hundred yards from the radio studios. That kindness enabled me to be on station without complication. I cleared and sponged the damp decks and placed a piece of polystyrene on the mast step for the interviewer to sit on.

Following a precarious embarkation, and despite Epic sitting low in the water, the interview was a buoyant affair. Accompanied by unusual interference – rattling oars on rowlocks, spasmodic traffic noise and parrot-like squeaks from Ted's foam seat, we chatted for a while about the trip. Within a minute or so it began to rain.

Pride Of The Fleet

The GCE (General Certificate of Education) year at Stourbridge was a time of impatient expectation. Though really at school, we were creeping from our chrysalises. Still in limbo, we felt the presence of our destiny – downstairs. Prior to mutating, we glimpsed paint splattered older students moving huge canvasses into their tangy turpentine lairs. For the time being we contented ourselves with poster paints. The life-room door was closed. We had to curb imaginations, particularly when pretty, dressing-gowned models flitted by.

Though jeans and jumpers set us apart from regular sixth formers, there was still a fair amount of academic work to contend with. English language and literature, art history and architecture, all had to be digested; and I had my fill. Getting to grips with that side of things was a bit of a drag. Mighty as the pen may be, I could not wait to swap it for the paintbrush. Though doing my best, I still managed to fail both Englishes. Somehow I slipped through the net without obtaining the 'compulsory' 'oh' levels.

The following year I became a First Year Intermediate – metamorphosis complete. Of the two main subspecies, the jangling, pendant-sporting tribe, whose assorted metalwork would include the mandatory Ban the Bomb symbol, were the majority. They would be beaded, and bedecked in bright multicoloured, oversized clothing. So different to the 'Beardsley black', minimalist dressers, floating around seemingly deep in thought, their only adornment a small Ban the Bomb badge. Much time and thought was taken cultivating the 'I don't care what I look like' look.

There was so much to be discovered. I immersed myself in drawing and painting, ceramics and sculpture, anatomy and painting from life. I delved into the lives and works of painters, sculptors and architects. All held me captive. I could not get enough. There was fascination in subjects not listed for examination. There was time to return to the studios and work until late – when the caretakers locked us out. There was even time to fail English language, again. Duty also called for plenty of recreation. To miss the odd night's sleep was almost obligatory. How else could you manage to hitch a lorry ride to London to see the exhibitions?

Bear Pit

21½' x 14½' 1960

'For the time being we contented ourselves with poster paints. The life-room door was closed. We had to curb imaginations, particularly when pretty, dressing-gowned models flitted by.'

Horizons expanded. Train travel for me virtually ceased when I became the proud owner of a hundred and fifty cc Frances Barnet motorcycle.

In due course I became a Second Year Intermediate. Still retaining the Frances Barnet, I got into cars (not with the motorbike of course). Before the ill-fated Wolsey came along, I had brief associations with Austin Seven and Morris Eight types of transport. All my vehicles were reaching the end of their useful life – whether they knew it or not.

To supplement my educational grant, and help finance my addiction to clapped out cars, I undertook weekend and holiday jobs. One position which took a bit of getting used to was the milk round. Early starts in sub-zero temperatures were bad enough, but having to load up from the cold store was sheer misery. There followed a stint working in an out of town bakery, assisting Jim – 'Cottage Loaf' patron to be. There was a similar nocturnal start at four in the morning. Compensation for turning out at such a gruesome hour on cold winter mornings was the comforting warmth from the bread ovens. Being involved in production gave great job satisfaction. Being responsible for rows of doughnuts creeping across greaseproof-paper lined wooden trays was very satisfying. The ring doughnuts were coated with sugar, and the round ones inseminated with jam – there was never a dull moment.

On the subject of employment (triggered by jam doughnuts), I am reminded of a comical (in hindsight) situation at a police station, following a fracas on the steps of a dance hall. I imagine we were rejected and ejected for not wearing ties – shameful. To defend our friend, who had been caught up in a fist scuffle with a bouncer, to the satisfaction of the constabulary, we first had to give our names and occupations. Scott was a carpet tuner and Rob a turkey inseminator – truly.

Having a driving licence increased work opportunities. I became a grocery deliverer on Saturdays, serving the district round Tenbury Wells. I was seventeen, with weeks of driving experience. Though too young to drive, Brian was on board as navigator, qualifying as son of the grocery store manager. It was an old fashioned emporium, displaying sacks of foodstuffs, and mahogany-lidded tin chests graced with fancy 'fairground' lettering, advertising teas, coffee, etc. I kept my little used motorbike in an old stable off the entry that led from Teme Street (the main-street) to the shop's garages. (The horses were long gone.) The business had just acquired a new mobile shop – the pride of the fleet. Not having a particularly large chassis, it overhung in all directions – imagine a mobile shed. Most vans at the time had bonnets, but this one had a flat front. The dark green monster swayed about alarmingly, particularly off road when making farm deliveries. Heavy items were positioned low down for stability, and to eliminate serious head wounds. Bread was kept in the rack above the driver. Early into the round it was not unusual to be attacked by the odd cottage loaf or bloomer.

On an isolated farm track one afternoon, I was having problems with a snowdrift. We had nearly completed the round when it became necessary to use the van as a snowplough ('me lud'). After a few charges, the non-angled front built up an impenetrable barrier before snapping, leaving a jagged, spiky edge, a foot above where the bottom of the mobile shop had been. With the aid of a few shovelled heaps of ash spread around the wheels, ramming procedure was repeated in reverse gear, creating another impenetrable barrier, finally trapping the beast. The ash was not a stock item; it was taken on board for such an eventuality.

The farmer, whose wife was expecting a couple of large sandwich loaves, fixed a chain from the front of his tractor around our back axle and slowly dragged the swaying van, ignominiously, back down the track. At one point, wishing to help and show I was not completely useless, I did a spot of reversing. The farmer, in straightening up the tractor was moving forward. Our combined speeds enabled the lengthy gearbox protrusion on the front of the Massey Ferguson to penetrate the aluminium back panel of the van. With dismay, I looked over the melting snow and ashes that caked the floor. Occupying space inside the rear of the 'pride of the fleet' was a large portion of tractor. At least it was dark, and the shop closed, when I drove quietly up the entry to the sanctuary behind 'Gaius Smiths, Grocer and Baker – Deliveries Undertaken'.

Being an art student, one was expected to be a little different. I fashioned my hair in what some termed the French style – later called a Beatle's haircut. A short while after the van incident, I was fortunate to watch a pop group performing at the Saturday dance, held at the Bridge Hotel, by the river (the other end of Teme Street from my pottery workshop). On that day, the group reached number one in the charts for the first time. We were honoured that they fulfilled a long-term booking commitment and performed their brand new hit along with a few other numbers. Yeah, they were great, with neat, no collar jackets, and hair done in the French style. After forty minutes, they pushed past us with their guitars, heading for immortality.

Red Admiral, Blue Bosun
Ruan Lanihorne to Smugglers' Cottage

Half a mile from Ruan Lanihorne, a narrow lane runs alongside the little Ruan River. There is an abundance of green and quiet, and a riverside lay-by is not all it seems. Twin stone bollards suggest an occasional wharf, available when tidal water rises above the mud to infiltrate the reedy grasses.

Freshly painted and gleaming brightly white, Epic was tethered to the upstream bollard, ready for the voyage to continue. Raising the mast and attaching the shrouds and forestay after the long intermission seemed like a replay. Though a different tidal river, it was the same date (5th July) but two years later. Upstream, by the side of the lay-by / quay, the bank was cushioned with soft lush grass. From that natural slipway, watched by a pair of gleaming white swans, Robin and I launched the dinghy, soundlessly into still water.

Realizing food was not in the offing, the swans glided off downstream interrupting the calm surface that reflected the clear evening sky. Robin thought he would join them. We set the Bosun (of which more later), fitted the centreboard and rudder, and with a light wind occasionally providing steerageway, he crept down the creek. When it became apparent the tide was turning, Robin did likewise and rowed back to the lay-by.

The falling river level hastened our loading. With buckets and bags on board, and the red jib secured at the base of the forestay, I cast off. Exchanging 'See you soons', I rowed away from Ruan Wharf. Soon the old Ford was out of sight. The engine sound faded. Silence.

Red Admiral

Robin was nineteen, the same age as Toby had been when he ferried me to the Tamar at the beginning of my Mirror meanderings. Robin had transported Epic and me to the quiet lay-by location, five miles south of Truro. High (spring) tide was around eight o'clock that evening. Butterflies prevented a morning start. It was not a fear of the 'north five, occasionally six' shipping forecast, for I would be in sheltered waters for a while, but two five by five feet canvasses. One depicted a tortoiseshell, the other a red admiral. The large oil paintings seemed fairly abstract at first glance – the 'sitters' bringing their own powerful, personal arrangements to the compositions, leaving me little more than managing magnification.

I had overseen the hanging of the paintings in the new Crown Court in Truro. The building preceded the new Tate Gallery (opened two weeks earlier in St Ives) by a few years. The same architects were employed on the projects which featured expansive white-walled interiors – hungry for paintings. Judge Taylor thought it a good idea to enhance the Court with works of art. So it was thanks to the 'hanging Judge' that my mind was taken away from my return to the tributaries for a few hours (including the 'elusive' Fal – almost explored two years earlier).

Where was Epic bound? Nostalgia suggested St Ives where I spent that long hot summer. From the kitchen window of the second hotel in which I worked, when stockpot tending allowed, I gazed over Porthmeor at scenes captured by a plethora of painters over the last century. The assistant chef, with doughnut experience, did more than avert his gaze from the simmering bones. A descriptive oil painting depicting a 'Tateless' view of the beach, buildings and Island, accompanied me home after an exciting and varied six-month sojourn.

As a destination for Epic, St Ives, though desirable, seemed out of the question. Wild water, off the Lizard, Land's End and Cape Cornwall, was reason enough to suggest a South Coast destination.

Blue Bosun

Light wafts ruffled the river surface as I reached the junction with the River Fal, a couple of hundred yards on from the wharf. It was a good feeling to finally arrive at the upper reaches, even though navigation was car assisted. In the lee of the hillside alongside the Ruan River, I had been protected from the fresh north wind that suddenly blew up. I unfurled the Bosun from round the mast and held the short line that Robin had used as a sheet. The wind gained a little more puff and soon Epic was racing downstream. A lake, about a mile long and half as wide, is formed at the tidal limit of the Fal. As I entered the empty stretch of water, a strong gust detached the sheet from the sail. Though the short sheet Robin attached was a temporary measure, I should have checked the knot was not. That hectic few minutes taken to restrain the thrashing fabric, wrapping it back round the mast and attaching a longer sheet, not only tested the new Bosun, but shook me from my reverie. Pondering probable destinations could wait awhile. With two turns round the mast, reducing the sail area by two thirds, I carried on, paying greater attention to the matter in hand.

Epic was in a backwater, left of the main channel, while the 'lake' was rapidly draining. Heading for deeper water, where the river narrowed, I started to negotiate a one hundred and eighty degree bend round to the left. Progress seemed to have slowed. It certainly had. The centreboard had imperceptibly buried itself into soft mud, trapping the dinghy. Not wishing to test the squidgy depth, while wearing my new green wellies with pristine soft linings, and with thoughts of my Tamar mud experience looming large, I frantically heaved out the muddy board and set to with the oars, digging them into the mud, forcing Epic through the receding few inches of water. Mission accomplished, I let Epic drift to the outer edge of the river, out of the wind in the protection of a high wooded bank. Partly submerged dead trees, 'lichened' light grey/green, formed half hidden obstructions. I carefully looped the painter over a brittle branch, bringing the dinghy to rest. I stowed the gear, making Epic as shipshape as a 'ship' that shape could be.

Cut off from all outside pressures I was happily adrift. My physical

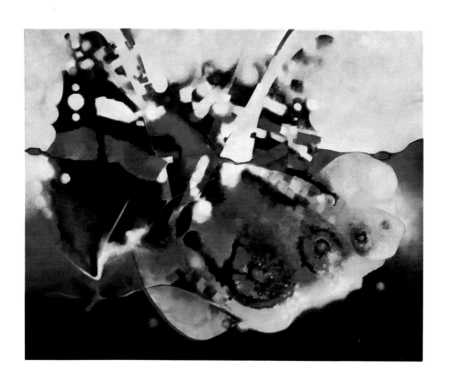

Red Admiral, Blue Bosun
Oil on canvas 6'4"x 5'2"   2001
(The details of the 'Bosun' are in fact taken from a Blue Pansy, tropical butterfly.)

responsibilities for the time being were within arms' reach. The changing 'riverscapes' would again remind me of past happenings, as had the launch site – taking me back to a time when another full river invaded grassy margins. Aged eleven, armed with a newly acquired tank (as in military) aerial fishing rod, I was on my first solo sortie to the mighty River Severn that was heavily in flood. From the brown cloudy water, where cows had grazed a few days before, I pulled a monstrous fish. I recall the thrill of an invisible power bending my aerial into a tight curve. (It snapped later.) My chub, in reality, weighed only a pound and a half-ounce, but to me it was a leviathan compared to the bullheads and minnows previously taken on stick and thread from the little brook nearer home. In the following years I made weightier conquests – flicking flies, low under branches, tempting wary brown trout. ('Brown trout' – more like, 'gold flanked with rubies, trout'.) That incongruous happening on the Severn, grass carrying on being grass despite being under water, still brings back that happy recollection.

Totally unwound and without schedule, I wondered whether to spend the night hitched to the tree or to carry on down to the Smugglers Cottage. Though I wanted to take time adjusting to the floating life again, I harboured a tingling impatience to cross the track of the previous voyage. I opted for a lazy, tide assisted row down to the Smugglers, three miles away. Soon after reaching the Truro River junction I turned left, tied Epic to the pontoon and made my way up the gangway. Entering the inn again, I relaxed to enjoy a bowl of minestrone and a nightcap pint. Soon I would be heading seaward, starting another adventure. It all felt so familiar, and very exciting.

Epic had been laid up for two winters prior to the lay-by launch, necessitating a thorough seeing to. (You may not find the critical mix of glass-fibre, folding sections and double skinned boxes gripping. If that is the case, feel free to skip a page or two.) When cleaning the bottom of the dinghy in preparation for painting, I noticed cracks where the plywood panels almost met. After a trip to a 'do it yourself store', I did, and became a second-class, glass-fibre repair exponent. The kit consisted of two square feet of coarse glass matt, a tin of sticky resin, a small tube of hardener, one mixing beaker, one brush and a sheet of black sanding paper. Having cleansed the 'wounds', I prepared my first mix. Within minutes, the equipment was depleted disproportionately to results. A hard hot lump of resin claimed my beaker and brush. (A smaller smidgen of hardener was required.) Never having been fond of clear resin paperweights containing hapless livestock, such as crabs, I was even less enamoured finding my brush encapsulated. Having mastered the critical mix, manufactured disposable brushes from broom bristles, and acquired a quantity of foil take-away containers (I had beef curry and fried rice), I administered patches, rendering the hull sound. Rubbed down and painted, the surgical quality, texturally speaking, was surprisingly acceptable. Further treatment inside the hull was required where glass-fibre tape seams had come adrift. The most acute I repaired, resisting the temptation to treat them all. A probing fingernail suggested many remaining seams were of cosmetic value only.

To make sleeping on 'board' more comfortable, I cut a hinged section from a portion of the hinged floor of a defunct rubber dinghy. This removable unit fitted between the foredeck and thwart (seat), and each side lifted independently for access. A bright red, double-skinned picnic box replaced a lidded plastic bucket. The insulated container, as well as preventing Mars bars melting, was used with the centreboard and folding section to form a relatively flat sleeping surface.

An indispensable addition to the inventory, worth almost its weight in gold, was half a battered polystyrene surfboard – one of those small rectangular ones, used for body boarding. I hoped not to require the floatation properties of the ultra-light, thermal cushion-cum-lifebuoy. On previous occasions, while sitting on the floor of the dinghy to aid stability, a mere trickle of water on board would find its way to my backside. Soaked jeans take so long to dry.

To retain the two jib system, dispensing with the boom and gaff again, I required a second sail. A high price was paid for being a jib short on my last sea leg. Being unsuccessful seeking a second Mirror jib, after visiting several dealers in second-hand nautical bits, I eventually purchased a specimen that had been parted from a Bosun dinghy. It was blue, in fair condition and only three feet too long. I cut the wire edged side towards the top and secured it round a cringle. (Cringle – an eye at the edge of a sail formed from a thimble. [A thimble is like a cringle without a hole, except in nautical terms when it becomes a grommet, also known as a cringle.] And there you have it.) After trimming away excess material, it was a simple matter to fold and tape the cut edge.

My new sail was christened Blue Bosun. The red Mirror jib, for obvious reasons, I named the Red Admiral. It was fitting that the butterfly sail, having served longer, should hold higher rank.

From the groundsheet of a tattered and torn two-man tent, I fashioned a rudimentary detachable shelter. After two wet summers, the cover seemed a useful addition. The opening end was fastened to the mast, and the sides fixed under the gunwales with loops over small round-headed screws. Large knots in the heavy material kept the stern corners in place. The end result was far from chic – a veritable Vivienne Westwood – the colour clashing awfully with the Bosun's blue. To provide limited crouching, the aft end was raised by halyard. The smallness of the enclosure was of no consequence, for I intended doing very little crouching.

Raw Chips
Smugglers' Cottage to Penryn

After a pleasant hour ashore at the Smugglers', as dusk was deepening, I rejoined Epic and continued down the Fal. Half a mile on, on the right hand side of the river, I hitched to another dead tree that overhung deep water. Unlike the previous 'tree stop', the location would not dry out. In near darkness I arranged my bed. Within five minutes of wriggling into the sleeping bag, the moon, large and intensely white, rose above the treetops, bathing the riverscape in silvery half-light – heaven. After five minutes the blessed silence was shattered. A generator on one of two cargo vessels anchored a quarter of a mile upriver, just past the King Harry Ferry, erupted into life. In a short while, the diesel fumes, having travelled four hundred and forty yards got right up my nose. With my hearing and sense of smell invaded, I prepared to exit before an outbreak of blindness ensued. After rowing a mile or so downstream, round to the right, I eventually tied to a mooring buoy in the large pool below

Trelissick House. It was about eleven thirty when I re-bagged. Outside my cosy bag, the temperature dropped to an uncomfortable chill.

My first night in Epic for two years was a cold affair. The thermal properties of the sleeping bag diminished as it soaked up the dew – which I should have expected. By the time I listened to the shipping forecast at five to six, the lower part of my bag was sopping. The northerly wind would back to the northeast, putting my planned excursions up Restronguet, Mylor and Penryn creeks in jeopardy. There was no hint of wind as I breakfasted on Old Jamaica and water. (Old Jamaica is a chocolate bar. I had not broached the rum cask.) By six thirty five a slight breeze enabled me to boom out the Bosun and head towards Restronguet. Progress was sedate, graced with the low sun over the stern. The odd fish rose, and little birds cheeped from the trees on the shoreline. Unwelcome accompaniment came from raucous rooks – they should have known better at that early hour. The warmth of the sun soon eliminated the wrinkled puffiness of my feet as they rested on the transom. Epic moved well over the calm, near flat sea, passing tree covered mini-cliffs to starboard. I had just passed Feock when a seal popped its head above the surface, gave a cursory glance, and popped it back. There was nothing of interest up-top, its taste being savoury no doubt. The 'visuals' it left for me.

A little after seven, I beached Epic on the gently shelving, stony Loe Beach. There I painted a group of waterside buildings. The unusually early start I found most rewarding – the low sun angle providing strong contrasting sunlight and shadows. Not wishing to drag Epic's thin, newly painted plywood very far over the stones, from where the draining tide had settled the dinghy, I worked at great speed. Tonal composition complete, I pushed off. As is often the case, a work executed without too much fiddling retains vitality, which can be lost with over fussing. The forecast wind wafted away the stillness, hastening me on towards Restronguet Point. During my hurried withdrawal from the scene, I inadvertently left the watercolour on the foredeck (a habit of mine) and was lucky to retrieve it before it was whisked into the briny. Epic came out of the lee, oars replaced sail and I rowed into the wind, struggling against the outgoing tide. Energetically I edged upriver, passing the Pandora Inn to port, a few hundred yards into the creek. A little way past the pub I was forced by fatigue to grab a mooring buoy to save being driven back. (Oh no; not driven back to a pub.) I fed the painter through the handle of, what was in fact, a square, barnacle encrusted, white plastic container (one gallon capacity). There was no way on that tide I could reach Devoran, a mile and a half away at the head of the creek. My sleeping bag which had been on the foredeck in the sunshine, was still soaking wet, so I hoisted it up the mast.

Being out of action for a while, I took the opportunity to rig a cord on my new sunhat – there was never a dull moment. The white cotton replacement was the type cricket players tend to wear these days. It was not so 'Jack Tar' as the previous oatmeal coloured, strong canvas number claimed by Neptune west of Fowey, but I hoped to remain attached to it. Waiting for the tide to turn before trying to head up to Restronguet again, I lay down in the boat for a while, to warm up out of the wind. Rest rendered me restless, so with time on my hands, I decided to pop down to the Pandora for a pint. After lowering the sleeping bag, I cast off from the plastic bottle and arrived post-haste at Pandora's pontoon.

Although low water was at half past one, I had to leave two hours earlier to avoid grounding outside the pub; which would never do. In no time, Epic was back down the creek, sheltering off Restronguet Point, tied to an authentic, large, round, red buoy. A pair of serene swans paid me a visit – at least they appeared serene as they sailed over to me. Their combined neck spans was greater than the dinghy's beam. With probing swans, port and starboard, I thought it best not to attempt bonding with my visitors, for it was not a social call. I was extremely happy to see them huff off after they had thoroughly sampled the textures of my clothing. They were an odd couple with scraggy necks discoloured through dipping in dirty water. One had a torn upper bill, a piece about the size of a child's little finger sticking out at a most uncomfortable looking angle. Poor thing.

Impatience got the better of me. Though the tide had another hour to run out, I decided to set off up the creek again. The wind was stronger than ever, so to reduce drag I unwrapped the Bosun from round the mast, lowered and stowed it. A quarter of a hard fought mile further on, the shallows through which I had been rowing drained away, leaving Epic marooned on a reddish-brown, hard mud spit that divided two channels. With all options taken away, I lay down out of the wind and listened to Radio Four. There were other diversions. I became aware of two men in a boat as small as mine. They came slowly downstream as they vainly attempted to head up, to reach, I assumed, one of many larger grounded boats clustered upstream. Eventually, to save being washed into Carrick Roads they pulled into the shore just below me. My last sight of the ensemble, after they negotiated the mud, was the lurching upturned hull lumbering into bushes like a giant tortoise.

A spit or so away, a man was digging in the mud. There was a remote chance he was digging for treasure, but most likely he was seeking rag or lugworms for fishing bait. Tiring of watching the worm prospector, I returned my attention to Afternoon Theatre on the radio. Through my earphones came the story of a trapped traveller. We had nothing else in common – he being on a train, and in no way to blame for his predicament.

The wind was gusting stronger than ever down the creek. Had I waited for the incoming tide, it would have been very difficult, if not impossible, to row up to Devoran and on to the Norway Inn at Perranarworthal. Epic finally floated. I quickly retreated, rounding the point and rushing two miles down to the harbour at Mylor Churchtown. With Epic tied alongside a heavy wooden pontoon in a sheltered corner, I popped up to the office and asked if my boat could remain there for half an hour or so, as the adverse wind ruled out a visit to Mylor Bridge. As I sat at an outside table at the nearby Lemon Arms, taking lunch of coffee and a toasted cheese sandwich, I felt it more than likely that I would not be heading up the third creek to Penryn. The sea condition was too rough to allow myself to be blown past Pendennis Point into Falmouth Bay, so it was with uncertainty that I set off for Falmouth Harbour. With the Bosun set, Epic hurtled a further two and a half miles against the tide down to Trefusis Point, opposite Falmouth Docks. Up to that point I had been sheltered on flattish water, and to some extent that was true until I began tacking towards Flushing. Little did I realize, I was about to earn my cheese sandwich.

The channel leading up to Penryn, two miles away, was the same heading as the previous two. Still the strong wind blew. Flushing, like

Looe from where I was flushed unwillingly on the last trip, had all the makings of another Waterloo. The waterway was cluttered with boats on moorings, many of them large cruising yachts.

Epic needed a boost if she were to head more into the wind. Feeling the addition of the Admiral would be too much, I broke out 'Son of Bosun'. The four foot long sail was fashioned by sewing tapes to a triangular portion of tent remnants. Though rather flimsy, I hoped it would be 'boy' enough to help Epic – ever the optimist. All went well at first as I threaded the blue-sailed dinghy, back and forth between the boats. I seemed to be pointing well upstream, but made a lot of leeway (sideways slip) and had to slacken off the sails from time to time to pass behind vessels or mooring buoys. Half an hour of frustrating tacking, familiarizing myself with certain craft, particularly one with a large bowsprit just lower than Epic's masthead, gained me no more than a couple of hundred yards. My performance became agonizingly abject when, shortly after disentangling my starboard shroud from the familiar bowsprit, my little sail blew out. An embarrassed Mirror operative, flying a shredded blue 'burgee', headed reflectively to the quieter north shore to take stock.

With the Bosun down, and 'Son of' ready for the first rubbish bin, I commenced rowing. It was tough going, even with assistance from the ingoing tide, until I eventually crept past Flushing where the creek turned a little westerly. In a quiet backwater, I stepped out onto a shingle beach to stretch my legs. Apart from brief pit stops, I had been on board for twenty-four hours. The sky was blue and the wind seemed to be dropping. In good cheer I rowed up to Penryn.

While I was floundering around close to the roadside wharfs, the resident of the Humber Keel, Harlequin, invited me to tie up alongside. The Keel is an oddly named boat – being flat bottomed and having no keel. The barge was the home of Simon, a singer and musician with a theatre group. His floating home contained a cavernous hold, converted into living space, boasting a solid-fuel stove, piano and spiral staircase, and plenty of room to swing several cougars.

Over the road and up the hill a few yards, I chanced upon the Kings Arms from where I phoned a progress report home. I stayed on for supper and a beer, but had no wish to remain till closing time. My fix was the uncharted day ahead. Intoxicated by thoughts of heading seaward again, I rejoined Epic and rowed to a quiet pool a few hundred yards back down the river. With surprising ease I rigged the tent. Soon I was asleep in the privacy of my own small blue world.

I felt secure inside the little tent, a bit like an ostrich burying its head in the sand. (Not a good analogy. I don't think they actually do that. As a survival ploy, it seems a most unlikely tactic, making breathing difficult for a start.) Children love hideouts and dens – I know I did. You feel safe in your own secret place. My friend Colin and I must have been about ten when we went to our camp in a nearby hedge. The intention was to rustle up some chips. The sound of chips sizzling in a baked bean tin was not exactly immediate. In fact, as you might expect, it took a great deal of time for the lard to melt. The pieces of potato coated in luke-warm fat were still totally raw when the candles expired. It was part of life's learning curve. From that episode I learned what terrific value four pennyworths of chips were.

Such experiences must have in some small way contributed to my minimalist approach to voyaging, particularly in the Spartan catering department. Not for a moment did I think to attempt even the simplest form of cooking, and certainly not chips. Peeling bananas and breaking into crisp packets can be taxing enough.

Silver Sardine Band
Penryn to Helford

Epic grounded around midnight and re-floated about four. I cannot be exact, for I slept soundly. The soft mud gently claimed then cradled Epic, and in due course released her to swing against the incoming tide. At five to six I listened to the force three to four forecast. A wind blowing down channel (Atlantic bound) was expected – that would be ideal. It had been another dewy night and the canopy was dripping with an incomprehensible amount of water. The same was true of the varnished interior, as if it had rained inside the tent during the night. If there had been onlookers, it would have appeared I was boat-proud in the extreme as I sponged all surfaces and hoisted the dripping 'rain machine' and sleeping bag. Chores complete, I breakfasted on a couple of bananas.

Before utilizing the fair wind, I decided to paint the buildings towards the head of the creek. By seven o'clock, with moist items up the mast catching the sun, I headed back up to Penryn. To starboard, moored bow to bank, were a couple of dozen varied craft: some laid up; some occupied houseboats; others, terminal cases with submarine tendencies. In close proximity to the 'boat-park', I tied to a mooring buoy and began a painting featuring a large boatshed. Sunlight on boats in front of the dark, open-ended building was the main element. As I worked, cloud cover increased to seventy five percent. During a spell of waiting for the sun to return, I found myself being perused by a river dweller. He may have wondered why I was producing a picture of a ramshackle shed, and why my sky was predominately blue. After a while my scrutinizer popped back down his hatch, knowing I was harmless, and 'what I would take away would still remain', so to speak, give or take a few clouds.

By nine thirty, having packed away my painting equipment, I was exploring the top end of Penryn Harbour. Clouds were dispersing – typical. All was serene as I drifted downriver past the Harlequin. With a following breeze I 'Bosun'd' on down to Flushing. With Epic tied up close to the Fisherman's Jetty, I climbed up onto the quay and ambled over (as if I had just completed the homeward leg on a tea clipper) to the Quay Restaurant. Sitting outside, outnumbered by the congenial staff of two young ladies, I enjoyed morning coffee in the sunshine. It was extremely pleasant just 'being'. The remaining little white clouds sidled away in the direction I would soon be wafted. My caterers assured me Epic would not be in the way while I went to restock the picnic box with crisps and Mars bars. That carefree attitude was the norm. (The unfortunate encounter when I was turned away at St Germans was a rare occurrence. Since then, members of the Quay Yacht Club who were displeased with the non-representative, have contacted me. Visitors are now welcome, and there is a sign to prove it.)

Opulent Flushing looked well cared for. Even a gigantic redundant oil rig, moored close by, seemed to know its place, lurking discreetly just around the headland.

While crossing over to Falmouth I scribbled in my logbook / diary. *'Stopped while rowing (11:51) over to Fal. To say I'm the luckiest person alive'*. Had I not stopped to jot, that moment of utter contentment would have been forgotten, filtered from my mind by later passages. My happiness then, overflowing with optimistic eagerness at the prospect of leaving Carrick Roads, was as great as two years before, when finally entering those sheltered waters after the long haul from Mevagissey – funny old world.

Keeping close to the Falmouth foreshore, I idled by various slipways and quays, both private and public. Grandly restored or derelict, the hop-scotch structures exuded a 'sailory' excitement. From the empty air I conjured sounds and smells from the age of sail: cracking canvas on straining spars, and the tang of tar and oakum. My imagination filled the comparatively empty waters with Tuke's three or four masters at anchor. (Henry Scott Tuke 1858–1929. Newlyn School painter who moved to Falmouth – painted nude boys bathing; also beautiful, accurate presentations of sailing ships. He sailed his own yachts.)

A real taste of bygone working sailing boats is still presented off Falmouth. From the rear of several shops that front the main street, a panoramic view of the vintage racers can be seen. I cannot be the only weekend shopper to abort a mission, tempted away by sails observed through the back window, drawn to the harbour-side to enjoy old gaffers jousting, awed by the graceful, delicate dancing of weighty, straight stemmed, bowsprit sporting craft carrying multitudinous canvas squares and triangles as they race in thunderous flocks through crowded moorings – can I?

A hundred yards or so offshore, at the end of the town's waterfront, I hitched to a mooring buoy off Custom House Quay. It was on the stone steps of that very quay, in the summer of sixty-five, that Robert Manry stepped ashore from his thirteen and a half foot, clinker built, Tinkerbelle, having sailed from Falmouth, Massachusetts. A joint venture in his friend's twenty-five foot yacht was called off, so he used his own little boat for a solo voyage. Having added a tiny cabin to the miniscule family boat, he spent eleven weeks crossing the Atlantic. The story of Tinkerbelle is my favourite sea adventure. Around the time of reading the inspiring account of that voyage, I watched the return to Falmouth of Robin Knox-Jonston in his Ketch Suhaili (hull length – thirty two and a half feet). He also climbed ashore at the Custom House Quay steps. How I wished that I could make a solo ocean voyage.

In the docks nearby, several ocean-going ships were being refitted – vast antifouled hulls, empty, elevated slabs of burnt sienna. When returned to commerce, their destinations would be more distant, but unlikely to be more beautiful than Epic's next port of call – the Helford River, just round the corner.

The wind, quite fresh away from the shelter of the buildings, reminded me to put on my lifejacket. The jacket, comprising front and collar only, is secured round the waist with tapes (imagine me demonstrating the tying, also indicating the whistle with a pretend blow). Do not think of the Michelin man, for virtually deflated it is not at all cumbersome. The backless little number can be worn under a jumper and quickly inflated by mouth if the need arises. I hoisted the Bosun and furled it round the mast ready for rapid deployment. After tidying away loose gear in the foredeck mini-compartments and beneath the folding section, I was set to sail. Within a few hours, the wood-fringed Helford waterways would begin to fill with a new tide – my gratis ride to the upper reaches. I was off to the creeks of intrigue, designated by Daphne.

First I had to escape from the dock area. Oar power was required to negotiate the five hundred yards barrier of bays that hemmed me in. The structure was composed of ranks of huge timbers. The shady labyrinths seemed an ideal setting for mysterious operations; there was space to spare for Mr Big's lair and any number of mini Bond subs. My feverish rowing was mainly to counteract the wind and outgoing stream. Together they made me fight for freedom. Though short of Herculean, the task of passing the pillars was pitifully slow. The reward, when escape from the docks was eventually achieved, was more than fair compensation. With the oars resting along the gunwales, the Bosun eased me past the be-castled headland of Pendennis. Soon Epic and I were chuckling across Falmouth Bay.

I lay with head on hands, elbows on the foredeck, torso on the folding deck modification and legs on the red picnic box. The prone position presented less resistance to the offshore beam wind, and provided me with a great deal of fun. I steered with my feet, and for better vision held the lower edge of the sail up with my hat. Hands free, I was able to use the Ordnance Survey map to determine direction. Although only four miles distant, the mouth of the Helford River was not apparent as I looked obliquely along the coastline. It was not a problem finding my way, but I was in play mode and indulged in a little Captain Cookery. With map and compass I practised navigation. Not surprisingly, for my eyelevel was little more than a foot above sea level, I received the odd face-full of spray as the flat hull slapped the little waves. My spirit was not the slightest bit dampened though.

Before the playful spray ceased being a novelty, the breeze lessened. Arrival off the river mouth was completed with 'just one further ado'. The August Rock is situated a quarter of a mile off Mawnan, between Rosemullion Head and the river. That point is the only blemish on the large blue area of Falmouth Bay depicted on OS 204. To be fair, the sole hazard to be avoided was slightly underwater at the time. There must have been telltale signs of agitated water, but I was too busy navigating to notice. The slight contact was a salutary lesson that left Epic unscathed.

In dying wind I enjoyed a pleasant sail to a point where the river narrows to three hundred yards. I had no wish to chase the yachts that motored past. I was enjoying the delay provided by the fitful breeze. Sedate tacking presented views of details on both shores as the tide moved Epic slowly onwards. Discreet, small-scale structures on the southern side of the river entrance added sympathetic additions to the wooded hillsides and rocky foreshore. A circular fortification and octagonal mini lookout were perfect focal points for paintings. Man's geometry, particularly rustically aged examples, complemented nature's pretty competent arrangements.

At the narrow point, just before Helford Passage on the right and Helford village to the left, I downed sail and commenced a spell of lazy rowing. All was quiet. With inns each side of the river, I resisted the temptation to stop, having succumbed to soothing tranquillity. At five o'clock my idyll was interrupted in a most engrossing way. Three miles into the river, off Frenchman's Creek, a hissing tide-race sound captured my attention. The sight of two or three hundred square yards of broken water, composed of rushing, swirling arcs, was totally out of order. Had I been able to look below the surface, I would have seen, no doubt, a large shoal of fish feeding on very tiny portions of aquatic foodstuff.

Soon I left Groyne Point to the right, opting not to head towards Constantine, favouring the Gweek over the Roman creek. Upriver a few hundred yards, a group of young people were enjoying a barbecue. They had travelled to the secluded spot in dinghies that were tied alongside Tremayne Quay. I increased my row rate and rippled on upstream, leaving them in peace. The quay was built for a visit by Queen Victoria, though she did not make it (the visit that is, not the quay). Something more important than a trip to Helford must have cropped up while the work was in progress. It was pleasing to see that a century and a half later the effort had not been wasted. (Please forgive the lack of historical and architectural information. Had I mentioned all the sites from large stones to old mine workings, and the famous and infamous who trod, or like Queen Vic. nearly trod, I may have lost the gist, along with the will to live.)

Gweek is at the head of the river, six miles from the sea. The ingoing tide slackened, making the final two-mile row into a fresh breeze a hard slog. Until then I had been protected in a tree-lined section. At a fork in the river I turned right, ignoring a sheltered mysterious looking creek that led to Trelowarren Mill, half a mile away. My instinct for adventure was put on hold, for I was famished. An inn, which I hoped to find at

Gweek, was my objective. At a quarter to eight, I tied Epic close by a varied collection of larger craft. Intermingled with rugged houseboat types, which started life as fishing vessels, were serious sailing cruisers undergoing extensive refits.

For a while I sat outside the Black Swan listening to live brass band music and wondering from whence it came, whilst also wondering why I was the only outside patron. It came to me, as my hot vegetarian curry arrived – it was rather chilly (not the curry). Sitting for a while, cooling down after the exercise, rendered me oblivious to the falling temperature. I hurried my curry and withdrew to sup a pint in congenial warmth. Alas, I could not dally, for as my glass was empting, so too was the river.

Boats and banks became silhouettes. The lower sky reflected burning orange onto the water. As I made my way back down to the river, the band blew up again. Gweek Silver Band (not brass as I thought at the time) was practising in a small building just down the road from the pub. Though I saw no alternative venue, it seemed inconceivable that such volume should come from that tiny place. If the structure did not have a 'Tardis tendency', it must have been jammed packed with metal and musicians. With accompaniment from the distant silver 'sardine' band, I boarded Epic, then helped by the wind and falling tide, rowed into the chill dusk.

From deepening darkness came another sound. Far from musical, it was akin to noise made by an unhappy cow. The barking moos, I realised after a spell of confused imaginings, undoubtedly came from Gweek's famous seal sanctuary. Whatever the cause, there was no excuse for the racket. Given the fact that it had free fish, the inmate could have at least been melodious. Peace returned as my enjoyable day drew to a close. I continued rowing into the silent night, wholly content.

It was extremely dark when I arrived at the junction with Frenchman's Creek. Again there were a great number of small fish rising. At several splashes per second, I assumed the shoal was midnight supping on flies – yummy. Leaving the feasting fish behind I entered the narrowing stretch of water, seeking a berth for the night. The creek was quite eerie. From dark crowded banks, limbs from dead tree obstructions faintly fingered the inky sky – oooh. With Epic once again hitched to a dead deciduous, I lay down in my sleeping bag under the bundle of tent that I had no desire to rig. An hour or so later, the Mirror grounded at an extremely uncomfortable angle, due to a build up of creek bed round the submerged boughs of my make-do hitching post. On that slope I suffered. The water rapidly receded from the shallow creek. I dared not move, lest I roll over the three-inch protective freeboard into the ooze, which I imagined to be soft and bottomless. At some point I expected to step into the mud, but meantime, forced myself to endure broken sleep until daylight.

At five, after gingerly extricating myself from the wet bag and tent, I found myself at low ebb. The only way was up; and so it was. I slipped my icy cold feet into my new fluffy lined wellies and, avoiding squelchy areas, stepped onto a surprisingly firmish surface. To counteract the cold, I wandered along the wooded waterside for a while in the twilight. The early half-light of the new day revealed a setting dominated by large rounded root-tops (tree bottoms), upholstered with spongy mosses. It was a place where hobbits and other nether-world creatures might be encountered. Having reminded my legs of their purpose, I headed back to resume my seafaring roll. Glimpsed between trees I beheld a Tolkien-like illustration. The mist-shrouded river crept towards my tiny craft that appeared gripped within a sinister entanglement of weed festooned branches.

The exercise lifted me to the warmer side of freezing. Under a clear sky, coldly holding a half moon, I returned to the listing dinghy as the incoming tide lapped her undersides. By the time my wellies were swilled and glistening on the dewy stern seat, I was afloat. It was a quarter to six. Every item that was not in a polythene bag or on my person, was wringing wet as usual. Seeking the sun I headed to the mouth of Frenchman's Creek.

Anna Hill's early morning shipping forecast came through my earphones. First the good news, '… north-west three …' a wind to take me out of the Helford River, round Nare point and down the coast. Then, '… backing south-west, four to five …' a wind that would blow me speedily offshore. Anna could be wrong; after all, I was on the up.

At six fifteen a lone swan arrived on the scene. It surged down the creek, supercharged by the sound of a breaking bar of Bournville, I assumed. Terminating a period of total calm, the intruder disturbed the glassy surface in a totally unnecessary manner. The swan closed in. Having earlier survived attention from the dishevelled pair, I was not at all intimidated, but to be on the safe side, and keep in the swan's good books, I placed a precious square of chocolate on the gunwale; it was his neck of the woods after all. Without deliberation, my peace offering was beaked off to the bottom of the creek. We elevate them to protected bird status, yet they have absolutely no consideration for others.

A little while later I was floating around in the creek mouth, warming myself in the early sunshine. The dripping bag was hoisted. Like raising the flag, it was becoming a custom. The fish returned on the tide and I was again in the centre of a splashing, flapping circus. Shortly afterwards, a flock of small gulls with black heads (no pimples) joined the fray, adding their link to the food chain. There are times when you have to escape the hurly-burly, so I headed back up the creek to explore the upper reaches. With my back resting against the painting stool and my naked feet raised to the sun, I made my way back up past the submerging mooring tree. Keeping to the sunny side, I watched my 'pennant' sleeping bag cast a moving shadow, 'contouring' the trees above the darker waterline area. Less than a mile on, the inlet petered out in a confusion of fallen trees. I turned Epic round and took my leave of Frenchman's Creek.

With wind assistance I rode on down to the pontoon at Helford Point, disembarked and wandered round the headland to picturesque Helford village. Dwellings, including the waterside Shipwright's Arms (the thatched inn, I nobly left in my wake the previous evening) are situated on the protected slopes of an inlet. I strolled through the village to the top of the hill, and strolled back down again. While reconnoitring I noticed Rose Cottage tea garden, and felt it time to eat.

Checking my watch for the nearness of lunchtime, I found it four or five hours away. Enquiring into opening time I was fortunate to meet Kate, who kindly opened half an hour early, inviting me to take a seat in her sunny retreat. At the onset I intended to take a simple breakfast. My request went something like – "Perhaps a little toast?" Soon I was exercising a most rewarding lack of willpower. The mention of something cooked in a pan or under a grill tipped the balance. The great outdoor fried bacon aroma, wafting from the kitchen, served the coup de grâce.

Eggs, beans, buttered toast and marmalade, a large pot of tea and a glass of fresh orange followed, putting me in sublime cheer. Fully fuelled and feeling on top of the world, I left the small terraced garden – an Eden by another name (Rose Cottage).

In a prominent position, on the point at Helford Point, stands an old wooden seat. Before making my way back to Epic, I sat for a while, looking downriver towards the English Channel. There I would turn right, but where I would end up, I knew not. To my left, clouds were gathering, the lower ones deepening to a darker hue. It seemed Anna might be right. 'Butterfly-time' again.

Beaten Back
Helford to Porthoustock

By eleven o'clock there was full cloud and the wind was getting up, blowing down-river, pressing Epic against the pontoon. I attached both sails but left them furled while I rowed into free water. Soon the Red Admiral (as jib, on the forestay) was taking me out of the Helford River. Fifteen minutes later it was raining. A sharp right-hander out of the estuary and you are in Gillan Harbour. This natural inlet at the mouth of a mile long creek has a lesser St Anthony on the north shore and a lesser Flushing on the south. A stranger, blundering into this peaceful backwater, may wonder at the rearrangement and shrinking of Carrick Roads. It was pleasant pottering around the sheltered confines in the light greyness. A group of hardy youngsters, quite beyond the call of duty to my mind, were swimming. Perhaps their stalwartness aided my decision to sail the three miles to Porthhallow for a rain check. I would utilise the last of the outgoing tide and the offshore west wind that was reaching its useful maximum for me. Rounding a lesser Nare Head (the proper big one is to the east of Carrick Roads) I headed south.

Feeling my time at sea might be coming to an end for the time being did nothing for my spirit. It had reached its zenith and was starting to dip. The continuing dreary weather was partly to blame. My short passage to Porthhallow was satisfyingly uneventful, and the offshore wind made beaching a simple, dry operation. It was two thirty. With the

Porthoustock

7½" x 19"

'Porthoustock awaited my pleasure (though I did not know at the time).'

tide almost out and Epic tethered to a heavy stone on the grey shingle, I was free to wander. A row of fishing boats had been winched above the high tide line. Beyond, as luck would have it, stood a pub. From dipping, my spirit level angled upwards; then sadly nosedived. The notice board outside the Five Pilchards read – 'Closed 2:30-7:00'. If chalk could talk, that sign would have whispered, 'So there'.

A little way up the hill I entered a secluded teagarden (a phase I was going through) and was soon taking tea together with a large piece of homemade fruitcake. Again I was the sole customer, as if on a crusade not to allow seaside caterers to be without custom. While weighing up the chance of wind moderation with the lady of the cake, a passionate horticulturist, one of her numerous potted plants was blown off a nearby wall. Omen-like, the pot smashed before me. Had it hit me on the head I may have taken heed. Back down on the beach a small group of fishermen were standing by their boats. I asked the most senior if he thought it safe for me to be sailing on the two miles to Porthoustock. Receiving an OK, with qualification that I keep well inshore, I set off.

Swift progress was made till abeam another grey shingle beach. Porthoustock awaited my pleasure (though I did not know at the time). At both ends of the beach stood large concrete constructions. A forty-foot high rectangular silo, built for loading crushed stone into ships, guarded the north side. The silo was defunct, its sombre presence suggesting a stark fortification. Ahead was Manacle Point, ending in four or five pointy pinnacles stepping seaward. The tide was turning against me (how true) but there was plenty of wind to counteract its early contra-flow, so I decided to carry on.

When supposedly rounding the series of ten to fifteen foot high outcrops, for some strange reason I aimed at the gap between numbers three and four (in from the sea). Losing the wind in the narrow channel coincided with the swell lowering Epic onto a previously submerged rock. Swiftly hauling out the centreboard I soon had the chaos in full swing, with the oars making contact with both sides of the gulley. The laces held the oars to the rowlocks and rowlocks to the gunwale (as they should have done) causing great hindrance as I tried to push off with one oar and paddle Red Indian style. Progress was tortuous. With restricted manipulation of oar, and galvanised rowlock clanging against rock and hull, Epic was lucky to lose nothing more than a touch of her new white paint. She could so easily have tipped over on projecting ledges when scraping down the barnacled sides of the passage. The silly thing is, I was not even trying to save time – just having fun. What a foolish thing to do.

Once in the clear I tacked down the coast, close inshore, well inside the Manacles – a group of sinister rocks that lie one mile out to sea. The hazardous cluster, mostly hidden at high tide, is the graveyard of numerous vessels. Many masters of commercial sailing ships in the past came to grief there, paying the ultimate price for corner cutting.

Black clouds were congregating, spreading gloom. Pushing against the tide slowed me down. Three miles on from Porthallow, through a gap between Lowland Point and Great Wrea – a group of rocks just off the Point – I sighted Coverack. Three times I tried to pass that final barrier. The sails provided plenty of power and I was well in control, but alas, the tide was too strong. Offshore tacks had to be terminated within a few hundred yards of the shore, for sea conditions were too much to cope with further out. The tide was extremely rapid at the Point, each time ending my inshore tacks inside the Great Wrea. Perhaps it was as well, for had I got round, the wind that had backed southwest could have cast Epic ashore, short of our destination. Coverack was tantalizingly close. Another mile and we would have reached an area protected by high land around the little harbour; but it was not to be. I could do no more, unlike the time off Falmouth when I should have used full sail to push Epic harder, so as not to make such a spectacle of myself.

I did something rather foolish on my last tack out, close to Lowland Point. To reduce wind interference I lay down and steered with my feet. The jib sheet was locked in the portside clam-cleat (a device with spring loaded toothed cams that grip lines when under pressure, and will release with a reverse pull.) Because the Bosun's sheet was squeezed into a flimsy 'polytheney' type plastic fitting, I put a turn round the rowlock for good measure. I crashed along at a fair pace, grasping the gunwales to stay on board. Both sails bulged tautly under the strain, tipping the boat to starboard, utilising the few precious inches of freeboard. A gust dipped the lee gunwale into a wave. I tried to push the tiller down to head into the wind and release the pressure on the sails, but my foot slipped. As I yanked the Admiral's sheet free, I tumbled into the watery, starboard side of Epic, along with the red picnic box and other odds and ends. Nothing was lost. The shroud (don't worry, its one of the three wires that stay the mast) helped me stay on board. Broadside to the wind, I spent a few frantic seconds releasing the dangerously secured sheet. Though damp, I was instantly safe. Apart from flapping sails, order returned. I drifted to the northeast with plenty of time to take stock before the odd Manacle could intervene. Deceptively quickly, and under jib alone, I headed back down the coast, keeping well inshore of course.

For the first time since leaving Morwellham Quay I was forced to retreat (or second if you count the 'faffing' around at Restronguet). On my struggle out to Lowland Point I passed a pier, alongside which a large cargo boat (or should I say ship) was waiting to take on board a load of crushed grey stone from a conveyor running along a high gantry. The pier, half a mile from Lowland Point, has a small sandy beach on the south side where I landed. As the hull touched the sand I jumped from the dinghy and, with help from a breaking wave, hauled Epic a few yards up the beach. The loading of the cargo ship (you can put a boat on a ship but not a ship on a boat) had just started, and I wondered how long it would take to convey ten thousand tons or so of stone into the hold. At the time I was hoping to leave Epic at the quarry. My intention was to make the request after the ship was loaded. While the operation continued, I untied the sails and removed most of the gear, stacking it at the top of the beach. The waves at the time were little flippers, no more than a foot high, but I repeatedly had to go to Epic's aid as she turned broadside and bumped against the beach, taking fountains of sandy water up the centreboard slot.

With my charge tethered to a long line, I passed a depressing hour fending off. I landed at seven o'clock, hours before high tide. To cheer myself up, as I stood in the drizzle watching the surprisingly rapid loading of the chippings, I munched Old Jamaica and Bournville. The stern of the ship sank low in the water, then the bow, then in great haste mooring lines were slipped and the vessel reversed out to sea – leaving a totally deserted scene. Being alone, I felt no embarrassment standing on an empty beach tending several gallons of salty water in the bottom of a Mirror dinghy. Moving Epic to a safe position on my own, up the steep slope at the back of the beach, would not only have been a strenuous proposition, but rather presumptuous. Epic might have been claimed as salvage (if that happens ashore). Taking the sensible option I bailed out, reset the Bosun, reloaded, pushed off and shot back to Porthoustock. On a patch of soft grey sand, behind the giant silo, I beached Epic. When I was sure the tide had turned, I left to phone home to see if the 'reliant' Robin could collect me.

As was the custom, a handful of fishing boats about fifteen feet long had been winched above the tide-line. Higher up the beach, where the grey pebbles were large, two fishermen were working on a boat. They were sure it would be in order for me to leave the dinghy close by till fair weather returned. They also directed me to the oddly named public house, the '3 Tuns' at St Keverne. I arranged to meet my chauffeur there. A stroll over to the pub, one and a half miles away, would help me pass the time. As the first half mile required gaining considerable altitude, my need for refreshment moved from, 'I don't mind if I do' status, to, 'Perhaps if I lie under the tap ...' Later, after turning Epic over on the big stones, we loaded the car with mast, oars and the remaining damp sandy clutter, then headed home.

My long eventful day, starting at Frenchman's Creek, had been punctuated with disappointment and pantomime. Despite being battered, bruised and beaten back, I was surprisingly content when returned to Mevagissey a little before 'pumpkin time'. 'Oh yes I was.'

Into The Frying Pan
Porthoustock to The Lizard

I waited for fair weather. Week followed week. Favourable conditions were required for rounding Lizard Point. Four full weeks went by. I waited patiently. Following an early shipping forecast on August 5th, the waiting was over. Walking down the garden later that morning, on my way to collect the mast and oars from the studio, I found the wind still quite strong. The few white clouds, high in the heavens, were certainly not hanging about. Pondering, I picked and ate a handful of dark red, wild strawberries – a taste of real summer. In a few weeks the buddleia bush/tree would be bedecked with butterflies. Many a frustrating hour I have spent trying to photograph a red admiral and peacock butterfly on the same flower, posing for that elusive, perfect composition. A few successful pictures have helped me produce many paintings incorporating those stunningly dramatic 'sitters', and dozens more solo portraits, favouring the red admiral (the eyes, do not, have it). The sun felt hot on my back. I hoped the wind was enjoying its last gasp. Epic called.

While enjoying a bacon sandwich, served by a man from a van in a lay-by, en route to Porthoustock, I jotted '… *west northwest 4 – 5 occasionally 6, decreasing 3. Bacon sandwich good, wind direction good, decreasing three – delicious'*. Edward, Robin and I continued on our way. A week or so earlier, Julia and I visited Epic, still in place, upside-down on the big stones. It was gratifying to find her still there, unmolested. Thank you Porthoustock.

Hardly helped by a very light offshore breeze, the boys set off from the grey shingle for a sail. Robin was unlucky again in the wind department, so to speak. For half an hour or so, mostly rowing, they cruised the bay while I sat nervously in the car worrying about leaving behind the distress flare, lent by well-wishers who knew I was heading towards the Lizard. Like the Dodman, the Lizard has a cruel reputation, only more so. My extended absence from the water had allowed a modicum of pessimism to manifest itself. It would be all right when I was underway.

Sometime after four o'clock I stepped into Epic, rowed out a little

Red Admiral

Oil on canvas 4'6" x 5'

'Many a frustrating hour I have spent trying to photograph a red admiral and peacock butterfly on the same flower, posing for that elusive, perfect composition ... favouring the red admiral (the eyes, do not, have it).'

way and hoisted both sails. As the car was driven away, I waved goodbye to the boys. We were leaving behind a relaxed holiday scene. Other small dinghies provided fun afloat, while a dozen or so folk, mostly children, were doing their own thing at the waterline. On leaving the bay, my concentration was forcefully knocked out of neutral when I missed by a mere foot, a tip of rock just breaking the surface. It was a not too distant, small offshoot relation of Manacle Point. With many a look over my shoulder, I rounded the headland for a second and hopefully last time, giving it a respectful berth.

Alone again. No worries for a while. The simple pleasure of sailing from A to B, not knowing where B is till it becomes another A. After passing close to the quarry pier, I 'déjà vu'd' along to Lowland Point, the previous point of return. Soon I was leaning against the sail-bag, sailing fast, feet first between crab-pot marker flags to B – Coverack. Off Coverack I noted shorthandedly, *'WNW 4 5 DC 3 MFG.'* (MFG = 'mainly fair, good' – referring to visibility.) I liked to think the 'good', that often ended an area sequence, was the presenter saying 'that's alright then'. The weather prediction was almost identical to the bacon sandwich forecast, but thankfully without the 'Occ. 6'.

Just past the harbour entrance I came alongside an old timber lifeboat slip. There was just room to ride to a short painter between slip and rocky shore. I tied up and found the wind held the dinghy away from the solid wood structure. A perfect arrangement, for I was able to step ashore easily, and later, as the tide fell, re-hitch to the slip lower down.

After four weeks delay I was anxious to get on, staying just forty-five minutes in Coverack. It was time enough to inspect the pretty little harbour, filled with floating boats, strung tidily in lines, bow to stern. The retreating tide would drain away, leaving lifeless, stranded craft. The scene was one of total peace. Twenty or so smaller boats were out of the water, dotted about the inner slipway. Sheltered from the breeze by the harbour wall, there were just a handful of people carrying out their inactivity in the sunshine. Though tempted, I did not dally. At the Parris Hotel, situated close to the harbour, I refuelled with apple pie and cream, a large mug of coffee and a half pint of Newquay Steam. *'Yes, just a half'*, I noted in the log.

The next leg of the voyage did not turn out as I expected, the experience continuing to be a learning process. High tide was about a quarter to eight in the evening. I left about an hour before that, expecting little contrary tidal movement. It would not be too long, I assumed, for the English Channel to start to flow towards the Atlantic, helping me cover the five or six miles to Cadgwith. Just half a mile on, there was quite a swell running onto Chynhals Point, considering the sheltered aspect. It caused surges to rise much higher up the rocks than one would have imagined.

Looking back I saw the Dodman, still faintly visible though twenty miles away. I was pleased to be no nearer the source of a potent cow manure odour that drifted my way. To land persons, what we think is the smell of the sea, is to those who venture out to sea, the smell of the land. In fact, it is neither – it being the seashore aroma, often featuring rotten seaweed – cows permitting.

Another mile on, after taking a sharp right round Black Head, I lost sight of the Dodman. Then, between Black Head and off-lying rocks, I sighted the Lizard (Lizard Point) for the first time – that really made me feel far from home waters. The sun shone from behind tall rock pinnacles that spiked from the sea. Like statues in silhouette clinging to a cathedral, elongated black seabirds perched motionless, austerely decorating the 'Gothic' cliffs. That point marked the fiftieth parallel. Just three miles of the British mainland – the end of the Lizard Peninsular – lie to the south in the 'fair fifties' (degrees, north latitude). Fortunately, our waters do not have the fearsome reputation of the southerly roaring forties or furious fifties.

At seven o'clock I set course for (aimed at) Cadgwith, imagining a swift passage, for Epic cut satisfyingly through the water. Darkness fell imperceptibly, making it difficult to gauge progress. The land became indistinct as I headed towards the setting sun. Though time was slipping by, I thought nothing amiss till a fixed buoy trailing a gurgling wake appeared to overtake me. Expecting a favourable tide and finding speed through the water insufficient to compete with a stationary buoy, was a bit of a shock, I can tell you. The session of 'perfect' sailing was a rare delight. I enjoyed my dash into the dusk, till delusion dawned. Action was required. I was going nowhere fast, losing ground on a treadmill sea, being taken back to 'A' – Coverack. My position, half a mile offshore, was not the place to be, even on such a pleasant evening. To rectify the setback, I downed sail and hurriedly rowed in close to the cliffs to escape the full force of the tide.

'8:15, sighted the Lizard again'. The landmark reappearing between rocks off Black Head was reassuring. I was heading in the right direction, re-crossing the fiftieth parallel and heading west. Rowing as tight in against the hostile coastline as I dared, I set off between the rocks and mini islands to cover the three miles to Kennack Sands in the corner of the bay. A fresh cold wind blew on my back, sentencing me to an hour of uncomfortable rowing, which seemed much longer at the time. It was virtually dark, with just a touch of pink in the sky, as I approached the beach. Guided in by a small fire, I was fortunate not to collide with a low reef, glimpsed at the last moment against the dwindling flames. Having rounded the obstruction that protruded a mere foot above the surface, I was about to run onto the beach when a man out walking with his family shouted instructions for me to head in a few yards to my right. I was waved over to an area free from rocks. Having taken off his shoes and socks, he stepped into the sea and helped Epic in on a little wave. Most unfairly, the paddler was rewarded with wet trouser bottoms. I was in no danger, the kind man just wished to save Epic from damage.

After bailing out the few gallons of sea that entered over the stern on landing, I headed for the phone facility, which the helpful gentleman informed me was situated a few hundred yards up the steep hill, inside the Kennack Sands Hotel – most convenient. The tide was receding and would return to meet Epic after the early forecast the following morning – which was also most convenient. On leaving the hotel/pub an hour or so later, I was greeted by a huge round orange moon rising from behind the hill to the east. Moonlight grandly silhouetted more of the sinister reef as the tide fell. A fiery lunar path, pointing towards Mevagissey, reflected off the calm sea. I felt a bit lonely. In an area of rough grass beside a little stream behind the beach, I lay down in my bag, enfolded within the mutilated tent.

At the beginning of each leg I was always over optimistic, expecting to be wafted effortlessly to each new B. The rhythm of the voyage had not returned and I was still at 'half' with nature, out of tune with the tidal flow. I slept fitfully, waking several times during the night. *'V cold night. No gloves.'* My cursory observations in the 'twidark' suggested huge Bondi Beach breakers were pounding the beach. Needlessly I worried, blindly multiplying the difficulties of launching through giant waves. Overriding the temptation to remain recharging in my bag, I decided to confront the problem of launching. From the beachhead at an unearthly hour, I viewed the scene in amazement. There was jaunty little Epic, blunt bow slightly raised, pointing a stumpy mast towards the Lizard. Of giant rollers there were none. Periodically, a token wave formed and collapsed in slow motion down the length of the beach. That such a timid act of nature could produce such volume was quite extraordinary. Relieved at not being beach-bound again so soon, I awaited the shipping forecast. In clear, low-key morning light, I enjoyed the fleeting second of birth and oblivion of a prize shooting star.

At half five, wearing headphones under my woolly hat, I stalked the beach. With logbook at the ready and pen wedged between frozen fingers, I waited to jot. The Walkman delivered, 'Danny Boy', 'Up She Rises' and 'Men of Harlech'. The rousing band music preceded the perfect prediction, '… variable three', followed by an equally perfect, light offshore beam wind that would take me towards the Lizard.

The tide was approaching Epic's stern as I was loading the soggy bag and tent. Close by were a number of rocks and large pebbles, excavated by the little stream as it meandered down the beach forming a mini sand canyon. The angular rocks, up to a foot or so across, was the hazard I was diverted round the previous night.

A small amount of water entered the boat up the centreboard casing as I launched. It was not long before I was happily reunited with the sun that had been shielded behind hills during my early hours on the beach. In no time, the groundsheet/tent and sail bag were hoisted to dry. On an oily calm, I rowed towards Enys Head. *'7:01 EPIC LEAKS!!'* my pen exclaimed, as if Epic's life expectancy could be measured in minutes. I sponged a pint or so of gritty water overboard, repeating the process a few more times. Then, to my great relief, Epic became dry. After beaching at Kennack Sands, water must have drained into the rear buoyancy/seat compartment and seeped out after re-floating, when the dinghy was horizontal again.

Luxuriating in sunny silence, I hugged the coast. Less than a mile on

I chanced upon Carleon Cove. Twin stone buildings, a lone three-storey warehouse and a disused, circular structure, tempted me to land with a view to paint. Rocky outcrops on the scrubby hillsides and shadows cast by the low sun presented a fine composition. The plan was to step sprightly on to a boulder; then, as the slight swell receded, push Epic away with my foot. I would be ashore with the dinghy bobbing about on the end of a long painter. Alas, it was a larger than average surge I chose for the manoeuvre. As I disembarked it surged on, filling my left welling-ton. Precariously maintaining balance, I tottered, tumbling back on board with the next swell. At ten to eight, a hundred yards offshore just below the fiftieth parallel, a lone mariner with white legs 'pinkening' in the sunshine, sat rinsing a sock in fresh water. Jeans with one wet leg dangled from a halyard alongside a tent and life jacket.

After a leisurely row to Cadgwith, I pulled Epic onto the shingle and wandered a few yards up the beach to sit at the bottom of a slipway wall. It was nine fifteen-ish. I breakfasted on tangy cheese and sweet spicy homemade chutney sandwiches prepared at home the day before. The welcome feast had matured into a succulent amalgamation. In my state of ravenousness, the lumpy fare was a pure delight. A handful of people came and went while a lone fisherman worked on an engine in one of the thirty or so smallish boats on the beach. I fancied a hot drink, but had to wait for an hour for a café to open. In the meantime I wandered round to the Devil's Frying-pan. Passing between stone cottages, some thatched, I soon arrived at the site. I looked down into a very large, crater-like hole with a pool at the bottom that led to the sea via a cave of story-book wonder. The pan was barely simmering. In rough weather, the giant cauldron becomes a confined maelstrom with angry seas surging through the tunnel creating a hellish scene. Hoping for heavenly conditions later, I left to have a cup of tea.

The fine shingle beach was quite steep, so it was a simple matter to drag Epic back into the sea. At eleven o'clock, it was out of Cadgwith and into the Frying Pan – a magical experience. Sunlight shone down into the crater, reflecting light underwater, indicating the special cave entrance from other dead-end caves nearby. The rocky ceiling seemed to offer too little clearance at first (as the bridge at Looe) for Epic to enter, but getting nearer, I reckoned the masthead might just squeeze through, and so it did. The dark water inside the cave rose and fell lazily, making me anxious lest the mast be pushed through the hull. There was just enough room to manipulate the oars and squeeze through onto the bright, watery stage of that natural amphitheatre. (I am speaking extremely loosely, for even standing with crampons would be quite a feat, and popping out for an ice-cream could involve cliff rescue.) In such a peaceful setting I had no wish to break the spell and refrained from acoustic testing. I was extremely lucky, being in the right place at the right time to gain entry into the delightful Frying Pan.

If charted, my progress would have described a meandering line up to the left side of the salt-stained, sticky-taped Ordnance Survey Landranger 204 that had guided me from Mevagissey. I unfolded map 203, the fourth and most dramatic used since setting out on the Tamar. A photograph on the cover shows rugged cliffs at Land's End with agitated white water at their base. Though I wished to take Epic round that most westerly tip of England, it was still in the realm of fantasy. Sea charts were less useful to me than the OS maps for pinpointing position. The descriptive sheets included many landmarks, even differentiating between churches with or without spires. They were a valuable aid for one so intimately involved with the shoreline. Landranger 203 also featured the Lizard, the most southerly point of the English mainland – just two and a half inches, or two miles away.

How different it was then, rowing gently with tide-assistance, than had been the battle to Kennack Sands the previous evening. Apart from Epic, all I beheld was nature's own spectacular creation. It was an unadulterated coastline of powerful grandeur, easy on the eye with harmonious combinations of mostly muted colours. There was a band of purple/black above the sea-line, topped by saffron yellowed, salt-sprayed lichen; then flashes from newly fractured granite, punctuating scarred stone outcrops of greys and burnt sienna that led up to dry yellow/green draped cliff tops. An audacious backcloth canopy of perplexing hue topped the striking landscape. How, I wondered, could such light sky be reflected so darkly, creating that bluest of Prussian blue sea? Only a serrated band at the foot of the cliff, where the ocean lapped barnacled ochre, did the water pale to turquoise.

Burnt Out And Fired Up

Burning a candle from both ends exacts a price. Subdividing the candle and burning from many ends accelerates the process. With two years of art college remaining, I suffered a pretty decisive burnout – a rather sudden extinguishing.

Though the Francis Barnet had been handed down to younger brother Michael, a control force decreed I should 'take off' on the machine, Steve McQueen style. (Remember the film, where his bid for freedom on a motorbike included a cross-country chase in which he, with bike, leaped over barbed wire.) Just a few memory fragments remain of that fateful day. Was I escaping, or just sightseeing? I will never know. For what it's worth, here are the pieces.

I collected the motorbike from the stable and rode out of Gaius Smith's entry. Though I was the rider, the real 'Yours truly' had already entered another dimension. The events following the demise of the old Wolsey I clearly remember, but of my dive into the ditch with the Francis Barnet, leaving it behind while I staggered off into the country-side, I remember nothing.

The people at the farmhouse, who mercifully took me in, must have been shocked by the arrival of a dishevelled, zombie-like visitor. They did not turn away the rambling stranger. Without identification or meaningful articulation from me, my parents were not informed of my predicament for a while. Virtually all my time back then was spent away in digs, or on painting missions, so it was not surprising that an art student losing the plot had largely gone unnoticed. Seated in the back of a police car, between two officers, I was conveyed to a hospital where I was (I quote from records) '… given a course of electrical treatment …'. Such drastic measure, in that type of situation, I am assured by the medical profession, is a thing of the past.

For a year or so I overworked, candles guttering by the bucket load. I paid the price and required time to recuperate. Medication slowed me down. I wandered round in a state of lethargy for a while. The desire to record my surroundings did not cease. Several drawings, executed on backs of Christmas cards and cheap fluffy paper (off-white, not grey) using pen, pencil and chalk, remind me of the incarceration. Corridors with 'cell' doors feature, along with studies of a few fellow inmates. There is a drawing of cars outside in the snow – one an Austin A40. Another drawing portrays a man in a white coat.

Thankfully it is with hazy recollection that I dredge up these memories. Drugged, restrained on an iron framed bed; something in the mouth to stop swallowing or biting the tongue; a wooden box, wires, electrodes to the head; thrashing, convulsing; a pathetic queue in the corridor; my turn; open mouth – checking the capsule swallowed; heavy metal door clumps shut; a key turns. Confused, alone; remove hidden capsule from under tongue. I want to go home.

After release, I slowly re-engaged, feeling my way back, painting subjects close to home. Horizons reopened by degrees. Water based pigments captured a sunset outside the window. I took further 'therapeutic' steps to paint a barn being reconstructed a few yards down the hill. I still have the sketchbook with 'renaissance' pictures.

A couple of months later I packed the Vauxhall with my oil painting gear and set off for St Ives, and summer sunshine.

In December of that year, I enrolled at Birmingham College of Art. The Fine Art course was overflowing and my late application was unsuccessful. Not wishing to delay my final two years training, ceramics became the route to qualification. Pottery had been part of my Intermediate training. That messy clay business, along with tedious hours of plant drawing for design stimulation, might have been, but for a happy crowd of captives, a rather tiresome sentence.

Fellow student Martin brought in the young Bob Dylan's LPs to help combat boredom. A diversion of less duration was the creation of 'the giant snake'. Clay was mixed and reconstituted using a pug mill – a powerful electric mixer that extruded four-inch diameter lengths of clay. A dozen or so fledgling ceramicists combined to feed into the machine every last available ounce of clay in the department. The weighty, lengthening serpent, borne on the shoulders of a team working in unison, may not have been all that creative, but was testament to bonhomie and collaboration.

At the time, my becoming a potter seemed as likely as men on the moon. Chemistry lecturers from the University visited, but did not fire my imagination. Chemical formulas for clay and glaze mixes just caused confusion. You could not buy a bag of KO_2 or SiO_2; you purchased mineral substances such as felspar, china clay, Cornish stone and other earthy stuff. I could not relate to the invisible abstract compound numbers and symbols.

Following the final examinations, and much to my surprise, I 'contracted' ceramics. Clay from under my fingernails had seeped into my veins. The self-prescribed treatment was to rapidly acquire knowledge to enable me to set up my own workshop. My changed regard for the craft could not have been instantaneous. During the months of examination fever it must have crept up on me, hovering out of reach as I worked to meet deadlines for thesis, design and production requirements.

Unlocking the magic began with an empirical approach to glaze creation – mixing varying quantities of the most common ingredients used in the high temperature glazes I had been using. Starting from scratch to create my own individual glazes seemed a logical approach which eventually bore fruit. Tiny shallow bowls thrown on the wheel, from the top of a large centred lump of clay, were produced in great numbers. Small, varying percentages of combinations of colouring oxides were added to my perfected range of base glazes and applied to the little pots.

Copper oxide will produce green; but there are exceptions. Reducing oxygen in a firing can radically change a glaze as replacement oxygen is drawn from the ware. Rich blood reds can be produced using copper in reduction firing, but it is a tricky operation. Centuries ago, a Chinese potter produced a glorious red glaze. He was ordered to reproduce the same beautiful effect. Try as he might, repeated disappointments put him in fear of his life. His final failure caused him to climb into the kiln to end it all. [He fired himself]. That did the trick; that batch provided the most magnificent red wares.

Without undue pressure, my trial (and error) tests were tweaked, resulting in a satisfactory selection of glazes. Those few weeks of endeavour before I left college gave me the confidence to ask a Tenbury butcher if I could set up a pottery workshop in his cowshed. The fact that my thrown work up to that time consisted mainly of very small bowls with rough bases, did not deter me. Clones of the little glaze test bowls, but with finished bottoms, became best sellers in a later pottery.

One of my first orders was for a number of ashtrays with handles and spouts for the Tea Pot Café, situated at the other end of Teme Street. We all have to start somewhere.

Cruel Shower
The Lizard to Porthleven

Wondering where to seek advice regarding suitable tides and times for rounding The Lizard, I sighted a lifeboat building and slip between Whale Rock and the mainland. Consulting the map, I found I was approaching Church Cove, which was somewhat perplexing. Where were the church and sandy beach? It was a location I had been advised not to miss. (The recommended cove is on the other side of the Lizard, beyond Mullion.) A rash of Gull Rocks I was aware of, but an outbreak of Church Coves on the Lizard was quite surprising.

As I slipped through the inviting channel alongside the big black Whale Rock, rascally little rocks broke the surface. With frequent glances over my shoulders, towards my destination, I headed the half-mile to the Cove 'for orders'. (Perhaps I should have fitted wing mirrors.)

There was a bit of a swell running in, making me think twice about landing. Fearing to approach the Lizard without receiving local knowledge, I dithered a while before heading in to the rough shingle area below a steep slip leading up to half a dozen stone dwellings. Annoying, spasmodic surges of sea prevented my leaving Epic for more than a few moments, thwarting my mission – acquiring information for doubling the cape (as we mariners say), not to mention solving the mystery of the missing church.

In no time, unbelievably good fortune befell. A little way along the coast, off the lifeboat slip, I chanced upon a fisherman aboard his boat anchored just a hundred yards or so out to sea. It was as if I had been granted a wish – 'Small Sailing Boat Advisory Bureau, how can I assist?' The fisherman was 'doing' something to crabs – something best not to know when ordering a crab sandwich. (Mine is not to criticise the harvesters of the seas. In any case, the poor crabs would not need their legs again.). My good fortune was 'go' – to immediately row round the

Lizard. The lucky chance – right time, place and conditions again, was seized upon without delay. Before even completing my sincere thanks, I was rowing with gusto, along with a measure of excited apprehension, towards the southern extremity.

Half a mile on, half an hour past noon, I arrived at Bass Point and began making a long right hand turn, entering an area of irregular waves. The Lizard is but a point on small-scale maps. In reality, it is one and a half miles wide. Large independent bodies of water diverted by the land-mass caused great disturbance when coming together. After a while I rounded a large leaning monolith. It stood below the sunlit, white Lizard Light buildings – probably the Lizard itself, though Bumble Rock appears on the map. Before me, an awesome barrier of low-lying jagged rocks stretched seaward. But for the crab-man, I could have been over-awed. Even so, as I approached, all thoughts of threading my way between the hazards evaporated. Angling past the most southerly tip, I was surprised to see a slipway, tucked away in a cove (Polpeor) by the side of a small beach. On reflection, I am sorry not to have put in to that unexpected, inviting haven, for conditions were perfect for landing, which I am sure is not usual. However, being psyched up to reach Mullion Cove on the tide, I headed joyously, northish.

Thankful that I had been dealt the kindest hand, I hastened on, away from waters seldom so lenient. Off Kynance Cove I ceased rowing to listen to the lunchtime shipping forecast. The 'light, variable wind' was eminently acceptable. As far as 'fog around dawn' was concerned, I was not, for I was happily bobbing about close to another Gull Rock, and a Lion Rock, which from my vantage point actually looked like a lion, complete with sun-goldened, lichened mane. The land/seascape I knew well from the brushwork of artists, capturing the scene over the past hundred years or so. At the time I had no wish to attempt a landing, for there at the bottom of England, I wished to be alone, savouring a personal high.

The painters' paradise slipped astern. I made the most of the remaining favourable tide to row the five miles to Mullion. With about two miles to go, the tide began to run back towards the Lizard. It was about that time I was offered a tow, which I declined, citing my masochistic bent.

The considerate fisherman asked if I had been at sea in the area of Kennack Sands the previous evening. Unknown to me, my safe landing had been overseen. My far from convincing performance had been witnessed by the Lizard Coastguard, of which he was a member. Without even an implied 'tut-tut', the part-time lookout puttered off to Mullion. Half a mile 'later', I received another tow offer, with a reminder of the increasing speed of adverse tide. I thanked boatman number two, saying I would make haste under my own steam and keep close to the cliffs to escape the strongest flow. After my recent experience I should have been hugging the coastline, away from the 'return ticket zone'.

As I crossed the fiftieth parallel, finally heading north, I became aware that the top outsides of my calves were being lightly roasted. When rowing in feet back mode, as opposed to out in front, my lower legs stuck out sideways to avoid knee contact with the oars. Exposed leg portions, not protected by a towel, were punished mercilessly. In the lee of a rocky outcrop I wriggled into my coarse dried jeans – belatedly bolting the door.

Eventually, achingly, thankfully, I sighted, between the mainland and Mullion Island, a cluster of buildings on a hilltop. Soon other dwellings beside the sea became apparent. There was still plenty of strenuous rowing to do, but the visual incentive eased my mind. At half past four Epic nonchalantly nudged the sand within the arms of the harbour walls at Mullion Cove. Was it really only twenty-four hours since I left Porthoustock? Yes.

A willing helper assisted in hauling Epic a few yards onto the newly washed sand. My arrival kindled the sense of adventure. To the sound of 'Swiss Family and Swallows' chatter, I left to climb the grassy slope on the south side of the harbour. Over the next half hour or so, as I looked down with relieved satisfaction, the sand round Epic was being turned over by tiny feet. Between two 'pinnacled' islets, just beyond the harbour, I glimpsed St Michael's Mount, floating in the hazy distance. Within the trodden circle, my little ship was waiting to transport me to a real 'castle in the sky'.

Returning to the beach a little while later, I was helped by Bob, from whom the second tow offer came, to carry some gear above the tide-line. During the operation I managed to fall over an outboard motor, ending up sitting in evil smelling, mushy seaweed. That was but a mild blip, for fortune smiled immediately.

Having helped me move the dinghy up the beach, Bob, a man of many showers, offered me the use of one at his holiday camp. In little time, after a short walk up the hill, I was standing expectantly in a cubicle. My bag, clothes and towel festooned the hook on the door. Other accoutrements, including a sample bottle of bright blue shampoo, were crammed onto a small shelf. (The sole reason for having the blueberry and cucumber, eco friendly goo, was the miniature size of the container.) The eagerly awaited cascade did not materialize. My ten pence piece had primed the mechanism in an adjoining cubicle. After transferring my impedamenta, and suffering for a few seconds an unavoidable blanching of my partly cooked parts, I luxuriated beneath the hot caressing spray. In a blue lather I eased away the strains of fifteen miles of rowing. That such heavenly bliss should then, without warning, be so cruelly taken away, seemed most unfair. My ten pence allowance of hot water expired all too quickly, causing an abrupt cessation of flow. After rinsing myself, and washing the smelly portion of my jeans in cold water at the sink, I set off damply for Mullion village. There, in an old inn (The Old Inn), sitting on OS 204 to protect the upholstered seat from slowly drying denim, I dined.

It was getting dark when I collected my bedding from the boat. I headed up the grassy slope to bed down (or should that be up) for the night. Lying in my bag, which was inside the orange survival one, I looked across at the lights stretching from Marazion to Mousehole. To the left, I picked out the odd twinkle. Left again, blackness, concealing the empty Atlantic – an ocean I may or may not visit. Night progressed with a three-quarter moon keeping me vaguely in the picture. A shame my burnt calves were too painful to allow weariness to convey me straight to the land of dreams. The slippery bag eased itself gently down the slope. It was not a problem, just annoying, for the direction was not towards a cliff drop, and minor obstructions ruled out a rendezvous with Epic. The plastic covering kept me warm at first, though through perspiration I became increasingly damp. As the night advanced, cold crept in. (Burning legs plus cold feet did not equal comfort.) Moisture increased, ruling out more than fitful sleep. Periodically I reached out to bring the painting bag down to my new elevation. Awake at half past four, thinking it much later, I prepared myself with torch, radio, book and pen for the six o'clock forecast. Waiting for the lark (oh what fun), I endeavoured to ignore the chilly conditions and doze away till dawn.

The cold eventually drove me from the wretched bags. I wandered down to warm my hands in the sea. After stowing the inadequate bedding, I rigged the sails ready for hoisting; *'I should be so lucky'*, I noted. At five past seven, under a clear blue sky scrolling down to pastel peach, I rowed out of Mullion Cove on a sea of glass. Though twenty miles away (three miles before Land's End) Gwennap Head appeared invitingly serene in the early morning mist.

Though sun barrier-cream, hardened by the low temperature, was difficult to apply, I was not tempted to forgo application to my hand backs and face. My untrustworthy legs were confined to jeans for a while. Out of the quiet came a loud, roaring sound like heavy surf breaking on a beach. Surely that could not be in such mild conditions, I was thinking, when it turned out to be just that. Unnoticed waves from an apparently flat sea funnelled into Polurrian Cove, creating large breakers. The amplified sound rebounded from the cliffs. Such a powerful manifestation, conjured up in so tranquil a setting was quite amazing. (It seems I will never cease to be amazed.)

I hoisted the wet bag then breakfasted on Mars (out of this world) followed by banana and water. Epic barely stirred on the near flat sea. My attention was drawn to a light disc that sat on the surface close by. There appeared no rational cause for the strange phenomenon. I sat pondering the physical riddle for a while. Perhaps this lone sailor was the chosen one, a stray, earthling specimen to be transported to an alien world. The mysterious, pulsating disc might metamorphose into an encapsulating sphere… Without interstellar intervention the mystery was solved. A drip from an oar blade set the daytime moon's reflection scattering. Like the cold sun barrier-cream, my brain needed coaxing into useful service.

A landing at the second Church Cove seemed possible until the last minute, when a single, large lolloping wave suggested otherwise. (There were other waves of course, but only one at a time.) Landing on the beach would have been tricky, but more to the point, re-launching would have been an extremely wet affair. A pair of dolphins entertained me for half an hour or so as I travelled to the next cove. Every time I took a picture of their joyous cavorting they were thirty or forty yards away. My record of umpteen empty seas, with disputable distant dots, served only to boost Kodak sales.

When the dolphins left, I took advantage of calm conditions to explore a secret grotto-type place. It was situated at Pedngwinian, below a cliff at the end of a little cape. (Please excuse the following digression – the 'cape' word reminds me of when I dressed as a type of Bat Man hero one New Year's eve – chest logo, an oven ready bird with the caption, 'Couldn't Get A Turkey This Year, So I've Got A Capon'. That was a few years after my 'Fish In Abundance' – a headband with cardboard fish dangling from wires among simulated rock cakes made from pieces of torn sponge dotted with black felt-tip spots. A recent presentation – 'Lemming Meringue Pie' – a hinged meringue disc (polystyrene) hat, raised to release a shower of lemmings dangling on threads.) The grotto could have been a hideaway where war canoes lurked in ambush. It was nine thirty when I eased Epic onto the patch of still water behind protective outlying rocks. A shaft of sunlight penetrated the depths, revealing, like an eerie green hologram, a mysterious subterranean world. The site was reminiscent of the Frying Pan. Fascinated, I leant out for a better view of the sub aqua rock formations. From under the boat snaked a giant conger. My heart almost exploded as I rapidly withdrew from the side. Unlike the previous mystery, the aberration was fleeting. The 'monster' was in fact the reflection of an oar. As I tipped the boat, the distorted reflection sprang onto the surface. Caution; hours alone in a small boat may impair reasoning.

Shortly after setting off for Porthleven, three miles further on, I was rowing past Gunwalloe Fishing Cove at the beginning of the two and a half mile long Porthleven Sands. At the time the beach was mostly hidden beneath the high tide. Half way along is Loe Bar, which bars access to the Loe – a mile long Lake leading towards Helston. Earlier, when studying the map, I had in mind to step ashore at the Bar, haul Epic onto the Loe, explore a little and possibly do a bit of painting. It would have been a pleasant change, not being pushed around on tidal waters, and satisfyingly low on the fear and getting wet factors.

Looking at the bar I revised my plan of action. Even raising my small boat the few yards up the steep shingle seemed too much. Had I been able to land safely, the procedure would certainly have demanded expending a great deal more energy than is sensible. There are other ways of spending time on a hot sunny beach. The size of slow-motion roller waves, forming against the steep shelving shoreline that repeatedly pounded Porthleven Sands, were not obvious till almost on the beach. A hazardous bar beaching would have been in total contrast to the peaceful beer-garden landing executed at Tresillian.

Rowing on to Porthleven Harbour was a strenuous affair. The slightly lumpy sea, combined with an increasing onshore breeze, slowed Epic considerably. With great relief I eventually passed rocky shallows off the entrance and headed towards the inner harbour, in the protection of a long, stone breakwater. Having been tantalized long enough by a tall turreted church tower, topped by an 'afterthought' stunted spire, it was gratifying to finally row past it.

When arriving at a new harbour it is customary to immediately inform the harbourmaster. Without delay, after tying Epic alongside steps on the east side, I headed over to report at the harbour office. I was a bit miffed to read the sign, 'CLOSED TILL MONDAY'. (It was Saturday.) Returning to Epic I moved her further along to a metal ladder. Even with an absent harbourmaster it is bad form to hog the steps. With my little boat tied to a line, long enough to allow it to settle when the harbour emptied, I climbed the tall ladder that twisted disconcertingly, being economically attached at the top by a single shackle on a short length of chain.

While waiting for the lunchtime shipping forecast I sat alone on a cliff ledge, north of Porthleven, looking over Mounts Bay. Only fifteen miles away, ahead and due west, lay Gwennap Head. Just before it and almost in line were the Logan Rock and Pedn-men-an-mere headlands, which enclose a small bay, set back between towering cliffs. There, built into the cliff-top, is the open-air Porthcurno theatre. I listened to the radio to see if a seafaring role was in the offing. 'Northwest three; occasionally four.' To the northwest, at the top of the bay, stood St Michael's Mount. I would wait in the wings.

Michael doth blow so I can't go
Just my luck he did not suck

Epic was to stay at Porthleven for a while. Robin would collect me in the early evening. I left the dinghy on the mud by the high harbour wall, twice the height of Epic's mast, and set off to walk to Helston via The Loe. The three-mile excursion was most therapeutic. Dinghy journeying greatly exercises the mind; so it was natural I suppose, given half a chance, that my legs would take the initiative when returned to land. My stroll took me along the fringes of the beautiful wave-less lake. Within the hour I was passing a smaller, more formal stretch of water on the edge of town.

Helston's Coronation Park Boating Lake was reminiscent of a Birmingham lake, not far from my home. (I have returned to my toddling years.) Though not a large stretch of water, to me it seemed like the sea, complete with tiny waves lapping two feet wide mini beaches. There, shortly before Queen Elizabeth II's coronation, the older boys grappled with great big gudgeon, whilst I stalked the wary stickleback with net and stringed jam jar at the ready. Post-toddle, and pre 'three-legged gold', I was taken boating on the lake. I picture now the ranks of sleek clinker rowing boats tethered bow to landing stage. They were classy constructions – high seat backs, and steering ropes attached to rudders set on fine triangular transoms. They jostled each other, ready for cast off with wavelets slapping their slim hulls. A crafty 'captain' would make sure he was up at the far end of the lake, behind the island, when time was called, thus gaining five minutes extra voyaging. I obviously had no inkling then, that when grown, I would be weighing up the possibility of taking an even smaller craft to an adventure on the fringes of a real ocean. Brookvale Park now nestles in the shade of stilted motorway intersections at Spaghetti Junction.

On the subject of small boats, I recall an episode from those early years featuring even smaller boats. I was standing up, working the pedals, unable to reach the seat of a grown-up's non-crossbar, black bicycle. My mission seemed of the utmost urgency at the time. I was on my way to a large indoor market where my Dad had a stall. The roads were wet, following a downpour. Sunken tramlines threatened to ensnare thin-wheeled traffic. Beware of the gobbling, rattling, whining monsters. The great hall was a cacophony of babble and banging, aromas and colours, fruits and bright fabrics. The floor accumulated litter throughout the day – cast aside orange trays, feathers and straw. My business was at the sagging trestle tables where treasure chests (once ammunition boxes) were packed with numerous desirable items. No bullets now, just cap bombs, marbles of all colours and sizes, rubber balls and miniature viewers showing six scenes of London. My mission was to take home a coveted set of four plastic sailing boats. I was captivated with my prize – half walnut size, with a slot for the flat plastic sail/mast. The shiny ships were recessed into a card. Pristine, red, blue, green and yellow, the fleet floated in the sink. I blew and they all fell over. Lately, as you must have noticed, I err towards under-canvassing and extreme reefing.

A few years after my disappointing miniature boat purchase, good fortune struck our family. Father worked several markets, selling mainly dress and curtain materials. Quite out of the blue while he was tending his outside stall in Market Square, Tenbury Wells, a farmer unknown to Dad, offered a low interest loan to purchase the shop behind his stall which was being auctioned that very day. It was destiny – the family would not become 'Spaghetti Westoners.'

Back to Helston (or should I say forward), and my arrival at four forty five. Following a swift walk round the town, and a brief stop for a toasted teacake and mug of tea, it was time to return to Epic. I took the road back in case Robin should chance along; little knowing he had chanced along earlier and was waiting for me down at the harbour. Robin was in a bit of a hurry, so we set about making a speedy departure. While he drove the car down to the waterside at the inner end of the harbour, I descended the rickety ladder and quickly rowed to the slip where we transferred the boat's contents to the car, tied the oars, along with the mast wrapped in the Bosun, to the roof rack, then carried the overweight, waterlogged Epic to a yard across the road.

Robin's urgency could not compete with the temptation wafting from a nearby fish'n'chip shop. Dormant taste buds frenzied as banquets were eagerly unwrapped for transference to deprived stomachs.

Dracula's Castle
Porthleven to Lamorna

The early forecast, six days after retreating from Porthleven, '… variable, decreasing three, occasionally four, fair, good'. With an incredibly itchy right leg, still a bit tender after the roasting, I stood impatiently queuing in a St Austell bank. Diverting my mind, I glanced round the interior. The digital clock displayed 13:00, on Friday 13th. Consulting the tide tables earlier, I noted, *'High tide 13:00 GMT'*. The correction for my area, Plymouth (time advances along with the tide as it flows up-channel) was minus one hour, leaving 13:13 British Summer Time. As I am not superstitious there was no earthly, chronological or astrological, reason preventing my return to Porthleven.

There was quite a swell running down the inside of the south side of the outer harbour wall. (Not a gravity defying toff, legging it out to sea.) To head out was a daunting prospect, but Epic coped admirably, riding over the surges. Progress down the harbour channel was a slow, faltering business. Confused rocking made oar strokes a hit and miss affair, but eventually the hits drew Epic clear. The state of the sea outside was ordered, though slightly choppy, due to the fresh southerly onshore wind that produced sharp little waves close to the headlands.

There were reminders of past industry. Disused mine workings stood mournfully on the sloping cliff-tops. The empty sea gave no indication of scale. Old engine houses and chimneys, one side bright with sunlight, punctuated a manicured toy landscape dotted with building blocks, awaiting tin soldiers.

By four o'clock, Porthleven was just a smudge in the distance. It was a delicate and interesting smudge, mind you; as unlike a blot as could possibly be imagined. Life on board was perfect. It was not too warm and I enjoyed myself to the full. *'The sky was mostly blue …'* I wrote in joggling scrawl, on joggling waves; and now decipher with difficulty. It took even longer to make sense of the *'Hard to write'* – possibly the most pointless remark ever penned.

Through rather choppy water, with the sails set to starboard, I made steady headway up to Cudden Point. While watching surf break against the outcrop, I had reason to jot, *'5-20 see St Micks'*. Set against the hazy mainland, St Michael's Mount was rather understated compared with the dark rocks and white water close at hand. Even so, it was still unmistakably the most charismatic of Cornish landmarks.

For much of the next hour my gaze was drawn to the Mount. Gradually, the mysterious form dominated the background hills. Architectural details on the summit became more defined. Behind me, the distant giant dishes of Goonhilly Downs were visible in the clear air. Fascinating as the radio telescope dishes were, they did not hold my attention for long. Ahead, the dramatic structure atop the steep-sided island demanded precedence. Within half a mile, the intriguing castle still retained mystery. It was impossible to distinguish between constructed and natural formation, for I approached the shaded side. Had I been in sombre mood, the scene would have seemed quite eerie. Dusk, with a double bass bowing sighing moans, would have done the trick. Having skirted left, the castellated towers and tall ornate chimneys appeared in a cheerful light – the sun bathing the stone.

On the sunny side, in the lee of the outer harbour wall, I downed sail and rowed into St Michael's surprisingly large harbour. On my right, towards the outer end of the wall, I tied up close to a sturdy wooden ladder. It was from the top rung a few minutes later that I dropped my only jumper into the water. My visit to the island was not a chance gate-crashing. The previous year, a couple who live on the Mount called at my gallery and invited me to pop in after I had mentioned my proposed trip to them. The invitation was more genuine than a casual, "We live by the harbour, drop in next time you're passing." I called. They were out, but would be back at nine o'clock before the causeway disappeared beneath the waves.

I wandered over to Marazion to be impressed once more by the majesty of St Michael's viewed from another angle. Mainland cod 'n' chips was next on the agenda, and that too was magnificent. The waters rose, urging me to re-cross the slippery stone causeway, to call again at the terraced cottage behind the harbour buildings. After an enjoyable chat over cups of tea, Richard and Maggie offered me a bed for the night, but I had to do what a man had to do and settled for my wet woolly going in the drier. They must have wondered at such odd behaviour.

I wandered from their cosy cottage into pitch darkness. Wearing my warm tumbled jumper, I fumbled round the harbour and descended safely into Epic. Bagged and happily without the need for protective plastic, I floated comfortably aboard Epic.

Mevagissey had been depicted as Whitby in a Count Dracula film produced in Cornwall in the seventies. St Michael's Mount, with little transformation, became the vampire's Transylvanian haunt. Floating in my 'plywood box', I faced the Mount, topped by the floodlit 'Dracula's Castle'. The appearance of a crescent moon and bats flitting softly, all but transported me to 'Bram Stoker Land'. (It is all perfectly true; even the bats.) With the absence of 'sighing moans' and no thought of Friday 13th, I fearlessly drifted off – to sleep.

I woke early to catch the forecast. The day dawned clear and calm with the possibility of a force four to five from the southwest later, which would rule out my heading towards Land's End. Such speculation could wait, for I had been invited to look round the Mount. The island hamlet was silent at that early hour. Not wishing to intrude, I mooched round the harbour end for a while enjoying the beautiful setting and rare stillness. Faint day noises began on the mainland. The causeway/road, being submerged more often than not, results in minimal motor vehicle disturbance. At a quarter to eight, the Penzance helicopter droned off to the Isles of Scilly.

After marmalade and crumpets at the terrace cottage, Richard guided me round the gardens and buildings. The island seemed much bigger when being explored. The seaward side, not usually open to visitors, is more rugged than the sheltered, greener and more formal harbour side. The half tamed, steep, grassy, granite outcropped terrain, incorporated secret terraces, walled with brick and stone. Varied foliage burst around scattered urns and partly over-grown steps. It was a pleasing partnership – nature tolerating man's intrusion – without shaved lawns or tortured, topiaried shrubs. Enough; I will not even begin to describe the fascinating atmospheric interiors. You must walk the causeway, or be taken over by boat, and see for yourself.

From battlements close to the top of the building, I looked down on tiny Epic. There was no mistaking the Mirror tucked inside the harbour entrance. She was the smallest craft and the only one with a sleeping bag

St Michael's Mount
19"x 19"
'St Michael's Mount, with little transformation, became the vampire's Transylvanian haunt.'

dangling from the masthead.

Lord St Levan was on a higher terrace (I looked up to him) changing a flag in favour of a lightweight one, hoping to induce a flutter in the virtually still air. I was introduced to his lordship, having been told that he also enjoyed boating. As we approached the head of the ancestral home, Richard instructed me to address the islanders' landlord as 'My Lord'. Though thinking my leg was being pulled, I did as requested. The conversation proceeded in a serious manner, and I was so pleased not to have made a flippant remark. Those working on the Mount were happy with the formality – they liked and respected their Lord.

As I was leaving, my hosts and another couple of Mount dwellers boarded a boat for the short hop to the mainland. As I was taking 'leaving pictures', they asked if I would like them to take a photo of me aboard Epic. I passed my camera over to them. Till then, the only photographic evidence of myself at sea in Epic were my own pictures, usually taken feet steering, showing feet and legs interfering with the Cornish landscape.

At half past eleven, as the helicopter returned from Scilly, I commenced the two-mile row towards Penzance. The town was emerging from a slight blue haze. I was prompted to raise the Admiral on the forestay and the Bosun against the mast as a faint breeze materialized. To the blue mainsail I attached a handy length of thick springy elastic in place of a sheet (I really do not know why I did that). Wafting onwards, I enjoyed a spot of perfect sailing with the Bosun gently heaving in and out.

The breeze increased, stretching the Bosun's elastic sheet and spilling the wind. Taking the sail in hand, I held on as Epic was rushed into a corner. The 'trap' was formed by Penzance Harbour wall, and the beach end piled high with huge, angular granite blocks. Rowing the few hundred yards to the harbour entrance was a slow, strenuous affair. I made my way to shelter through rapidly forming little waves, sculpted by the forecast stiff wind from the forecast direction. A more sensible sailor would have positioned himself upwind in anticipation, avoiding the tight corner. A more sensible sailor would have overlooked a piece of elastic when seeking a sheet. (The sheet, preferably a non-stretching one, is attached to the sail at the clew. All sails have clews, even when the operative is deficient.)

Inside Penzance Harbour, all was pleasantly peaceful. The Scillonian passenger/cargo ship was just popping off to the Scillies. My mini cruiser was anonymous amid the bustle and general pottering. Leaving Epic secured on a running line, between the iron-legged coast road that spanned the shore side of the harbour, and a small sailing boat, I climbed a ladder and stepped between railings onto the pavement. The sun shone warmly. Feeling carefree, I strolled into the metropolis.

Penzance is graced with fine architecture of various styles. The main street is built on a hill and oozes character, above the retailers' tasteless sabotage at ground level that is – which just oozes. The plastic shop front blight is ripe for salvation, and could be restored to former glory.

From a pleasant lady in a small café, up a few steps in a side street, I ordered a tuna sandwich. I was delighted to receive an ample lunch, heavy with tuna and generously accompanied with fresh salad. Though the town is well endowed with art galleries and antique shops, my mission was merely gastronomic, so on that occasion I gave them a miss. Culture was shelved; my thoughts were beyond the lighthouse. At four o'clock, as I left Penzance, the southwest wind outside the harbour seemed as strong as ever. I headed for Newlyn, just a mile away.

At the time, Newlyn held possibly the largest fishing fleet in Britain, although the fishing industry was in crisis. Fish quotas were being cut along with the size of the fleet. Broken ships were left in sorry piles – their keels sawn through. The same was true in Mevagissey; one sturdy looking vessel was being broken up outside the boat-building shed, while inside a new boat was taking shape. Strange times. Hopefully the tide will turn and fishing will bounce back as it did after hard times at the end of the nineteenth century. Then, the Newlyn School of painters portrayed fishing families enduring hardship. Titles such as, 'Men must work and women must weep', and 'Never morning wore to evening, but some heart did break', told the sad tales.

Arriving in Newlyn after a gusty trip I spent a while rowing round, hoping to locate the Lentern Rose, a smaller than average fishing boat from Mevagissey. The harbour was extremely busy. Boats were manoeuvring – arriving, taking on fuel and ice or berthing. I spied what I thought was Nick the Greek's boat at the far end of the harbour. It was a pretty pea-green boat, but not Nick's, who is no more Greek, than Rupert his crew is a bear.

Rounding a more 'lighthousey' looking lighthouse than the Penzance example, which is perched on top of a Doric column, I headed onwards. Half an hour or so later, Epic lay off old concrete structures – silos of some sort I imagine. In the lee, I awaited the forecast. A helicopter dawdled overhead as 'Thames, Dover …' was interrupted. Fortunately, the nub of my area (Plymouth) was audible. '… occasionally four … thunder developing … isolated fog …'. (For fortunately, read unfortunately). When passing the big pink doors of Penlee Lifeboat Station, a mile from Mousehole, it began to rain. It was still raining when I rowed into Mousehole Harbour wearing my yellow oilskin jacket. My joyful demeanour on arriving at Penzance had waned somewhat.

Most unexpectedly, I received a shouted greeting from a couple standing on the quayside. They were the crew of Windsong, a twenty-four foot, bright yellow sloop that was leaning against the wall at the other (south) end of the harbour. The pair had visited Mevagissey in their boat a few days before. By chance they called at the gallery and we chatted about things nautical and arty. Brian taught navigation, and Cheryl painted; so we had something in common – painting. A falling tide hastened their departure. They were heading west and rushed off with a, "May see you later". They did. My outlook immediately brightened as I edged Epic onto the harbour-bed.

Mousehole Harbour was emptying, leaving Epic safely stranded for a while. In the company of artist and navigator, I settled my harbour dues with the handy harbourmaster as he chanced by. "Half a day; eleven feet; no charge." Thank you again, kind harbourmaster. In a nearby restaurant, divested of our wet weather gear, we span salty tales. Dining-chair sailing was as easy and agreeable as armchair sailing. The intrepid couple described their journey down from the Isle of Man. After a couple of pints 'yarning', both Land's End and Cape 'Hornwall' were in the bag.

Back down in the harbour, in my own good time, I rigged a pair of running lines from bow to harbour wall and back to boat, and from stern to nearby punt and back to boat. In my slight state of befuddlement it was a drawn out procedure, but it would make casting off a simple matter, with just one minor drawback – the dinghy would end up full of wet rope. Later, alone on my damp thwart, I found the prospect of 'doubling the Cape', as we mariners say, by no means cut and dried.

The night started well, for it stopped raining. At one o'clock I lay down in my sleeping bag. Soon I was warm and snug as a bug. Lying down, afloat in a very small boat is a pleasant sensation. The boat rocks as you adjust position, compensating to some degree for the hard, uneven surfaces. Exhaustion, and minimal hours of sleep can also enter the equation. Floodlights at the harbour entrance, together with harbour-side lighting, illuminated the scene; which was rather inconvenient. Ripples radiated from Epic as I extricated myself sufficiently from the bag to perform an undercover operation requiring the bailer. Feeling myself the target of hidden eyes, I was relieved when re-zipped.

An hour later (no, not the bailer) rain began to fall on my unprotected bag. I willed it to stop; oh how I willed. Minutes passed. The bag soaked up fine rain. As I willed I got wetter, finally deciding to vacate my delightfully warm, cosy (why-didn't-I-take-any-bloody-notice-of-the-thundery-showers-forecast) sleeping bag, before it got too saturated and heavy to stuff into a polythene bag; where I should have been. Clammy, chilled and miserable in my wellies, oilskin jacket and thin crackly waterproof trousers, I waited for dawn.

The illuminations 'concealed' the fact that Sunday had sidled out of the gloom. My preparations for leaving were almost complete when I noticed Windsong, not yet discernibly yellow, silhouetting towards the harbour exit. Thinking how surprised the crew would be to see me up and about at such an inhuman hour, I rowed over to wave them off. Surprise was mine. Windsong was being strategically tied up in deeper water towards the harbour entrance (also the exit).

It could have been a mistake to accept the offer of breakfast aboard the sloop, for I was becoming at one with the outdoor life. By that time I was accustomed to 'Spartan class', finding it stimulating in a warped kind of way. Windsong's cabin was dry, warm and definitely 'indoors'. 'Cosy' would be a yacht broker's appraisal, but to me it seemed palatial. The facility to muster tea and hot rolls was a strong selling point. Had sizzling bacon been on the menu I may have jumped ship. Epic, though midget, had a lot going for it, including standing headroom, and access to many more channels than a large yacht with television.

At quarter past eight I bade farewell to Brian and Cheryl, upped jib in anticipation, and rowed out of Mousehole Harbour. There was *'Half cloud cover …'*. Had I not been in sombre mood, assuming the voyage was nearing its damp death throes, I may have optimistically opted for, 'Half blue sky'. The early information from the Scilly station included '… northwest by west, five …'. Keeping close inshore I headed towards Lamorna Cove, two and a half miles distant, hoping the wind would behave for an hour as I was rushed along under Admiral power.

St Michael's Mount with its top tower lost in low cloud came into view from behind St Clement's Island – an islet positioned protectively a few hundred yards off Mousehole. Imagining a heavyweight flag straining behind the ominous stratus above the hidden castle I headed towards Porthgwarra, a mile from the inland hamlet of St Levan – of personal interest to 'our' Lord. Porthgwarra is the last stopping place on the South Cornwall Coast (the first for anticlockwise mariners). The final bolthole is only accessible in fair weather, and for small boats.

Half a dozen or so wave sculpted caves in the fractured granite cliffs, to the south of Mousehole, is/are, I presume, the Mousehole/s. Further along at the base of a ferny hillside, that sloped down to the sea, were stacks of wave-worn blocks around which surf surged noisily. Heavier swells receded leaving a few off-lying large rocks, just breaking the surface. The potent warning encouraged me to steer a little further out. Epic sped on. A vague sun disc attempted to break through the blackened sky. Clouds closed in. A few minutes reprieve – swathes of sunlit brightness raced across sea and land. The northwest wind hurried me along more swiftly. I put on my lifejacket.

The hectic ride up to Carn-du, a protective headland to the east of Lamorna Cove, was quite invigorating. Carn-du was behind, leaving me in open water. I noticed a few white buildings in the Cove. A wicked wind blew down the valley, taking me away from Lamorna. The enforced heading would have taken Epic outside Tater-du – a little white lighthouse a mile away on the lower slope of the next promontory. I feared being swept back into windblown Mount's Bay. I recalled the 'force five'. Quite invigorating became quite frightening. During a precious lull I was able to claw down and lash the sail, then row towards the protection of the cliffs. For a few strength-sapping minutes I hauled Epic against the wind into the lee. I was then free to row back towards the breakwater wall that at first seemed part of the shoreline. Areas of large quarried blocks lay on the hillside. The angular monoliths gave the landscape a severe edge. There was ample craggy charm without those jarring additions. A shaft of welcoming sunshine broke through as I rowed round the arm of the stone jetty. In calm water I guided Epic onto a patch of sand between a scattering of stones and mini-boulders. It was nine thirty.

Few people were about when I landed; but very soon a Japanese gentleman materialised, asking if he could take a picture of his three small children standing alongside the dinghy (without the crew). I had arrived just in time to add a point of interest to an otherwise empty beach. After quickly de-masting and unloading, I left the mast, oars and other gear at the roadside under the watchful eye of Bob, the car park man. Having moved a few stones and pulled Epic a few yards up the beach, I hurriedly walked the half-mile or so up the road to the public phone box. Julia must have left home, which meant waiting till lunchtime to arrange a lift. Quite happy to be landlocked, I spent a few hours enjoying Lamorna.

My photograph of the beached dinghy, backed by a heavily overcast sky, is but a sad silhouette. The man from the Land of the Rising Sun chose a better moment. Maybe, on a lacquered sideboard in Tokyo, there is a portrait photograph of three beautiful smiling children standing on a Cornish beach alongside a sunlit Mirror dinghy.

Help was on hand to assist carrying the dinghy up onto the jetty, beyond the reach of possible rough seas. The story could have ended at Lamorna. Sound reasons for calling it a day were pushed from my mind by a growing obsession to round Land's End. My little boat would be safe while I waited for winds of a gentle disposition, and sought plausible reasons for continuing.

In a café, a few yards up from the beach, I poured myself a cup of tea, inadvertently loading it with tea leaves. Preoccupied with the Land's End map, I had overlooked the strainer. From the window I glimpsed the distant Lizard, a darker grey form beneath a ceiling of low cloud. My mind was on an area six or seven miles in the other direction. Wistfully, avoiding off-lying rocky hazards, I threaded a course round the westerly tip of England. Would I pass inside or outside the Armed Knight? How would I cope with Kettle's Bottom? Speculatively, I charted the future, knowing full well that the sensible option was to restrict further interest in OS 203 to two-dimensional fantasizing. Tea leaves in the bottom of my cup were no help in predicting the future. Into a fresh cup I poured another tea.

Before addressing more than a nod to the Lamorna Wink, a pub ten minutes walk along the valley road, I explored woodland and the tumbling stream which I had rushed by on my way to the phone box. Huge granite boulders, around which the little stream raced, were clothed in rich yellow/green moss, adding softness to the sheltered scene. Nature was in the process of claiming neglected artists' studios, ironically adding a touch of 'rustic' to the mysterious woodland landscape – typical 'Lamorna Birches'. (Lamorna Birch, 1869-1955. Famous Newlyn School painter and founder of the Lamorna Colony of artists and writers.)

Move To Mevagissey

It was around Easter time, 1969. Julia and I stood in front of a large black door on the harbour-side in Mevagissey. The barricade, which had a small door set into it, hung on wheels from a rail. The small door was locked. We wondered what lay behind, our curiosity aroused by the two words, hand painted in black letters on a fresh white card a foot square, FOR SALE. It was by default that we were on hand to read that temptingly precise statement. Could the card be a talisman and turn up trumps?

Let me explain. Starting from a point on the coast, due west from our home in Shrewsbury, Julia and I, over the previous twelve months had taken the road south, seeking premises in which to set up a pottery workshop and showroom. The property had to be within easy reach of the sea, and bear some relation to the value of a tiny terrace house with gasometer and prison views.

Having crept round Wales over several weekends, without seeing a single large stone building at the head of a creek going cheap, we continued our coastal creep round the Southwest Peninsula: Somerset, North Devon, North Cornwall, South Cornwall and South Devon. That final weekend of property hunting (though we did not know it), having found no joy in the Plymouth area, was the turning point. On a whim we turned round and headed back over the Tamar River into Cornwall. We returned to the fishing village, with narrow streets and cottages clustered around a double harbour, that we viewed the previous day in glorious sunshine. The tide had been in, endorsing our highest rating for the location. We felt our quest, finding a property for a pittance was doomed, so we decided to spend a day in Shangri-la. Strange that it should be for recreation, not property prospecting, that we retraced our steps; and a happy coincidence that Piper had just nailed up his sign.

Piper and his brother Alf owned the large three-storey building with the big black door. The ground floor was mostly taken up with Dunn's Walkaround, a gift-shop festooned externally with square yards of postcards, and run by Alf. We tracked Piper down. He lived in a house in an orchard, up a drive behind the village. We would meet at the black door. The little door was opened and we beheld, through the entry, a large sloping yard with a huge shed over to the left. Four or five yards ahead stood an open-fronted, corrugated roofed, defunct coal-shed. Utilizing a high stone wall to the right, and abutting a property to the rear, its only true wall was of naked breezeblocks. Platforms of concrete and railway sleepers, that once supported large paraffin tanks, stood amidst rubble and coal-dust.

Though in need of tidying, the shed looked a fair swap for 10 Victoria Terrace in the county of Shropshire. The open fronted-shed was not for sale. The large shed was not for sale. Nothing was for sale. We listened with crushed emotions as the ex coal merchant explained the meaning of the spurious sign. He then ushered us up to a vast old net loft above the Walkaround. With four large windows overlooking the harbour and out to sea, the old loft was, to a fledgling painter, pure, heart fluttering paradise. Obviously, one cannot purchase heaven, nor as it transpired, the loft. Piper thought a 'for sale' sign would create more interest than a 'for rent' one. How true. That was not to be the last time Piper would be proved right in matters relating to his property, and our involvement therein.

Without deliberation we decided to rent the studio of dreams. Had we not, we might still be looking, having trekked the coastlines up to Scotland and inspected huts on the Outer Hebrides. Towards the end of the year, after handing in our notices for release from secure paid employment, we would move to Cornwall. We would rent living accommodation of course, which would not be a problem, for it would be the end of the holiday season. It was all so simple.

The months ticked by. I would miss the blind children, and the education received from them at the castle. Colour was important to them. When glazing a pot for a sighted friend, it was essential to have chosen the recipient's favourite colours. In the future I would not take things for granted, and expect the unexpected. (So I was not too surprised when, a few months later, men landed on the moon.)

A large van was hired to transport my pottery equipment down to Cornwall. Also for shipment was a splendid old oak dresser, still our most prized possession, acquired for a song at auction – owing to foot and mouth travel restrictions. I had gone to the auction for floor covering for our new home in Shrewsbury. After successfully bidding fifteen shillings for a large Persian style carpet, big enough and more to cover the whole floor area, I had money to spare for bargain furniture.

With a person at each corner, the kiln was loaded into the van. Several hundredweights of glaze materials were packed, leaving room for the dresser and electric potters' wheel. Extrication of the wheel from 10 Victoria Terrace (pottery number two) was a relatively easy operation, for notches had been cut in the doorframe of the tiny bedroom, to squeeze it into possibly the world's smallest pottery. Pottery number three would have panoramic views over a Cornish harbour. What a glorious contrast to that bleak, cramped little bedroom, illuminated by a single naked light bulb that dimly glinted on the few visible square inches of tired green linoleum. Twenty months earlier the cumbersome wheel came out of the cowshed easily enough. The cowshed boasted a few more square feet than the mini pottery in the mini bedroom, but I had contrived to squander it by fitting the 'gift horse' counter mentioned earlier. My sales technique had been seriously defective, for I had to work hard segregating possible customers from my wares by removing and replacing the door and window to accommodate the enormous barrier.

Swans at Mevagissey
13" x 14"
'... the inner harbour slipway, round the corner from the gallery ...'

135

Brother Michael did most of the driving on the night trip down to Cornwall. The following morning, together with Piper, who could not quite lift the kiln on his own, we unloaded a ton of pottery equipment outside the old coal-shed. Though he was semi-retired, the great strength of the ex-boxer was to be invaluable over the next few weeks. While contemplating the transference of weighty cargo up a long flight of stairs, Piper proffered a solution that would save a lot of bother in the short term, and be a sensible move towards success of the venture long term.

"Why not take the coal-shed?", Piper suggested. The explanation, that customers were less likely to walk upstairs, seems so obvious now.

The premises would require more than a spot of dusting though. It was in need of electricity, water, and a shop front. It was true, standing at the front of the open shed that would become the sales area, one could look down the entry and glimpse the boats; but there would be no breathtaking sea and harbour panoramas. The dream of the upstairs studio had been uppermost in my mind over the preceding months, so it was with some pain that I opted to see sense, and rent the ground floor site. There would be fewer distractions in the back of the shed, and certainly no wild beasts shaking the walls. With a short intermission, I had shed one shed for another; but amid the shambles I sensed a silver lining.

On the day Julia and I secured the workshop/retail outlet, we also arranged, after being directed around the village to various 'probables', to take a small holiday cottage for the winter, with an option to stay in the summer at a higher rate. Our future residence fitted our dream cottage category, being situated in the heart of the village. In essence it was rather basic, but that mattered not one jot, for we viewed through wrap-round rose tinted spectacles. The floor area was possibly less than our old 'two up, two down', but that did not matter, for our possessions were fewer. We did not have to accommodate a pottery workshop or a boat. For financial reason, the Gremlin had to go. The sale, due to our moving to the seaside, was rather ironic.

The unusual 'one down, one up and one up again' configuration of our future home possessed other surprises. The kitchen, including the sink, was hidden in a cupboard on the ground floor – a tidy, if compact arrangement. The main bedroom held a secret cupboard also – a water closet. The limited area necessitated an open door policy when the facility was in use. It was a quaint feature, particularly as the master bedroom was en route to upstairs. The dwelling of surprising cupboards was situated at the bottom of a steep, winding and extremely narrow street, just a few steps from a vantage point overlooking the inner harbour and out to sea. The next day we went back to Shrewsbury. Very soon we would return.

Though we were setting off on a big adventure, we would not forget our first little home together in Victoria Terrace. The diminutive kitchen we enhanced with an unusual dresser. From a saleroom, less than a mile away, we successfully bid for a kitchen table with bulbous legs, and a wall cabinet with two glass doors. "Taking the Mrs out to dinner," shouted a witty bus driver as we headed home pushing our incredibly noisy, castor-wheeled table along the road. We rattled under that same railway-line, a short distance from the railway-bridge where I had struggled with a heavy green grip. Below the cabinet, which I screwed to the wall, I fixed half the sawn in half table. The other half, with legs sawn in half, I fixed on top of the taller section. Painted, in the then trendy bright orange, the cabinet and cannibalized table appeared a homogeneous whole.

The ground at the back of number ten was six inches higher when we left. Buried beneath the five feet 'long' back garden (it was about ten feet wide) was a pile of broken, dreary, creamy tiles and concrete rubble – the remains of a gruesome fireplace. The bathroom was five and a half feet long, the length of the kitchen, and six inches wider than the bath. The compact space meant raising your feet above bath height to turn round. Rather than 'risky orange', we chose 'safe white' for the bathroom. Unfortunately, the finish turned out an unpleasant off cream – a translucent, greeny brown type of cream, a bit like the fireplace tiles – tacky. A few days after applying the paint, I was quite surprised to find my feet stuck to the wall as I lay in the bath. The paint was still drying when we moved twenty months later.

The days ticked by. Finally, in early October, we closed the black front door of number ten for the last time, leaving behind happy memories, and a most unusual dresser. With the remainder of our worldly possessions, including a spin-dryer, we squeezed into our Fiat 600 and set off for Cornwall.

Pure Theatre
Lamorna to Porthgwarra

Let me yet know of you whither you are bound.
No, sooth, sir; my determinate voyage is mere extravagancy.

William Shakespeare 'Twelfth Night'

Three days later I was back at Lamorna Cove. My obsession prevailed – I just had to try to take Epic round Land's End. I can't really explain why. Evolution can claim a portion of blame – for our distant ancestors crept from the sea. 'Because it is there', though not very original, is the closest I can come to a reason. Windless weather was probably imminent. Whatever was bringing the 'non-wind', and how it would know when to stop, or should I say start, I did not dwell on. Meteorology is not an exact science.

At a very early hour, from a campsite near Mevagissey, I press-ganged brother Michael before he found something better to do. He and his Rascal (a small, slim, bright yellow van, eminently suitable for traversing narrow lanes with a dinghy on top) would transport me 'way down to La-morn-ah' (popular Cornish folk-song). Before heading west, we undertook a leisurely loading. There was no rush, for the distance between Lamorna and Porthgwarra, where I intended to wait for a period of extremely calm weather, was only six miles.

Physically I felt in good order. On most days over the last few years I had carried out a series of exercises. Though only lasting a minute or so, I used as many muscles as possible. The twisting, pulling and pushing included a 'hoist the mainsail' routine. Pressing fists hard together, one above the other, I slowly raised and lowered my arms a few times, alternating fist positions. Little effort was employed hauling ropes on my boat, but I had to be prepared for the unexpected. After hours of rowing over the previous weeks I was confident in my fitness to help

Epic round Land's End. There could be no real testing for the 'main event'. How do you practise being frightened? It was just a question of wait and see.

Friends told me of a couple, one a diver, who lived in Lamorna. It was suggested I look them up, to get the low-down regarding sea conditions in their area. With the Rascal parked tightly against the hedge in the narrow lane, Michael and I called at the little granite cottage. We stepped down into the garden, a treat of retreats, through which rushed the same boulder strewn stream that so impressed me a few days earlier. The secluded spot lay within protective wild woodland – a painter's paradise. Christine and Keith were at home. Keith's grandfather was a landscape painter who had lived and worked in the delightfully named 'Lily Cottage'. (Stanley Horace Gardiner 1888-1952 – one of the Lamorna circle, helped by Lamorna Birch.)

While taking tea in that tranquil setting, my resolve was severely tested.

"You've done well to get this far … stick while you're ahead … risky … bad currents …".

As you can imagine, Keith's repeated warnings did nothing to quell my apprehension. Later, down on the beach, I was attaching the oars to cleats on the gunwales using laces from a pair of my old running shoes. The laces were perfect for the job, being very long and strong. Keith looked on in disbelief.

"No one would think less of you if you called it a day. Phone me when you get round."

I took that as encouragement.

It was a heavenly day; warm and bright with a hazy sky over a calm sea, textured with slight rounded wavelets. With the Bosun wrapped neatly round the mast and the Admiral confined in the sail-bag, I headed westward. After the next stop my journey would no longer be a hit or miss affair – there was an ocean with rough edges to contend with. Having no wish to be 'overtaken' by a stationary buoy again, I had the tides pretty well sussed

From the beach and then the cliff-top, Michael photographed Epic's progress for a while. Apart from the departure picture at St Michael's, Michael's are still the only record of me at sea during the voyages. Those few photographs are a precious reminder; yet I knew nothing of them for quite a time. The first picture shows me in shirtsleeves, plying the non-matching oars, as if setting off for a row round Brookvale Park boating lake. Epic, with a white plastic bucket on the stern buoyancy compartment, is dwarfed by towering granite cliffs. There is nothing to suggest ocean aspirations. The series of five pictures ends with Epic, a barely discernible speck, three or four miles distant in front of the Runnel Stone – an isolated lump of rock situated a mile off Porthgwarra. It is a useful landmark and a danger to shipping – depending whether or not you run into it.

Lunchtime, and 'ta-ta' to Tater du. Where would I be the same time tomorrow? I wondered. Requiring local information, I gripped the oars and headed onwards, hopefully towards the answers. An hour or so later, my thoughts were interrupted by a faint buzzing sound out to sea. A large dolphin was leading two men in a dinghy in mutual entertainment. While I was more than happy escaping the 'pleasures' of the combustion engine, it seemed that sociable mammal was seeking them out. The dolphin made a final dive and the dinghy-men disappeared back east.

As I angled in towards the shore, a speck of white 'became' the gable end of one of a few cottages in the fishing hamlet of Penberth Cove. A large black structure, like an H on its side, was a mystery to me at the time. It turned (not recently) out to be a defunct capstan. A mechanical winch now hauls out the boats. Anchored a couple of hundred feet offshore was a solid little open fishing boat named Lily. I chatted to the stocky fisherman who was waiting for his boat to be hauled up the granite slip on the exposed beach that had been constructed between large boulders. In such calm conditions, I was informed, a landing at Porthgwarra would not be a problem. The boatman's upbeat information helped me forget the cautious Lily Cottage conversation. While I rowed on, Lily chugged off with the fisherman to join the dozen or so boats at the top of the beach.

Soon I was involved in a man/dolphin trio (there was a lot of it about). A pair of playful 'aquabats' kept company with Epic for ten minutes or so. I was reminded of the passing visit of a dolphin at the other end of Cornwall. I hoped the portent signalled a positive scenario. As you know, an hour or two after that first sighting I was very nearly shipwrecked. Dolphins and magpies may have more than livery in common. Perhaps a measure of joy was in store – for only three miles further on, I hoped to take 'the big right-hander' and head into the Atlantic Ocean.

After passing the jagged topped Logan Rock headland, a formidable landmark jutting into the channel, I became aware of a mysterious, distant sound. It was spasmodic, akin to muffled clapping rather than the more likely surf against granite – most intriguing. Turning round, I viewed a visual quirk of nature. There appeared to be a sizeable patch of predominately red flowers at the cliff-top. As I closed in and the sound increased, the mystery was solved. The floral arrangement synthesized into an audience enjoying a performance of Twelfth Night (I learned later) at the open air Minack Theatre, Porthcurno.

If boating be the food of fun, row on – slow exit, stage starboard.

Rowing for a further hour positioned me off Porthgwarra. Relieved to notice a lighter scar in the cliff, I headed into the last refuge. Unfortunately, the tide was in just too far for me to undertake a straight-forward sand landing. The milky green 'water colour' was a sure sign of sand below, but sea lapped the lower end of the sloping granite slip. Attached there, and running seawards, was a fixed line – a great help to me in landing at the edge of the giant 'cobblestones'. There was little scraping of hull as I hauled the dinghy up from the water's edge. After I had unloaded Epic, a bearded chap offered to help me lug her a few yards further up. The strenuous lift and hurried stagger pre-empted a rushed release onto a pointy projection, causing me to wince inwardly. Not wishing to appear ungrateful, I left checking the thin ply till later.

Four, 'fifteen-foot-ish', fishing boats lay a little way up the slip. Down at the lower end there lolled a handful of people. That was the gloriously minimal action of 'Downtown' Porthgwarra. Instead of taking the direct route up the steep slipway, one can reach 'Uptown' through an underpass. This tunnel was blown through the cliff by St Just dynamiters, back in mining times. The seaward side (slip-side) of the excavation features a perplexing, non-accessible, higher entrance. The miners' explosive skill was obviously in advance of their directional ability. Rough weather combined with onshore wind drives a fair quantity of seaweed into the narrow channel. The gratis fertilizer was carried away in carts, easily loaded via the tunnel, commissioned for that very purpose.

The 'shed cafe', beyond the slip in a more sheltered position, was closed by the time I wandered up there. In my quest for local knowledge I spoke with a gentleman a few years my senior. It transpired that Eric was the author of books for children, the harbour master, the café master and the very man to direct me to the skipper of one of the fishing boats on the slip. Les lived two miles away, up a long steep hill at Trethewey. Having walked less than a mile, I was fortunate to be offered a lift by the bearded man returning home with his wife and children. He was, or had been, a merchant seaman, and obviously more used to dealing with steel plate than plywood. Peaceful Porthgwarra was the family's favourite spot. Happily, my 'low quay' arrival had not made waves.

The man with local knowledge invited me into his home. He intended going to sea himself the following day and was fairly sure conditions would be favourable. Metaphorically speaking, the completion of the voyage was, as my walk back to Epic, all downhill. With a light step, only partly due to gravity, I strolled through a landscape shaped by the elements. Sparse, tortured trees, bent to the east, testament of prevailing winds. Evidence of lichen and mosses suggested surroundings often draped in damp mist. It was my fortune to descend through countryside wrapped in soothing summer.

On the outskirts of Porthgwarra I stopped to admire a vigorously carved stone relief. Set above a doorway, it graced a fine granite cottage situated a couple of hundred yards from the sea. Apparently, the large headed, open-mouthed fishy monster was a dolphin – a wondrous and rather fanciful representation. Seated in the porch was a gentleman, glass in hand, appreciating fine whisky and the pleasant evening. He had no objection to me photographing the beast, which was a relief (carving). I wondered if there was local significance in the work. There was none. Apparently, the heavy creation which must have weighed a ton, had been transported from 'way up country' on behalf of a previous cottage owner. Perhaps it was my sun-parched appearance that led kindly John to offer refreshment. Gratefully I accepted a tumbler of iced beer and was soon chilling out in the shade of the relocated dolphin.

Down on the slip I was kept busy for a while, making good with plastic wood – repairing the slight hull damage. The plywood was broken, and though the small break was almost closed up, the fracture needed sealing to prevent seepage, water logging and peace of mind. With Epic sound, and I equipped with information from the knowledgeable Les, I felt reasonably confident regarding the imminent mission.

Uptown I checked the other amenity, closing the phone-box door behind me. Acting on Keith's, "if you're at a loose end I'll drive you over to the pub", I rang to let him know I had arrived at Porthgwarra, and my 'end could not be looser'. A public house diversion was just the ticket to kill a couple of the remaining fifteen hours of countdown.

The evening was still and the sea beautifully, 'boding well', flat. A large seal entered the inlet, surfacing tentatively. It raised its head to con and sniff out intruders. Happily at one with the world, I lay quietly on the rocks watching the gentle giant. A young lady from Canada (via Lamorna Cove where she was doing summertime work at the harbour-side café) also crept down to seal watch, saying she often came to see the solitary seal. She offered me a piece of Highland shortcake. I will never know if I would have accepted the offer, for at that moment Keith arrived.

After an hour or so, supping in moderation at the First and Last at Sennen, we supped our last sup and drove back to Epic. The headlights faded. Alone in the blackness, I groped my way down to Epic. The slip slope was really too steep for sleep. At first, when moulding myself to fit the undulations between the large, smoothed blocks of granite, relaxation seemed possible. A little way down from the dinghy, just a few yards away from the calm sea, I was soon in the groove. Had I been able to remain stock still, all would have been well, but slight projections, that at first were mere irritations, became vengeful, causing me to adjust position, precipitating downward movement. (By then I should really have known better.) Though I tried, there was no arresting the slipping sleeping bag. Continually 'up-wriggling', pushing against crevice with my feet, would not halt the inexorable slide for long. My iliac crests (pelvis tops) would not be comforted. True, I had other things on my mind, but why, when the cause was obviously lost, did I not relocate?

Throughout the night I was lullabied, unsuccessfully, by rhythmic slow swishing of small waves on soft sand. (If only I had been in a hammock, slung between palm trees.) In the early hours my overworked mind was diverted for a time by a perturbing sound – perhaps the munching of thick seaweed stems by powerful jaws. The noise came from the dark sea a couple of dozen yards away. My straining eyes caught only a hint of silent bats – residents of the blasted caves, I assumed.

From inside my wandering, though comfortingly warm, sleeping bag, I noted – *'5:55 Thur 19 Aug V (variable) 3 or less F (fair) mod pos fog? L'*. 'Fog later' did not concern me at the time, the present being very much on my mind. The sea just below my feet was still calm – not even a riplet. All systems were 'go'. I intended setting off at around half past ten, using the remainder of the outgoing tide to help me along to Land's End, where the turning tide would ease me round. It was as simple as that.

With time to kill I had a lie-in. Passing time, I observed inch long, marine woodlice type creatures scurrying about. I was pleased to have been unaware of those little beings during the night. They were a light taupey colour, more 'feelery' and less shiny than the compact garden type. Though I was the intruder, they conducted themselves in a fault-less manner, happily remaining outside my quarters. The large head of the seal appeared close in. Had it been in the vicinity all night? Was it a vegetarian?

A lady swimmer, seventy years of age (she volunteered the informa-tion) came down to the cove to swim. Soon after, Les arrived to launch his boat. The steel-shod keel, guided in an iron stained groove, worn into the granite over the years, carried the white mock clinker boat into the sea with a rattling rush. Hitched to the rope that I found so handy when landing, Les prepared to go to sea. Leaving hectic Downtown, I walked up and across Gwennap Head to see what lay in store.

On my way up to the cliff-top, I stopped to look down into the cove. Epic, listing towards me, hiding white topsides and showing off her peeling varnished ply interior, presented all the charm of a cheap wardrobe. The sea, on the ebbing tide, just covered the gently shelving sand as it had on my arrival. The colour gradually deepened from light eggshell blue/green, imperceptibly darkening into deep steel. Nearing the headland I became aware of roaring traffic. That should not have been, for my OS map was quite recent and showed no new roads. The volume increased. Looking down from the cliff edge I saw no mystical motorway. I beheld a spectacle that blew my mind. To the east, the sea was but a millpond. Before me, hell boiled. Great swells, the product of a distant Atlantic storm, rose up the cliff ever higher, then sucked back down, forcing the tremendous weight to rejoin the turmoil. Tortured torrents tumbled down through the turquoise, churning out skeins of white warning that lingered on the surface a little way off the conflict.

Following the footpath towards H M Gwennap Head lookout station, I passed a 'flock' of twitchers. Grouped a little way down the slope at the cliff edge, there were adults and offspring. Most were attached to cameras sporting large telephoto lenses. The cluster remained motionless – statues overseeing the passage of time.

In a short while I came upon the lookout station. It commanded, as you would expect, a panoramic view of a fair portion of the sea I planned to venture upon. My tiny vessel would be tracked, at least part of the way. Feeling secure, I would give a confident wave to the team as I sailed by. On reaching the isolated building I was seriously taken aback. The place was locked and unmanned. For a while I was stunned. How many reasons did I need to abort the mission?

Though I harboured other thoughts at the time, the vacated facility would have made an ideal observation post for twitchers. I wondered if the bird watchers were set for an extended vigil, and if so, might they record the passage of an aquatic oddity. It was time to clutch at straws.

Gradually coming to terms with the empty lookout letdown, I strolled on across the remote headland. I was hoping to glimpse the Longship's Lighthouse that stands on a reef, a little over a mile off Land's End. The lighthouse was three miles distant, behind a veil of mist, restricting visibility to about one mile. During the previous few days I had wondered more and more if I would reach this westerly point. It was as well I did not see the final outpost. Turbulent seas, poor visibility and an empty Coastguard station were quite enough to be going on with.

Contemplatively, I meandered back to the Cove, walking on a springy, floral carpet. The rich random patterns equalled the subtlety of antique Persian harmonies. Heathers of fiery purple/reds and burnt orange, along with gorse flowers of the most intense yellow crowded the spongy grasses.

Perched on a rocky outcrop was a bird with ruffled brown plumage. It was reasonably defined, standing out for a moment against a patch of white ocean. Larger than a pigeon, it had characteristics of both owl and chicken. Before I could bring my camera to bear (bird), the unusual specimen took flight, dipping out of sight (definitely not a bear).

Passing close to the twitchers again I noticed a member, who, though sitting with the group, had ceased watching for a while. I approached quietly, bent over and whispered, "What are you looking for?"

"Birds," he whispered. There was a hint of hesitation, suggesting he was not too sure of my sanity. I slipped away without mentioning the chicken-owl.

Beyond The End
Porthgwarra to Sennen Cove

From Porthgwarra phone box I rang Falmouth Coastguard, informing them of my intention. They wished to know what safety equipment I was taking. It was a serious business.

"Distress flare; foghorn; compass; lifejacket; warm jumper; waterproof."

"Contact us when you reach Sennen Cove."

"I will," answered an adrenalin'd autopilot.

"Good luck," a cool professional voice ended the brief conversation. There was no suggestion I forget such foolishness. The die was cast.

Launch minus ninety minutes. Leave phone box in pensive mood. Perhaps a little vacant, but certainly not lonely, there being no room for thoughts other than practicalities relating to the task in hand. I wandered down and fiddled with Epic for a while. Les brought his boat back in.

146

Eric organized the winching up the slip. I chatted a while, then wandered up to the shed-café with the winch-man/harbourmaster (adept at filling a variety of 'rolls'). Eric, as caterer, opened the premises early to serve me a couple of mugs of tea. I was delighted to receive an inscribed copy of his adventure book for children, rich with happy-ever-afters. The gift seemed an ideal talisman. Happily, it was much later that I read the bit about the 'Supreme Ruler of the Underwater Kingdom'.

To sustain me on the journey, Eric insisted I take along one of his pasties. The specimen was large, pale, heavy and extremely welcome for I was low on victuals. Later, Eric helped me carry Epic down onto the sand. In order to photograph the 'master of trades' on the slip behind the dinghy, I made my way over to the rocks to the left of the inlet. There I managed to fill both my wellingtons. Despite cold feet, the countdown continued. Kindness shown that day helped me through what could have been an over anxious few hours. There was little butterfly activity. All things considered, I was relatively relaxed.

The time arrived. I eased Epic into the water and boarded with the necessary lunge to keep her upright. Hurriedly locating the oars in the rowlocks, I took the skin off the middle joint of my left little finger. There was no reason to hurry; I just wanted to appear confident. Normally, a scratched little digit is not a problem, but annoyingly, the nick caught on my jeans as I rowed and after a few strokes they were streaked with a little blood. Fortunately, man-eating sharks (or sharks eating men) were not rife in the area; and in any case I intended retaining my non-capsizing record. The seal raised its head to see me off. He was close enough to be photographed, but as I pressed the button he sank. The whiskery white tuft is difficult to spot in my picture. My wildlife studies up to that time were seriously lacking substance with no clue as to the species involved. Though the launch was far from perfect, I was half an hour ahead of schedule. One hundred yards out I stopped to take stock.

As Epic rose soothingly over the light swells I squeaked off my wellies, wrung out my socks and spread them out on the stern seat to dry. From the ice cream box I took my new Swiss Army knife, cut a square of Elastoplast, and applied it to my leaky little finger. It seemed fitting that a tool sporting a red-cross logo should be initiated in such a manner. With teeth and hands occupied, and a blade sharp enough to cut paper in intimate proximity with my nose, I watched the heavier and more streamlined oar slip silently overboard. How reassuring it was to observe the fail-safe system at work. Tied to the trainer lace that held the rowlock to the cleats, the long bootlace, with quick release half bow, safely restrained the wayward oar. I gingerly pulled the oar back within reach. If Eric and Les were using binoculars, they may have doubted my suitability for the task ahead. Over wet jeans I pulled my wet wellies – protection against sunburn. (I was not intending swimming any distance.)

Porthgwarra had been good to me. It seemed so familiar, as if I had lived there for a while, yet my occupancy had been a mere eighteen hours. Those hours were heightened by trepidation, resignation, and finally, excitement. As I rowed away, I looked back with fondness at deserted 'Downtown'.

I cast my eye along the low rocky cliff to the left of the cove (viewed from seaward). Hella Point stretched south for two or three hundred yards. Breaking waves rolled over the end. Although there was no wind at the time, the Point would provide Porthgwarra with protection from strong westerlies. Giving the rough water a wide berth, I rowed out into the Atlantic Ocean. A somewhat agitated sea greeted me. Had I not taken an early morning stroll, it would have been a more than somewhat confused mariner rowing out beneath the twitcher's gaze. My eyelevel being only thirty inches above the surface, I was spared the sight of most of the churning confusion. The view for me featured waves striking the cliffs. The sight and sound of the roaring, scouring swells was to accompany me for some time. Away from the granite walls, the sea surface was smooth with small rounded waves going my way – pretty much as I had hoped after two wind free days.

In what seemed no time at all, the sea behind me was empty. I assumed the tide was ushering me deceptively swiftly round Gwennap Head. Totally disoriented, I was confused to see, rising from the sea, a string of low-lying rocks that gradually 'became' the Logan Rock promontory. The swells were so far apart that I was unaware Epic was taking a switchback ride. Intending to continue half a mile or so out from the headlands, I made swift progress, but was soon over a mile offshore. I angled back in towards the barely visible Armed Knight, a rugged formation about a hundred and fifty yards long, standing that same distance offshore. The defiant islet, in a most inhospitable location from a seafarer's point of view, was just a mile and a half away – half a mile before Land's End. The Armed Knight I knew well, if only in two dimensions. It was portrayed clearly, set on a blue sea under a clear blue sky on the cover of my OS 203. Many times I optimistically fantasized – taking Epic through the inviting gap between islet and the mainland.

Headlands emerged from the mist to be swallowed after my passing. An area of short, sharp, non-breaking little waves caused a bumpy ride for a while – perhaps Epic was passing over shallows. It was about half past ten when I sighted white water breaking over the Longships's reef. The lighthouse, well over a hundred feet tall, remained obscure till I was nearly abeam. After thousands of miles free reign, the ocean's progress had been obstructed by the shelving sea-bed, forcing higher the stampeding swells. Huge waves formed, breaking against the reef barrier. There were breaking waves in a half-mile line. A two hundred yard wide block of surf rose in slow motion, hung in the air for a few moments, then faded. Other eruptions along the defensive line drew the sting from the invading force. Since rounding Hella Point, the increasing sound of the ocean's agitation had increased to the point where the booming, crashing cacophony assailed from both sides.

Passing behind the Armed Knight was no longer on my agenda – the darker form of the off-lying island was barely distinguishable. My earlier survey from Gwennap Head encouraged me to keep equidistant between the reef and the maelstrom around the cliffs. I had reached the end of Cornwall. In a charged state of euphoria I scribbled with shaky hand,

10.48 ROAR of Longships huge rollers! continuous ROAR 10.52 Lands End.

Surprisingly, running the gauntlet had been fairly straightforward and physically undemanding. The battle had been mental. Epic bobbed along quite happily, going with the flow. The noise at first was scary, but when I became accustomed, it added to the thrill. Motorized assistance would have lessened the purity of the adventure.

Half an hour after passing the westerly outpost I turned right. Epic brushed through bands of foam on less agitated water. Over diminishing swells I rowed on through the Tribbens – a two hundred yard wide channel inside the Cowloe rocks. Heavy waves crashed over that barrier, giving some protection to Sennen Cove's open harbour. The ocean backed up behind the Cowloe, forming a gravity defying higher level. It was a most disconcerting phenomenon, like a tidal wave in waiting, seeming set to roll on at any moment. To seaward the mist drew back. Sunshine and blue sky appeared. The roaring sound of the sea faded as I approached the seaweed draped, low-lying foreshore. It reached out further than usual, even though the exceptionally low tide still had over an hour to drop. It would reveal further fingerings of weed and rocks, enclosing a larger, shallow 'lagoon' at the end of a brand new lifeboat slipway. After a final pull on the oars, I crouched at the stern while Epic, bow up, glided over the clear water onto the concrete slip.

It was all over. I was safe, bursting with relief, floating in a heightened state of exhilaration. All thought had been focused on my tide ride to Sennen. Now free, my self-appointed taskmaster became redundant. He slipped from my shoulders as I stepped ashore at journey's end.

Sennen Cove was pleasantly quiet. Some distance away, a scattering of people sat at the top of the beach by a fleet of hauled out boats. A solitary child was building a sand castle. He seemed to be conjuring up 'a St Michael's'. The air was still. He would soon need a lightweight paper flag to fly from the top turret.

With nothing but a puddle at the end of the slip, and Sennen lifeboat moored a couple of hundred yards offshore, I felt sure the dinghy would not be in the way, but to be polite I strode up the slipway to check. The man overhauling winch gear inside the station said Epic would be alright for a while. I was free to phone Falmouth Coastguard to inform them of my safe arrival. I sat at a table, over the road from a café next to the lifeboat station, taking afternoon tea – quite continental. Holidaymakers were seated at other tables. Also feeling on holiday I removed my wellingtons to flex my white feet in the sunshine. With saltwater evaporating from my damp jeans, I bathed in luxurious idleness for half an hour. I found myself in conversation with a local fisherman. Having no intention of continuing the voyage, I do not know why I ventured, "Is a passage to St Ives possible in a small rowing boat?"

"Nearly five hours of tide left …"

Being one of the highest spring tides of the year also meant it was one of the swiftest. My irrational mind computed: twenty miles at four miles per hour; a couple or so miles courtesy of the big tide – no problem. I had gone insane. All rational, mental functioning ceased. Why oh why? Time was of the essence. At twenty minutes after midday 'an invincible lunatic' pulled on his wellies and strode back down the slip. 'He was just going to pop round to St Ives.' During my fifty minutes stay at Sennen Cove I had not strayed far from the lifeboat station area. My unplanned exit was not the most sensible decision I have ever made. What can I say? Hurried foolishness allowed no time for the usual 'what ifs'. I did not even make a second call to the coastguard – totally beyond the pale. I confess complete, unmitigated, imbecilic irresponsibility.

The Great White

Sennen Cove to St Ives

When a few yards out to sea I swapped wellies for flip-flops, tied on my lifejacket and tightened the floppy white hat cord under my chin. Air Point was my first target landmark. The fact that it was a mere mile away, the other side of Whitesand Bay and obscured by mist, should have been a warning; but I was already blinded by adventure. I made haste, leaving well to starboard a great sweep of dazzling light sand that faded into haziness. Large rounded swells passed under Epic to crash on the beach. Squealed delights from intrepid bathers, shepherded into safe zones by lifeguards, reached me above the sound of breaking surf as I sped quickly northward. The sun became lightly veiled. The distance between swells increased from tens to hundreds of yards as I propelled Epic obliquely away from the beach. Rowing conditions were perfect. With my course and afternoon mapped out, I set about expending the necessary energy to meet my, or should I say nature's, deadline.

Released from making major decisions for a while, my mind turned to the matter of refuelling. I took a couple of mouthfuls from my gallon water bottle – this was repeated several times an hour to counteract dehydration. Hollow feelings from my empty stomach prompted thoughts of the 'great white'. The Porthgwarra pasty had remained solidly in place, tucked away below my right-hand rowlock on the side buoyancy compartment. Cool and large, it was the ace of snacks for a ravenous rower – more than king-size. In rest mode, with the oars sticking out held by my 'under-knees', I bit off the first instalment. In the time taken to place a pasty on the side deck I was plying the oars again, savouring a portion of end pastry, eagerly awaiting the vegetables. Pasties provide both sustenance and lottery excitement. You never know when you will hit the jackpot. In lesser productions, meat is a mere token. Encounters with new species are spiced with an element of gambling. Expectancy to the end – will the 'stake' turn trumps, or turnip?

Five miles on from Sennen and one mile southwest of Cape Cornwall, twin islets rise from the sea. They mysteriously materialized from the vapour like freshly formed volcano tops. The map gave me the position of the Brisons and I could see they were no more than fifty feet high as I approached, but 302 could not warn of the angry area of white water to landward of the peaks. Reduced visibility, together with my low vantage point made it impossible to determine whether spasmodic waves were breaking against Cape Cornwall, the Brisons, or somewhere in the channel between. The tide hurried me into the risky unknown, triggering a healthy panic and an abrupt about-turn. Rapidly burning up pasty power, I forced Epic out to sea, away from the problem islets. The Cowloe phenomenon, only more so, pertained at the Brisons. As I rowed up towards the ridge I entered a large area of small breaking waves on the seaward side. A detour was required. Away from the threat I headed north again, pulling through 'shark-fin' wavelets – the result of backwash from the islets. Being tightly packed, the sharp little waves were more troublesome than those encountered just south of Land's End. I found the slow stuttering progress most frustrating and was mightily relieved to finally escape into clear water. The avoiding action placed me as far west as off Land's End.

I was abeam the distinctive Cape Cornwall, topped with an old mine chimney landmark. Leaving a healthy mile between Epic and the mist-shrouded cliffs of West Penwith, I continued rowing at a respectable rate of knots, passing a rugged coastline scattered with mining relics. The mist thickened, concealing the old workings and engine houses that clung to the cliffs around Botallack. Though I should not have been there in the first place, I was miffed not to view the stark ruins from the ocean.

If all went well, a heading between north and east would take me to St Ives Bay.

Approaching the powerful lighthouse-topped Pendeen Watch headland, three miles on from Cape Cornwall, I lost sight of land. The Sennen Cove fisherman had warned me to keep clear of the Three Stone Oar – one large and two tiny rocks, six hundred yards to the north of the Watch. From the lidded ice-cream box I took out my compass, and with map in hand, worked out a navigation strategy. I would head northeast till sighting or hearing something. Losing visual contact with Cornwall, whilst heading towards the unseen Oars, was a little disturbing. Trusting the compass was difficult, for my instincts suggested I was heading for Canada. I sipped water, took a bite from the 'great white' and plunged into the misty blanket in the direction indicated by the compass needle. Those ten minutes in the mist seemed so much longer. The faintest indication of a headland materialized, right where it should have been. Soon I was able to see a lighthouse, confirming Pendeen abeam. A couple of hundred yards off the starboard bow the sea broke white against the Three Stone Oar(s), revealing the troublesome rocks, which unlike the Brisons are extremely low-lying. Though it was for a relatively short period, my blind, faultless piece of navigation gave me confidence in the clever little compass – unerringly pointing the way, knowing nothing of fog, fear, or Canada.

Visibility to the west remained hazy. On a dark steel/blue sea, under a dusty pale blue sky, I headed into sunshine. Had I been heading the other way, the gradual onset of favourable wind would have been apparent sooner. Concentrating on purposeful rowing, for there was great incentive, I failed to notice the change. Riplets, the sign of good fortune foretelling the onset of welcome wind power, dappled the sea surface. Tide and oars had been taking me towards St Ives at around five miles an hour and it was not till a pasty pause that I felt the breeze. It was about three o'clock, with Pendeen Watch still powerfully present two miles astern, when I set the sails goose-winged (one each side of the mast). Epic made respectable progress, though no quicker than energetic rowing.

Besides welcome relief from pulling hard on the oars, I appreciated having my hands free. By that time I was particularly adept at feet steering. The ride was gentle enough for me to take pictures of waves breaking at the base of cliffs. Such interludes confirmed there was no safe place to stop before St Ives. It was imperative to keep up the pace. The wind eased and I row-sailed for a while to keep on schedule. The breeze strengthened. I willed away the miles.

The breeze increased, turning into a wonderful wind and continuing from dead astern. Epic surged on with the Red Admiral to port and the boathook holding the Bosun out to starboard, catching more of nature's favourable draught. Shortly after resuming proper sailing, my next objective hove into view. The irregular chunky outcrop of Gurnard's Head actually resembled a gurnard's head. (A gurnard is an ugly fish with a large head.) It is one of the few features to help identify position on that stretch of coastline. The headland, together with a few other rocks, caused the racing tide to throw up huge plumes of sun-whitened surf. Epic tilted and yawed as my overworked feet made belated corrections to the erratic course. While seeking a view between sail and gunwale, I took a series of superfluous photographs recording general boat clutter, sails and sky, together with a bloodied jean leg. Eventually a shot that resulted in a large painting – 'Headland and White Plumes' was captured. The picture of powerful contrasts is a reminder of that frantic race to safety.

In watercolour painting, white areas can be represented by leaving blank paper. Surprising perhaps that so few snow scenes are produced when imagined finished areas are there before starting. Quite the opposite is true of stone carving. Michelangelo knew his David was inside the block of marble, but he still had to chip the excess away. (That reminds me of a sad tale concerning other great artists and the disappointment felt by a poor man after he had put a painting and violin up for auction – a Rembrandt and Stradivarius. Alas, Stradivari was a very poor painter.)

Four inlets further on, west of Zennor Head, I bypassed Pendour Cove. A beautiful mermaid is associated with Zennor. I did not seek her out, for she has a reputation of luring mariners to a watery grave.

To calculate progress I had divided the passage into sections. Between Sennen and St Ives I sectioned thus: Cape Cornwall; Pendeen; Robin's Rocks (half a mile before the ugly fish, with no obvious ornithological attributes); The Carracks. That last feature, at the four/fifths mark, is a low rock formation – surrounded by crashing surf at the time. '4:00 The Carracks ½ ahead ?' The question mark is a sign of disbelief. Had I really made such good progress? "I am flying … stormy waters …" Alone on the ocean, in a pushing my luck sort of way, I sang with gusto to ease apprehension. Over the hours, the enormity of my utter foolishness sank in. Without that magical wind I could not have reached St Ives. True, the forecast wind was favourable, but to gamble on perfect direction, duration and strength was a bit of a long shot. Weather forecasting is not an exact science.

Under white patchy high clouds, with sunlight sparkling on waves behind Epic, I had that magnificent arena to myself. Other than a small fishing boat and a pair of canoes off Sennen Cove, I saw no other vessel at sea after leaving Porthgwarra.

I reeled in the remaining miles, and then, AND THEN, from behind Clodgy Point slid The Island. (Like man, it is not an island; although at times I felt a certain affinity.) My vision became a tiny bit blurred – the effect of that beautiful breeze I suppose. The moment I knew St Ives was within reach was the high point of highs, a chest-heaving pinnacle of elation.

'*4:30 Tate in view, I can't believe it !!!!*' I scribbled.

With sails set to port I headed in towards Porthmeor Beach. I looked for, but could not pick out, the Garrack Hotel from where I produced the oil painting mentioned earlier. Sailing alongside the isthmus, two hundred yards out from the sandy beach, I felt a wonderful feeling of reprieve.

By five o'clock my pace had slowed to what, on terra firma, would be a crawl. When rounding the eastern end of 'The Island', I realised the tide had finished slacking and, having turned, was starting to run back towards Sennen. Had I dallied during the race to St Ives, a tide against wind situation would have developed. Short steep waves would have taken Epic back, back wetly to the Gurnard, and eventual darkness.

Off the comparatively sheltered harbour entrance I pulled down the sails. As I tidied up, I cast a nostalgic glance towards the St Ives Bay Hotel. It stands to the south of the harbour overlooking Porthminster Beach. Before being elevated to assistant chef in the hotel over the hill, I spent a few weeks at 'The Bay'. There I washed up alongside Felix, who hailed from Madrid where his family owned a restaurant. When Felix arrived in Cornwall, his English was only a smidgen better than my Spanish which comprised little more than 'adios amigo'. Within a few days of dunking dirty dishes, reciprocal tuition enabled us to sing the ballad of Davy Crocket together using the other's language. I still have the name of Felix's family restaurant written on the back of a Players Gold Leaf packet. I would love to meet the 'King of the wild frontier' again. (It seems I have forgotten the Spanish words.)

After a leisurely row into the harbour I tied up alongside the light-house quay (Smeaton's Pier). It was an ignominious resting place, with

St Ives

10″ x 10½″

'Without that magical wind I could not have reached St Ives.'

wind driven, frothy off-white spume engulfing Epic. She appeared set in meringue, hardly just 'dessert' for the game little craft that danced over miles of pristine ocean.

At one point, while waiting for a lift home, I stood for a while near the slip, close to the Sloop Inn. Every minute or so a surge of salt water swished over the harbour road, soaking shoes and socks of the unwary, and giving immense pleasure to a mischievous young lad who stood nonchalantly in the danger zone until the last second when he would leap away, beside himself with enjoyment at the fate of the wet-footed people.

Carefree, lost in nostalgia, I whiled away a relaxing hour in the Sloop.

The Rascal duly arrived at the quayside. After locating the Mirror, dwarfed between fishing boats, Michael pulled up alongside. Quickly, without ceremony, we loaded the gear. Michael drove round to the Sloop while I rowed the last few strokes of the voyage. On a large swell that started life in a storm over a thousand miles away out in the Atlantic, and made my trip round Land's End so memorable, Epic was swept high up the slip a few yards from the Sloop – inn-keeping to the end. I nipped out dry shod. Michael helped me carry Epic out of the surge's reach. After sponging away meringue residue, we lifted Epic on top of the Rascal, tied her securely, and drove away.

Transported back into the regular world with emotions safely under control, I matter-of-factly mentioned to Michael that I had just rowed round Land's End. Of course, I knew he knew and knew he knew I knew, but I could not help but mention it a few more times during the drive back to Mevagissey.

ᘊ

ᕥ᠆ᕤ

Early Days, Mevagissey

Following journey's end, my logbook received just two short entries: *'Shivered when I got photos of Brisons back'* (five days later); *'... calluses on my hands with ragged white edges a reminder '* (twelve days later).

Ten months later I was back at sea, oar hardening my hands once more, setting out on a further adventure with Epic. Before then, under a metaphorical bridge, disturbed and threatening waters flowed. I wondered if I would ride again with my little dinghy.

A few days after the last logbook entry I felt twinges in my back, and the next day I lay prone, suffering from acute sciatica. "Do not move." "Exercise." Medicine is not an exact science. Never a casual user of painkillers, I deserve to suffer a little for the 'one too many'; but it was different then. Counting the minutes between big red pills, I urged the clock hands round to temporary relief. Days turned to weeks. By the time I hobbled, doubled, to a physiotherapist, the nerve-gripping pain had conquered my left leg, and the big toe was devoid of feeling and motive power. "Full recovery will take some time," I found out. The cause of the bother was probably my rowing in a sciatic-nerve-disturbing posture. Over many hours I had imposed an opening force on my lower back vertebrae. (So it's all my fault then.) Had I performed periodic back straightening, missing a couple of oar strokes now and then, I may have not become a red pill junkie. More importantly, I may have avoided the worrying time that followed.

That October, when I was able to walk in near human mode, Julia, Edward and I set off for two weeks, 'you-can't-afford-not-to-go-at-the-price', Turkey sunshine. My convalescence started off on the right lines – a relaxing train ride to Reading. There followed a minor setback. An overcrowded train, Gatwick bound, necessitated my clinging to the wire partition in a goods van for two hours. The flight was not an ideal precursor for the four-hour coach ride that immediately followed. Perhaps the femurs of future packaged fliers will be hinged.

Towards the end of the first week, after much lying around in the sunshine and occasional light bending, a Turkish doctor was called in the early hours. A chest pain rendered breathing increasingly difficult. The

September lie-in could have been related to my condition. The good doctor arrived promptly. After a swift appraisal and an injection, I was able to breathe freely. A week later I suffered the return travel triathlon – so ended my convalescence.

The first week of the New Year had not expired when I suffered a repeat of 'Turkey chest'. The complaint was less extreme, so while symptoms remained I made my way to the surgery for analysis. "Don't worry … maybe … heart attack." A little later, a kind young ambulance medic gave me calming reassurance as he wired me to monitors and fitted an oxygen mask (on me). Through tinted windows, I looked across St Austell Bay towards Pentewan. I managed to pick out our old home and gallery before grassy banks and trees sped past the darkened screen as I was transported to Truro.

There was anxiety for a couple of days along with X-rays and scans. The operative, guiding a lubricated device over my chest, brought up on a screen positioned between us a moving picture of my heart. While editing the video for the specialist, the linkman intimated that the pulsating organ looked in fine form. I noticed a lighter bit of workings getting in on the act.

"What's that?"

"That's your lung."

"Would it help if I kept it out of the way?"

"If it's no trouble." (Or words to that effect).

With a spot of shallow breathing I directed the lung out of shot. Another screen traced a possible blemish that I could not breathe away. "It may not be anything … blood thinning in case." Medicine is not an exact science. Spaceman: small steps; portable pump; intercept, lunchtime minus food and counting. Tracked into tube; flashing lights, clockwise – red, green; tunnel end; we have go – cool shepherd's pie, peaches and custard.

A week later, blood thinned to perfection, the cord was cut – reborn. Julia collects. We walked under the night sky. First stop, The Wheel at Tresillian.

"You're the chap in the Mirror Dinghy …" David remembered my beer-garden landing.

"Hello again. I rowed round Land's End last summer … hope to continue when the days are longer. A medium white and a pint of mild please?"

On that happy note, we will pop back a couple of decades to phase two of our joint adventure.

Our arrival in Mevagissey presented us with a near pristine canvas. The route to our dream was roughly sketched in, though we were in no hurry to complete the picture. At the onset, making our way from day to day was reward enough. We hoped to live from our own industry in our chosen location, enjoying life for the present. What more could one wish than to be your own boss in paradise.

Every night in those first weeks in October, Julia and I would wander round the corner from the cottage, to be thrilled by the harbour view. Rain and wind just added spice to the adventure. Being there seemed priceless, which was as well, for funds were getting low.

So it was that I became a self employed, coal-shed converter. The Wheelhouse Restaurant, next door but one, the other side of the entry from the Walkaround, was receiving a face-lift. Assisting the refurbishers to remove unwanted clutter, I gained several large sheets of marine ply. Cut into strips the 'donation' furnished me with a magnificent set of pot boards. I still have one or two bearing clues to their history – 'OCALLY CAUGHT FI' and 'RAB and LOBSTE', for instance. The handy reclamation source became cornucopian and I the benefactor of wondrous treasures. A pair of fully glazed, small paned, exterior wooden doors being the jewels in the crown. They added style to the frontage. Discarded pitch-pine church pews were transformed – starting a third life as showroom shelving, a mobile rack to accommodate pot boards and a base for a workshop table. A heavy flush surfaced door became the tabletop. It was amazing how useful the knob and keyholes were in the creation of sculptural, ceramic pieces.

Before commencing production, I had to remove a ton or so of concrete that had formed stands for the larger oil tanks. For 'I', read Piper. He brought, for my use, his sledgehammer. (Why would there be a special implement for hammering sledges?) The hefty tool was awesome – but only in the hands of one who could safely raise it overhead. Thank you Piper.

Dwindling finances were stretched even more (in the sense of getting less). The purchase of necessary equipment and materials, including a ton of high firing clay, ate into our reserves. A few weeks later, my unique pitch-pine pot rack, with pitch-pine wheels, was filled with shelves of glistening, drying mugs, awaiting handles. It is an odd fact that the mug, awaiting a handle (a vase), is more valuable before the extra 'handling'. Not many of us buy vases by the half dozen though. So began the transition of clay into spending money. The day before Good Friday our funds had dwindled to oblivion. That did not matter, for the pottery/painting showroom was opened for business. (I had brought a number of finished canvasses down to Cornwall.) The sale of two butter pots for four shillings and six pence equalled the price of two large pasties. Good Friday saw the sales rocket to over a pound. We were in business.

The Easter rush subsided and I settled down to build up stock, as we business people say. Julia worked in a St Austell boutique to boost funds until the summer season took off. Everything looked rosy. We were beginning to count our chickens. One day I developed a headache that gradually worsened. The following day, a deep squeezing of my brain intensified, necessitating my first ride in an ambulance to the hospital in Truro. Eden was playing hard to get. I had not fraternized with serpents, nor nicked apples, but the power that 'is' prescribed meningitis.

Julia left the boutique to oversee the dwindling pot stock and paintings. After six weeks of non-action, I emerged from our lair, appropriately named Underledge. (We had relocated following a dastardly hike in our summer rent.) Delicately, with the aid of gravity, I made my way down School Hill, then alongside the harbour to the pottery. I felt up to do a bit of sitting down. It would be some time before I could go to pot again. As there were too few items left for sale to satisfy our winter needs, I took a bus ride to St Austell to see what I could find. Plan 'B' (belts) came into play. Upstairs in the Market House I chanced upon a leather worker. Following negotiation, I took away a dozen of his fine leather belts – black, tan and natural in four sizes. They were an instant hit. After the first few satisfied customers, the range was of course

Cottage Angles – Mevagissey
Oil on wood panel 30˝ x 30˝   2003

incomplete, leaving vacant several of the twelve nails I had hammered into the top of one of the glazed doors. Two-dozen belts returned with me on the bus the next day. The simple solid brass buckles rattled all day against the small panes, as if rummaging visitors feared losing their trousers.

Less than a year later, Julia and I bought a rundown property in Pentewan, two miles north of Mevagissey on the coast, where we lived and set up a gallery. The dungeon-like subterranean level we let to a couple of young leather workers from London. Jim and David rented a small workshop and sales area in the shed across the yard from my pottery. The second year saw two workshops in Piper's yard. Along with a selection of ceramics, browsers could cross the yard to view fine leatherwork, including a comprehensive selection of belts, with choice of buckle.

The Pentewan premises – house with large shop area, across the road from the dock, was soon graced with a simple black and white sign – proudly proclaiming, 'DAVID WESTON GALLERY'. Stonewalls in the shop were laboriously uncovered from beneath clinging, crumbling plaster. The tenuously supported springy floor was 'made good' with a fine block wall built by Maurice, a stonemason from Zennor, who had recently moved to Mevagissey. He was so impressed by the 'crypt', which was basic even by our standards, that he mentioned 'a bargain basement in need of serious tidying' to the leather boys. Not everyone can boast having accommodated a bona fide cave dweller – for Jim's surname is Cave. Maurice, who solved many problems with an ultra sharpened axe that planed, carved, whittled and hammered, arrived one morning with rods and brush to sweep the chimney. After shaking out his soot-laden blanket, for some unknown reason inside the house, I opened the front door to allow the cloud to disperse.

"I should close that," offered the soft-hearted stonemason, "or your Mrs'll be, cold as a sssnnake."

The final touches, with spotlights angled from the wooden beams, and an incredibly cheap, dark brown carpet covering the stable floor (as opposed to unstable), finished off a perfect exhibition space; giving great incentive for the production of large oil paintings.

The second season started well and got better. I was working mainly in the pottery. Julia was selling her ceramic figures along with my paintings in the Pentewan gallery. It was 'a dream come true' – selling our own work in our own gallery in Cornwall. Paintings and pots were totally eclipsed by a joint production, proudly exhibited upstairs, reclining in an antique willow crib. The safe arrival of Toby completed our perfect world. On the way home with our precious cargo, I stopped the little Fiat on the back road to Pentewan while I picked a bunch of wild garlic flowers. The sight and scent of those simple white bells always reminded me of happy times, often spent by woodland streams when a young teenager. Now there is a greater happiness to remember.

Toby was five and a half weeks young when he left Cornwall for the first time. We accompanied him to Plymouth to view the start of the single-handed sailing race to America. From the Hoe we watched the melee of craft, including the fifty-five competitors' boats, cavorting round the Sound. It was not the biggest vessel by far in the race that most interested me, a one hundred and thirteen feet long, three-masted schooner 'Vendredi 13', but the smallest, the nineteen-foot 'Willing Griffin'. Julia thought they were all mad. Toby seemed to sleep most of the time.

I really wanted to take part in the next, or next but one race (they are held every four years). My workshop diary of kiln firing sequences and glaze recipes was interspersed with doodle designs for midget transatlantic sailing boats. The following year I wrote to a boat manufacturer and was offered, at cost, an eighteen-foot Bermudan sloop. At a sailing school, not a million miles from Plymouth, I attended an offshore sailing course. (The lessons were actually onshore; but you get my drift.) There were just three of us 'doing' navigation; the rest were learning how to fall out of dinghies. Those five days were thoroughly enjoyable, and totally non-instructive. I lost confidence when taking sextant sights. Accurate time is essential when working out one's position, we were told. An error of one second could be the difference between rounding a headland and running aground, we were told. The 'instructor' did not know if radio time signals were taken from the beginning or end of the last pip. There was obviously no danger, so long as we remained on the Hoe (ho).

It was about that time that John (Blythe) and I were 'baptized' during the clinker dinghy launching at Pentewan. A few months after that embarrassing, practical lesson, I was on board a much larger vessel. The captain (though not skipper at the time) was the renowned C Blythe. It was a case of the ridiculous to the sublime – from a J to a Chay and Aquilla to Great Britain II. With eight or nine other customers I set off from Dartmouth to experience 'heavy weather sailing' in the form of a trip round the Fastnet Rock. Because of extreme conditions, the four-day experience was, by mutual consent, modified. After rounding Wolf Rock, ten miles off Land's End, G.B. II put back to Falmouth for the night. 'Such a shame we could not go round the Rock', we all lied.

At first, as a crew member on that fantastic yacht, I really felt 'the part' in my large new white woollen jumper. Unfortunately, as the wool dampened and contracted round me during the trip, it gave off an unpleasant aroma due to its confinement inside my sweaty waterproofs. There is a worse experience than being thrown about inside a bucking hull while divesting oneself of a mound of wet, tight fitting clothing while feeling nauseous; it is, vesting oneself with a mound of smelly, chilly, clinging wet clothing, after sleeplessly warming up a sleeping bag for three hours. The smell of wet wool still makes me feel giddy.

With the seventy-seven foot racing ketch happily moored alongside the wharf of huge wooden pillars (where little Epic would pass by twenty years later) we rolled into town. Seated round a large table at a waterside tavern we exchanged 'embellished near truths' of a nautical nature for an hour or two. The following morning, the dark red hull slipped out of Carrick Roads. I took the helm (a huge steering wheel) of perhaps the fastest sailing vessel in the world at the time. With G.B. II under full sail, I was privileged to drive the powerful beast across Veryan Bay, past Dodman Point and on past Pentewan (where Aquilla was parked behind John's Pisky Cove).

Toby was two when Robin became the youngest family member. Because life was happily filled with baby, pottery and gallery commit-ments, I was more able to cope with disappointing news contained in correspondence from the Sailing Secretary of the Royal Western Yacht Club of England. The salient points being: '… too many applications … further entries must be refused.' Six years later, as the entrants were arriving at Plymouth for 'the one after that', I was away on a painting trip in Southern Spain and Portugal. Though keeping a low profile, the sailing bug had not gone away. Memories, along with the dream still lingered. How could one forget rounding Wolf Rock in heavy weather; holding on tight, clipping on the safety harness before clambering onto the listing, plunging deck? How could one forget peering into dark rain slashed night, seeking a light, and being amazed at the forty-five degree angle of the fleeting red beam? Senses were heightened; minds fully on the job; no time to recall the similarity to a revolving Wolsey's headlights. How could one forget?

Goose In The Oven

St Ives to Newquay

Five months or so after rebirth, 'the days were longer'. I was eager to continue my excursion – destination North Devon.

A rabbit hopped out. Confused, he dithered then hopped back. Stu' swerved slightly. My disinterested "What's up?" met an evasive, "Err, hmm… "

I was unaware of a kindly deceit. Legend has it, if a seaman on his way to embarkation sees a rabbit, he must return home or the voyage will be ill fated. (Months later Stuart came clean about the incident on an elevated section of the A30 near Hayle.) Awake, but with closed eyes, my tired mind was in overdrive. There was so little time and so much to worry about.

Dawn was breaking. St Ives was deserted and would remain so for several hours. We lifted Epic down from the van, parked near Smeaton's Pier, and carried her down to the sandy beach outside the harbour. There was little wind and the sea was fairly flat. I held the mast in position and clipped on the three wire stays, then raised the sails, securing the halyards to the cleats at the base of the mast. My heart, along with the sails, gently fluttered. I tried to appear intrepid, nonchalantly tying the oars and rowlocks in position with the long bootlaces. Stuart shared his flask of tea with me. The act performed on that empty beach had the feeling of a sombre ritual – a cleansed, plastic yoghurt container serving as a chalice.

After tying on my deflated life jacket, I exchanged low-key farewells with Stuart. The calm sea, along with my watertight green wellingtons, provided the luxury of a dry launching. My haulier headed to the south coast, I into the Atlantic. Wavelets ran over the sand, washing away all trace of the 'ceremony'.

It was before three o'clock that morning when Stuart arrived with roof-racked van at my home. Two and a half hours earlier, after several days of adverse forecasts, confirmation of favourable weather was delivered. Though early to bed, I had not slept, knowing the next week or so might not be all plain sailing. Daytime was fine, with thoughts of sunshine and balmy breezes. Nights triggered doom-laden imaginings, with me pathetically wishing for winds too strong for Epic to be out on the ocean. June 28th – no reprieve. The stubborn stillness of unruffled darkness prevented windy excuses. My goose was in the oven.

Perhaps it was understandable that a melancholic mood pervaded as we headed down west. The driver had no reason to be chirpy. It was pre-dawn, and he was dropping me off on his way to work. The sadistic timing of our journey, due to tide times, would make his start many hours early. On a Gorran Haven to Falmouth trip, particularly in darkness, St Ives is an unrewarding diversion. I should have tried to be more sociable, but found it difficult to chat.

A little before half past five, with a gentle breeze over the starboard quarter, I set out to cross the four miles of St Ives Bay, heading towards Godrevy Lighthouse. I looked forward to a close inspection of the prominent landmark off Godrevy Point. During my summer in St Ives, half a lifetime ago, I had painted the distant lighthouse. The Red Admiral and blue Bosun eased me away from the quiet town. The sky was clear, save for hazy sunrise pink above the mainland to the east. The church, lighthouses and a ribbon of patchwork buildings soon coalesced. Preparation and organization were over. I was free again. Twenty minutes later the sun rose over Godrevy. It was good to be back.

Anna Hill still captained the shipping forecast. Half an hour into the voyage she gave, '… southerly, four to five, occasionally six.' That was for area Sole. What on earth was she thinking of? Plymouth was better, '… three to four, veering westerly, five later'. (Land's End is the centre of four shipping areas – it was always tempting to choose the best one.) Conditions were ominously calm at the time. The wind, what little there was, far from increasing, died down, and I was rowing by the time Epic approached the gap between the lighthouse-island and Godrevy Point. It was a quarter to seven. The tide took us swiftly into the channel. One minute I was being conveyed on smooth velvety sea, the next, I was wildly manipulating the oars to gain purchase. Epic rattled around on short steep waves. There followed a confused few minutes with much pitching and hull slapping against choppy water. It was all so unexpectedly sudden. Being out of practice, I was worried for a while. Abruptly it was all over. Calm returned.

Together with a few small stone buildings, the octagonal white lighthouse stood solidly in a walled garden. It would be exciting to live there in rough weather, and pleasantly peaceful at other times. Visitors would have to be serious. Fair weather landing is obviously possible, for lighthouse keepers (who no longer keep) had to get to work.

For a further two miles I plied the oars, then with the onset of a slight breeze, row/sailed with the Admiral (jib) set. By eight o'clock both sails were up and in business. The tide was swift, and within half an hour Portreath was abeam. A fresh offshore breeze stretched the little sails, encouraging me to head on towards Newquay. Over the next five hours I enjoyed exhilarating sailing. The wind gradually increased and I became used to easing the Bosun sheet as the pressure brought the gunwale to the sea. Due to the offshore wind, the relatively flat ocean provided perfect sailing conditions. Even so, I still managed a near tipping off Perranporth. Another close shave off St Agnes hastened reefing – wrapping the Bosun one turn round the mast. As I should have expected, the main problems happened at headlands where tidal flows were deflected, forming larger, unpredictable waves.

Once past Perran Beach there were six rocky headlands to negotiate before reaching Newquay Harbour. My course, inside the off-lying islets off Penhale Point and Kelsey Head, was desirable in order to escape stronger winds offshore. In calmer conditions I would still have taken the same coast-hugging route to be more intimate with the cliff scene.

Penhale Point has Gull Rocks to seaward. (Gull Rock/Rocks abound around Cornwall and other coastlines too, I suppose. A few pages on I give a Gull Rock another name, partly because its form suggested something else, but mostly because there are just too many.) In the past, fishermen had no reason to range far in their small, sail-powered boats. Most communities would have their own local Gull Rock, never thinking of the confusion it would cause passing traffic in the future. Off Kelsey Head lies the Chick, larger than the tiny island off the penultimate promontory, Pentire Point East, which boasts The Goose.

The strength of the adverse tide increased, making wind-power essential. A rough ride awaited inside the first of the 'bird islands', causing me to chicken out when approaching The Goose. I bashed on outside in choppy water towards the final obstruction, Towan Head. The southeast wind was quite trying, strong enough for me to take in the Bosun. A great deal of huffing and tangling ensued as I slogged along for two miles off Fistral Beach – steering, trying to restrain the flapping sail and capture the halyard as it tried to escape. The unfavourable tide formed little waves, slowing Epic, forcing me to continuously play the tiller to maintain the correct heading.

With great relief, at a quarter to two, I passed Towan Head and hauled down the remaining sail. It was non-too easy lying across the foredeck with outstretched arms in order to keep weight aft. The wide flat bottom of the Mirror dinghy rapidly narrows as it folds round to meet the flat triangular bow, making the boat decidedly unstable if weight is transferred forward. In the confusion, while rushing to save being blown further out to sea, which would have meant extra rowing into the strong wind, the Admiral went overboard. With the soaking sail hurriedly retrieved and bundled in the bottom of the boat, I spent a strength-sapping fifteen minutes creeping up to Newquay Harbour. Rowing normally I would not have made headway, so I had to up the tempo and forego listening to the shipping forecast. That final mile took a great deal more effort than I would have wished, but having travelled so far along the north coast of Cornwall, there was satisfying compensation.

Epic grounded on smooth sand just inside the harbour entrance. It was so peaceful and quiet, and such bliss to be out of the wind. I could faintly hear the muffled sounds of huge rollers crashing into Newquay Bay a little way on from the harbour. The unruly sea, that made rowing so hard, was at the same time providing entertainment for a band of hardy holiday-makers having fun in the rollers.

Within twenty minutes of stepping onto the firm harbour bed, inside the protective walls, I was greeted by a victuals-bearing Ann, whose other half had purchased from me, sixteen or seventeen years earlier, a seven-teen-foot sailing cruiser christened BLACK ANT – because it was small and I had painted it black. For sentimental reason, I toyed with the name BLACKCURRANT, but there were rather a lot of letters for an impatient sailor to deal with. In the end (or should that be on the end) I applied the abridged ANT to the stern. It is a pleasant little name and so easy to apply. Epic nearly became ANT TOO.

We had kept in touch with Dennis, and fortunately for me, when he returned from Australia with Ann, they settled in Newquay. An ice-cool Fosters was immediately, lovingly, analysed by my grateful throat. Though I had not expected to arrive that day, Ann cast an eye over the harbour while passing, and chanced to notice the little white dinghy. In addition to canned nectar, I was 'hampered' with crisps, bananas, a bottle of water and a large fruitcake – summertime Christmas – quite antipodean.

After arranging to meet for a drink on the veranda of the Harbour Hotel, I was left to tidy Epic and report to the harbour master. A couple of hours later, as the tide came in, I was able to float the dinghy towards a tall stone bollard protruding from the sand at the top of the harbour beach. Epic would be safe overnight, fixed on a running line passing round the bollard and through a link in one of the many heavy mooring chains that lay on the harbour bed. At the time, I did not realize just how safe.

Between five and seven o'clock I periodically re-tied, further along the high quayside, the long line attached to Epic. It was a frustrating chore, for the Ireland v Norway, World Cup match was being televised in a pub just far enough away to make popping in and out non-viable. The game was half way through the second half before tethering was complete. I rushed off to spectate and enjoy a cut-price celebration pint of Guinness. Luckily, no goals had been scored before my arrival. Unluckily, no goals were scored in the match, putting Ireland out of the tournament.

The earlier shipping forecast had included '… southwest, five to six; rain, drizzle …' The five to six' (besides being the time) was too windy for me. The shipping forecast, along with the football result, dampened my spirit a little. That was soon rectified when I joined Ann and Dennis for a therapeutic pint. Drizzle drove us in from the balcony. An hour later we wandered down to the harbour to collect my waterproofs from the boat. We looked down on Epic, safely and serenely afloat, but of the bollard there was no sign, it being totally submerged. Clandestine plans had formed when being told earlier that the harbour was a no-go area overnight. Previously I had stayed on or near Epic, and my intention was, after picking up my wet weather clothing, to hang around for a few hours, then when all was quiet, sneak back to the boat.

"You'll get soaked. We have a spare bed; you must come and stay with us."

"… I always stay with Epic."

My proposed plan did not impress my psychologist friends. The more I fought my case the more lunatic I appeared. I did worry that accepting the kind offer would jeopardize the spirit of the voyage. On the other hand, I could not make them feel responsible for my suffering. My conscience, of course, could be talked round at my leisure. Obviously, a warm bed did not enter the equation.

Before going to sleep I received an encouraging, '… southwest four to five, becoming southerly three later'. Despite being in a comfortable bed, I dreamt of growling animals – perhaps the subconscious sound-track of my wild ride to Newquay. In the morning, hoping I was speaking to Dennis in his nonprofessional capacity, I asked if he heard unusual sounds during the night. Though I had noticed a higher than usual fence on my arrival, I assumed my hosts' garden abutted the countryside. A lion enclosure did not spring to mind. It is relatively peaceful living next door to a zoo. If you must have a little roaring, let it not be from road traffic.

Pintles Gudgeons And Noodles
Newquay to Padstow

Dennis gave me a lift to the harbour at nine o'clock the next morning. Les the harbourmaster was most helpful, so I thought it best not to mention the sunken bollard incident. Charts were studied and fishermen quizzed. The consensus – the wind might moderate sufficiently for my purpose. How I hoped that would be so, for I could not possibly go home after spending a single night away, particularly one of such pampered luxury. While optimistic glances skyward and doubtful shakings of heads combined to reach a unanimous 'Don't know', I noticed a fisherman sculling by using my distinctively taped, heavier oar. (I do admire the nonchalant ease with which fishermen, while standing in the stern of their punts, progress with a twisting, side to side wrist motion, using a single near vertical oar. My admiration is even greater when they use their own oar.) 'Communication' with the sculler followed, and I was duly reunited with the other half of my trusty propulsion system. Les was to tune into the professional shipping forecast at 13:40 BST. I would check the layman's version at five to two. If conditions and forecasts seemed suitable, I would set sail at four-ish.

Powerful surges pounded the wall as I waited for the 'southerly three' to arrive. I was relaxing in sunshine at the top of stone steps on the seaward side of the harbour. Had I not completed a passage in excess of twenty-five miles the previous day, I should have felt a complete fraud. The remainder of the Atlantic coastline of Cornwall beckoned. My impatience to be on the move took the edge off what should have been an enjoyable interlude. On the horizon, a mile off Trevose Head, I saw three small islets (there are more). I was eager to take a closer look, but had to be patient before making the seventeen-mile dash to Padstow.

As the harbour slowly drained, a couple of fishing boats set off to sea, leaving free space against the harbour wall. In order to be afloat at low tide, I tied Epic close to the entrance. Being too anxious to paint, I killed time strolling along the beautiful golden sands of Watergate Beach. I passed by Sea World, where you can pass through a glass tunnel surrounded by swimming fish, including shark-like specimens. There is a shallow pool, the bottom of which is carpeted with huge rays and other flatfish. For authenticity, submerged in the pool was a small wrecked boat – the remains of a Mirror dinghy that met its end off Newquay. Watergate investigation complete, I returned to watch over Epic.

Two hours after the lunchtime '… southerly, three to four …' I put on my lifejacket and rowed away from Newquay. It was still quite windy, but the sea had flattened considerably. The Admiral was hoisted, having been attached to the forestay while I was still in harbour. With the Bosun unwrapped from round the mast, I was hastened away towards the Quies – the previously mentioned islets. After a mile or so, having left the protection of the Newquay headlands, large swells became apparent. The whole sea surface was bedecked with little waves, adding sinister serrations to the crests of swells. The sea's aggressive appearance did not bother me, for I was going the weather's way. The waves slowly rolled past, rocking me onwards.

After approaching Trevose Head (nearly ten miles completed in two and three quarter hours) I steered towards the Bull, a small rock less than a quarter of a mile offshore. At times just its summit, 'a black sharks fin' would show, then it and the headland would be lost from view for a while. The state of the sea was how I imagined mid Atlantic to be. Shallower seas around the Bull caused swells to be steeper with breaking tops. Not wishing to push my luck, I set a course outside the islet but still found unpredictable waves closer together. All went well until, in an attempt to avoid a small portion of sea that came on board, I rapidly stood up – more a crouch really. The manoeuvre courted disaster. When making the foolish stand, I accidentally lifted off the tiller and rudder unit. In less time than it takes to say 'aaghh' I was lying prone, feet thrust against the dinghy's sides and elbows locked over the stern. Vice-like, I grasped the rudder-stock, forcing its pintles into the gudgeons on the transom. At the time, terminology was of no consequence – it was imperative the items were reunited, pronto. To be out of control in that situation would be an event of short duration – a preliminary to turning turtle. Those who have dinghy sailed know the difficulty of attaching a rudder while afloat. The water steers the blade till luck allows the wet-sleeved, red-faced contortionist to achieve relocation of the frisky blade. Rapid repositioning requires special stimulation – a rush of adrenalin released by acute fear will do the trick.

The Bull, along with the angry waves receded as I bore right, round the white lighthouse of Trevose. In the lee, I headed towards Pentire Point, some five miles away. Before reaching the headland, I would take another right-hander and head up the River Camel. An evening calm was setting in. Epic, a good mile offshore, glided past the village of Trevone, snugly tucked away. With its view to the northwest, facing the Atlantic that can display a meaner mood, it would not always be so peaceful.

My earlier cavorting had not prevented a slight sluicing. Standing to steer, I attempted to dry my jeans in the fading sunshine – a futile exercise, though I imagined a degree of warming to my chilled, damp backside. The setting sun cast the sailor's shadow upon the Red Admiral. Cue the music.

The peaked waves, faceted and accentuated by the low sun angle, held an austere grandeur as they ambled eastward. The helpful light airs ceased with the fading light. Turning south, I rounded Stepper Point and headed into the estuary. It was half past ten. Darkness fell as I rowed the final two miles up to Padstow. The last of the tide helped me into a slight adverse breeze. Thankfully, being high water, the infamous Doom Bar was dormant. It would be a different matter leaving at low tide. A mile from the harbour I sighted a silhouetted pack of moored boats. With frequent glances over my shoulder I steered between various pleasure-craft, until at ten thirty, absolute high tide, I reached the open harbour entrance. Wishing to leave in the early hours, when the lock gates would be closed, I did not enter.

Alongside the inner wall of the outer basin, close to the harbour entrance, I temporarily hitched Epic to a metal ladder while I tied ropes to bow and stern. After clambering up the ladder with bundles of rope, I secured the bow line to a huge iron ring on the quayside. Passing the extra long stern line through a ring, twenty yards further along, I fed the free end down into the boat. The warp seemed to have mysteriously lengthened. The end that should have been attached to Epic eventually came to hand, complete with a small galvanized eye fitting with two rusted screw stumps. It was a perfect time for a sheet lead to come adrift

– in harbour, with one end of the boat already secured. It could have happened off Trevose Head, while I was rudderless. Close by at the harbour office, I partly filled in an arrival form – leaving out gross tonnage but exactly recording length of vessel. As part of the shipping fraternity I was able to purchase, for a modest fee, a card to gain access to the shower block at the other side of the harbour. The official in charge said I could sleep in the facility, but I declined the kind offer, informing him that I would be sleeping on board.

Time in respect of Padstow nightlife was at a premium. Hastening into the village, I soon chanced upon the eminently sociable London Inn. After an enjoyable, though rather too swift an interlude with a slightly rushed pint of Guinness, I nipped into a handy Chinese take-away. In comforting darkness I dined aboard, doing justice to a tasty hot supper. *'Heaven',* I noted, after chasing the last slippery noodle round the tinfoil tray. In a state of complete contentment, following the midnight feast, I ambled round to the shower block and showered. Though very cosy compared to my airy accommodation, I was not tempted to stay. Not even for a second did I think of spending another night luxuriating in warm comfort, for it was not even raining. I would manage, unlike the previous night, without lion lullabies or floral printed duvet and pillows.

I had explained to the harbourmaster my need to be away a little before low water in order to ride eastward on the tide. A location at steps opposite, at the estuary end of the quay, was recommended. I had to move Epic lest she became trapped in the mud. Back at my berth (this is not another flashback) I carefully lowered the mooring lines into Epic as I climbed down the ladder, making sure they did not go overboard. Being squeaky-clean and salt free, I had no wish to share my limited space with a load of wet rope. I rowed over to my night station where I looped a line round a handrail in order to cast off easily when the time arrived – for there would certainly be drifts of glutinous mud around the lower steps. When relocated, I arranged my pristine sleeping bag on the picnic box, thwart and centreboard, zipped myself in then, metaphorically speaking, drifted off. All had been plain sailing since my fright off Trevose Head. It was a dry night and my luck seemed to be holding. The last time I slept on board was at Mousehole, when it rained.

Padstow
11" x 11"

Magwitch And The Doom Bar
Padstow to Port Isaac

It must have been about one o'clock in the morning when I entered the bag. Floating about in a little boat, being edged this way and that by mooring lines, really is most relaxing. The edging stopped. My rest period was over. After my two hours of slumber, Epic grounded, or rather 'sticky muddied'. There ensued a few moments of frantic action off that flight of steps. Speedily retrieving the muddy mooring line, I plopped it on the foredeck for swilling later. With the spade-ended oar, I set about spooning Epic off the mud. It seemed the harbour officials I encountered had difficulty assessing water levels.

"Wun'erd what you wus up to." A deep voice sounded from the darkness at the top of the steps.

I detected a vague form and thought of Magwitch. It was as well the tone conveyed no menace, for escape, had it been necessary, would have been a bit of a long shot. Having extricated Epic from the ooze, I rowed round to the estuary side of the pier. There I tied up against a sunken, leaky, pontoon-type structure. It gurgled and hissed periodically – draining and re-flooding in the slight swell.

"Duz zat zumtimes." Magwitch was still there.

I washed my lines and oar in the channel and returned to my bag for a further, rather pointless, ten minutes. It was not hidden eyes, but contemplation of the Doom Bar that was most worrying.

At around four o'clock, an orange and rose madder dawn was in the making. It was a little before low tide and time to exit the Camel (excuse the expression). On my way to the office, to return the shower block pass card, I briefly communed with the nocturnal one. He was a net fisherman, waiting for low water and incoming salmon. I phoned the coastguard, informing them of my imminent departure. An outboard motor coughed into life, heralding Magwitch's departure.

At a quarter past four I rowed into the channel that hugged the town side of the estuary. Acres of Town Bar sand lay exposed. In darkness to the east lay the village of Rock, where the palatable, mid-strength ale, Doom Bar is brewed. A mile on, at Gun Point, the net-man stood silently by his boat. Epic grazed by, touching the sand in the shallows, heading towards The Bar.

The first infiltrations of turning tide entered the river, materialising like smooth undulations of a gently wafted silken banner. The flow, pressed between headlands and constricted in the shallows, was barely noticeable at first. Small waves formed at the channel sides, the ends flipping onto the sand with a slight 'sssh'. The breaking extremities increased in length as the rounded swells grew. So began the eager advance of the flood. Epic no longer lifted over the steepening peaks, but pivoted sharply as breaking waves crashed noisily on both sides of the estuary. Soon white water stretched from shore to shore, save for a small mid section. With a 'last orders' enthusiasm, I rowed to cross The Bar before closing time. Both oars were close to tumbling surf as Epic broke through to calm water.

Had I departed immediately after grounding, I may have avoided the scary episode. The salmon fisher was obviously heading back upriver – ahead of the game. With pulse rate returning to normal, I hoisted the Bosun. Inside Stepper Point, a motor/sailer slowly tracked back and forth, waiting for deeper water and better odds before dicing with the Doom Bar.

At half past five, three miles out from Padstow, I rounded Pentire Point to be greeted by the rising sun. Though the seas were largish and lumpy, I had no trouble catching the shipping forecast. After slow progress round Rumps Point, I took shelter in the lee of the Mouls, a small islet a quarter of a mile offshore. I downed sail and finished cleaning the boat. Even at that early hour it was hot. Under clear blue sky I applied sun block, then put on my sun-hat. The wind was from the southeast, rather than the forecast south. Had the discrepancy been clockwise (veered instead of backed) I could have utilized wind power; instead I positioned the oars in the rowlocks and pulled to the east, towards Port Isaac.

'7:35 *Wind calmer – perhaps in lee of Portquin – Stop breakfast …*'. The tide was at last becoming favourable, '*… drift right way*'. Gently rocking, I crossed Portquin Bay, heading towards Kellan Head – the guardian of, the extremely difficult to spot, Portquin Channel. I munched away on Anne's cherry and walnut cake and sipped cool, fresh orange juice.

Scrumptious though the cake was, location was the most perfect element. Was ever a better breakfast taken? Such interludes of pure perfection were not an everyday occurrence. At times there might be a touch of fear, or discomfort in the form of cold, apprehension, blisters, or even sunburn that put a downer on proceedings. How pleasurable that day, drifting on a well-behaved, sun-drenched ocean. The only blemish was a plywood dinghy containing a contented fruitcake muncher.

A secret harbour is hard to resist (providing you can find it). The narrow inlet delineated on OS 200 looked so inviting; I had to investigate. Just off the entrance lie the Cow & Calf – small, low-lying, rocky obstructions. They must have claimed a great deal of shipping when Portquin was a commercial harbour in the days of sail. Other submerged formations left confusions of swirling water just beyond the rocks, towards the channel entrance. I held station for a while, to plot a safe passage, then gingerly rode the swells. Inside all was grandly serene and delightfully empty. Not a place for raised voices or outboard motors. A sign – 'By appointment only' would not have seemed out of place. The steep cliffs and precipitous grassy sides of the quarter-mile long 'mini fiord', were without human interference. Tucked away at the far end, huddled snugly together, were ten or so dwellings.

Set back, high in the centre of the undulating, grassy-topped Doyden Point, on the western side of the inlet, stands Doydon Castle. What appears to be the top of a crenulated tower is visible. On closer inspection, that is all there is. It was built in the early eighteen hundreds for recreational purposes – how discreet. As I made my way down the channel I noticed a movement – a touch of red on the distant slip. The lone figure may have been seeking solitude. There was no reason for me to intrude; in any case, there was sure to be some effect of ocean motion to make a landing all too energetic a task at that early hour. At eight thirty, I raised sail and headed out of 'tranquillity basin'.

Propelled by oar and sail, Epic lolloped along to Port Isaac, arriving at twenty past ten. The spacious harbour was not tightly bound with waterside lofts and cottages as many of the south coast harbours are. Being north facing would account for the extra long mooring chains that lay on the harbour bed. Powerful surges would certainly test boats teth-

11" x 11"
'Propelled by oar and sail, Epic lolloped along to **Port Isaac**'

181

ered with short reins. It was a surprise to find the place almost deserted. Getting up so early must have put me in afternoon mode. Though it was a little before high water I decided not to drag Epic further up the beach, for apart from the sandy patch where I had landed, it was quite stony. The time would soon come when pampering the freshly painted dinghy would cease. Epic took several bursts of gritty water up the centreboard case. *'I hate that!!'* I wrote, as if it was someone else's fault. Boat-lag was setting in. I wandered off to relax for a while.

Although the sole customer in the Golden Lion, I was treated royally. It was "no trouble" to serve tea. I consumed copiously. From the window I enjoyed the harbour panorama. The smallness of Epic was always a surprise to me when catching her unawares. I never felt constrained in my little world, for I was always heading to unknown waters, seeking new experiences.

I was helped to carry Epic down to the receding sea by one of the few people on the beach. Thinking positively, in order to continue the voyage without delay if conditions allowed, I rowed out to the east harbour wall. Before executing the manoeuvre, I consulted a fisherman about my plan. Imagine my surprise, finding three metal stanchions occasionally breaking the surface, close to the wall. They were the tops of safety rail uprights on steps leading from a mid-tide-level platform. How ironic would that have been, returning to find Epic skewered on a safety rail? The main purpose of the structure was to make loading and unloading easier around low water, for the inner wall sloped out considerably to the harbour bed. To save Epic from a severe rasping, I looped a stern line over an outer stanchion, then a mid-gunwale line along towards the harbour entrance. The arrangement was only partially successful at holding Epic off the wall. To counteract periodic grinding against the barnacles I required fenders. A sacrifice was required. (No live chickens were available, so) I broke my polythene surfboard/seat into four pieces. I feared the lines would cut through the polystyrene chunks, but the tethered jetsam remained attached, keeping the grating barnacles at bay. (My ingenuity was, without Houston help, in the 'make do and mend' mould of the Apollo Thirteen astronauts. Their salvation, by looping the moon, was a phenomenal achievement.)

Captain's log – half past four, *'Still V windy – lot of seahorses seems to be from the north* …' I had phoned Falmouth Coastguard at three o'clock to say I would carry on if the wind moderated and was favourable. The forecast was '… *variable, two to three becoming easterly three'*. The 'variable' was acceptable, but I was experiencing what seemed like a northerly five, whistling straight into the harbour. It would have been rewarding to carry on, and for the first time utilize two favourable tides in one day. There were only a few legs (perhaps two) before I ran out of Cornwall – so to speak. *'I'll wait till 5:30* …' Captain's log, twenty-five to five.

Following a walk and fish'n'chips on the cliffs, the deadline, plus a bit, had passed. No change. I arranged with John, the Harbourmaster, to leave Epic at the top of the beach. A 'voyage abort call' to the coast-guard was followed by a request for a lift home. With over an hour to kill, I wandered back up the hill (not to a Rose Cottage this time; or a limerick) to the Old School Hotel. Sunburn had rendered my face and the backs of my hands, stiff and red. My back was undergoing straight-ening pains, and my palms were oar blistered – still in need of further acclimatisation. The postponement was really peeving. There had been no more than four days free from disruption on my trip round Cornwall and I really had hoped to 'do the north coast' without further adjourn-ment. A feeling of slight melancholy, which had nothing to do with my clapped-out bodily state, set in.

Tea time again. From the hotel terrace I watched Epic, way down below, acquitting herself well in a standoff with the harbour wall. *'Suddenly looked on the bright side* …' (… when I was up, I was up …) The snippet, written at the tea table, continued '… *good distance. Have just phoned for a lift. Productive three days* …' My outlook changes like the wind.

Down on the harbour beach, a silver band was entertaining. Port Isaac was in party mood. My attention was not wholly captured, for I noticed Epic in danger of being cut off. In the nick of time I made my way along the rudimentary, cliff-hugging causeway which was being lapped by the rising tide. Aboard Epic, I disassembled fenders, cast off, and rowed towards the boats moored mid-harbour, intending to hitch alongside. A shout from Neil rendered the manoeuvre unnecessary. A few more oar strokes and Epic glided onto the beach. In no time at all the dinghy was chocked up beyond the high water mark, and mast and oars tied on top of the Fiesta. In no time plus ten minutes, my impromptu pick-up team, Neil and his brother-in-law Dave, joined me in the Golden Lion. We supped our pints as the band, booming out the Flora Dance, marched past the window.

ANTiclimax

Our three years in Pentewan were pretty idyllic: hot summers, with barbeques on the beach; Julia sitting outside the gallery working on her clay figures with Toby alongside – sculpting the future. Subjects were invariably pregnant ladies in flowing dresses, with infant in arms, or child held close. Because the village life we enjoyed so much was relatively quiet, regarding visitor numbers compared with Mevagissey, we dared not risk carving out a living solely from there. The pottery/painting studio was much busier and benefited from a much longer season. Following a five-minute, two-mile commute, I became accustomed to driving along the harbour to park in Piper's yard.

For my high-fired stoneware and porcelain work, I required the kiln to reach pretty near its maximum temperature – a white-hot, throbbing, thirteen hundred degrees centigrade. The final upward crawl to reach the last few degrees was often a long drawn out affair. This was not always so, for number of shelves and density of pots, along with variable power, made a difference. Sometimes there was an extreme power loss for no obvious reason. Many hours were whiled away at my door/table, doodling mini yacht designs into the night, willing the cone to bend. (Cones, set at an angle in the kiln, visible through a spy-hole, are slender, tapering pieces of blended materials, formulated to gradually melt at specific temperatures. They are used instead of a pyrometer and thermocouple – a sophisticated temperature gauge costing lots of money. If cones were good enough for the Chinese …)

Kiln watching required much patience for no immediate reward. Withdrawing the bung from the door to check the temperature revealed a disc of fire with the faintest of blemishes – the stubborn, leaning cone. The fact that a saucepan of water would boil on top of the kiln suggested an insulation deficiency. It was painful to hear the wasteful hum as I noted the galloping units zapping through the cable. Alongside the columns of figures recording kiln firings, I drew numerous over-complicated designs of self-steering gears for midget sailing boats. Perhaps I should have designed a kiln that did not double as a giant hotplate. Following the long awaited cone bend, a good day and a half would elapse before I was able to edge the heavy door open to glimpse the transformed treasure inside.

In fair weather I would sometimes walk to work along the coast path. Though further and rather hilly, it was a pleasant and invigorating exercise. On one occasion, shortly after we had moved to Pentewan, I decided to take a moonlight walk over to Mevagissey to oversee the final hours of a glaze firing. Following my nocturnal stroll, I arrived for kiln duty to find the big black door drawn across the entry, and locked. Mevagissey was deserted. I ran through my options: walk back to Pentewan and collect the key to the little door; knock up Piper; break in. The first may have resulted in melted pots. The second choice, on reflection, was out of the question, for I might have woken Peggy, Piper's wife, and even more likely wake the dog, and consequently, Peggy, Piper and other households. I conceived a plan of entry by stealth.

To the left of the Walkaround stood large premises of the remaining coal merchant. To the left again was a flight of steps leading up from the harbour to the steep, narrow road heading south out of the village. The wall by the side of the steps, at coal-shed roof height, was easy to scale, especially by one fearing the loss of two or three weeks worth of pottery production. Not wishing to be caught in the act of trespass, I crept silently over the shed's double pitched roof and down onto the lean-to roof above the leather boys' old workshop. Then it was just a matter of a few more yards before dropping down into Piper's yard to complete a successful mission. Had I taken my time on the final traverse, and had the roof not been of brittle asbestos, and had Harry been a sound sleeper …

Harry was an elderly fisherman living in the premises that completed the 'fortification' of the yard. Very early one sunny summer's morning, in our second summer season, Harry took me out fishing. We climbed down into his punt, tied up just over from the pottery, and he sculled us out to Maria, his twenty-foot boat that sported a cuddy – a small shelter up front with windows. (That type of boat is called a tosher in these parts.) We cruised around for a while, no more than a mile or two out, plummeting for mackerel. Once in a shoal the boat would be set to steer in wide circles while the poor fish attached themselves to one of a dozen or so hooks trailed on lines weighted down with a lump of lead (plummet). Three lines of hooks were trailed – two held out to the sides on poles. The gullible mackerel were tempted by nothing more than a strip of cloth or a feather. While detaching a flapping, flashing victim from a hook, I was astonished to see not five yards abeam, a massive black shark's fin keeping station with the boat. Ten feet behind the menacing triangle followed the tip of a tail, pushing side to side. Fear of what was situated ten feet ahead of the fin rendered me speechless. When finally I managed to alert Harry of our dire predicament, he nonchalantly informed, "Basking shark, quite harmless". At the time I knew nothing of the gentle, plankton-eating leviathans, naturally assuming the spectre had something more substantial in mind for breakfast than micro food.

… but Harry was not a sound sleeper. The asbestos roof exploded, dropping me down into a fishing net – a decorative feature bedecked with scallop shells and plastic lobsters. A first floor window shot up. Harry looked over the empty silent yard. After a few seconds a head rose up through the hole. In the dim light Harry could not know the identity of the intruder, but naturally assumed mischief was afoot. To allay his fear, I informed him of my presence with a rather ludicrous, "It's only me Harry". After a brief explanation of my 'break in', the vexed fisherman went back to bed. After extricating myself, I retired to the pottery to oversee the firing, and compose a note – explaining to my neighbour the 'hole affair', and my reason for dropping in out of hours.

Quite out of the blue, in the year following the roof incident, a large batch of moorings was made available in Mevagissey harbour. Having been far from the top of the waiting list I was taken by surprise at such good fortune. It was time to peruse yachting magazines with intent. The 'schooner drooling' pages were overlooked in favour of something befit-

Stoneware 'Fish' Pots

Bottle 7″   Wall Plate 4½″   1290°C   1975

'Along with my signature, I use the fish symbol to mark my paintings.
On oil paintings, I sometimes use gold leaf – to create a goldfish.'

ting my pocket, and handy for viewing.

ANT (yet to be named) was afloat in the Barbican Basin, Plymouth. The seventeen-foot Silhouette, a Bermudan sloop (what a captivating name for a class of boat) was of early GRP construction, incorporating some plywood. She sat forlornly in an oily backwater. Her once white topsides were yellowed and peeling, and the dark blue fibreglass hull had yielded its shine and some colour to the bleaching sun. (The matt finish was a perfect key for the application of black gloss.) Sitting on a mouldy plastic bunk cover, I inspected bilge water slurping below a lifted section of cabin floor. It was all and more than my heart desired.

Brother Michael, adept at things mechanical and electrical, came with me to refit and sail the pocket cruiser to its new home. We installed a newly charged twelve-volt battery, and soon had the red and green sidelights working. The white masthead light, ingeniously set inside a fish-paste jar, took a little while to fix. Night-time voyaging was on the agenda – it was all too exciting.

The trip to Mevagissey was planned with naval precision. Information was sought regarding tidal streams – the result was a departure time of three o'clock in the morning. We decided on an early night afloat in order to be wide-eyed and bushy-tailed for the voyage of a lifetime. We nipped out for a bite to eat. On the way we stopped for a quick one (you know what sailors are). The second one was definitely a mistake. The third pint of Guinness – well … Returning to ship we came upon a fish'n'chip shop that reminded us of our mission.

The reason for casting off three hours early was obviously not down to the fish and double portion of chips consumed. Progress out of Plymouth Sound was extraordinarily slow. Besides the problem of battling against an adverse tide, the future Ant carried a whole ecosystem below the waterline. The enormous accumulation of seaweeds and barnacles was quite a handicap – it could be likened to swimming in a fur coat. Still in the Sound (but not of mind), we counted, from several directions, the coded flashings of the Melampus buoy. For an hour or two the boat was carried around in the tidal flow. The bilge aroma, in conjunction with the unaccustomed motion, would have been enough to stimulate seasickness without the addition of excess stout, batter and lard-enriched chips. There was little conversation between two extremely chilled, miserable mariners as they took turns to steer the 'dreamboat' home. It was just not exciting anymore.

We bought a house at the bottom of Polkirt Hill – less than a half-minute amble to my workplace. Looking down the entry from outside the pottery, I could see the black Ant riding temptingly on her mooring. Just a glimpse of the little beauty gave me great pleasure.

On sunny days I could sail off for a few hours, returning for the busy evening trade. The quays were crowded with visitors till well after ten o'clock. To fulfil an urge to sail alone over the horizon, out of sight of land, I set off in Ant at six o'clock one evening. The coastline soon became a thin grey line. The mini sloop wafted along on a following breeze. The land sank below the horizon as dusk advanced. I happily hove to (fixed the jib to blanket the mainsail, spilling the wind and letting the boat look after herself, gently drifting downwind). I had always wanted to do that; it seemed such a nautical thing to do. Down below (sitting room only), after putting the kettle on, I checked the sequence of lighthouse flashes. The Mevagissey light and the Eddystone Rocks light both gave two flashes every ten seconds, which was a bit confusing at first. In reality it was quite straightforward, for I knew where they were, and I had a compass. It was comforting roughly knowing my position, and happily, it was not a foggy night. I 'unhove' and headed back to Mevagissey; or at least tried to.

The favourable waft that so easily took me away from land, could give me no better heading than towards Polperro. After several worrying hours at the tiller, I ended up in a bay twixt Looe and Rame Head. Ant's heading into wind ability was only a smidgen better than the zero-angle Epic achieves. Progress was pitiful. I zigzagged along the coast until the tide must have intervened. As you know, it was some time before I took advantage of the tidal gift. By about four in the morning the wind had virtually died. The tiny inboard engine was always reluctant to splutter into action, except when being tested. When in need, it would only start with a great deal of handle turning, swearing and threatening. With engines it is partly a matter of faith, and the little bastard knew I loathed it. The Stuart Turner, with cracked cylinder head (trust second-hand boat engine dealers as you would used car dealers), needed a dozen or so attempts before finally futtering into half-life to take Ant the remaining half-mile home. Many people do not understand the pleasure of sailing.

During our two years at Polkirt Hill, property prices plummeted, enabling us to persuade a bank manager to make up the shortened short-fall between the value of our house and that of the Harbour Stores in St Georges Square. So there we were, skippers of our own gallery, two little boys, Ant, an overdraft and villagers blaming me for ousting their purveyor of fine cheeses.

Donnella, a friend of a friend of Julia and lover of Cornwall, moved down to work with us and live in. The bathroom overlooked the harbour, and I think it was that proximity that caused our new head of sales slight hysterics on her first morning in residence. One of the family's goldfish had not been happy with the move (we all know it can be a stressful time). I thought we had sent it to goldfish heaven. The late night flush was a bit of a long shot, but I hoped the boys would not notice the shoal had halved during the night. Happily, having recovered from the shock of seeing a buoyant fish, lying on its side staring up at her, Donnella stayed with us for several years.

We Can't Force You

Port Isaac to Boscastle

Days with windy forecasts passed. A Monday, eleven days into July looked promising. Neil and I sat outside the Shipwright Arms above Port Isaac, waiting for the shipping forecast. The wrong sort of waves meant radio reception was not available down by the harbour. *'1:55 pm, S bec. var. 3 4 bec W'*. I would have been happy to cast caution to the variable wind, but it seemed to be blowing over freshly from the north, putting me in two minds. The sea appeared deceptively flat from our high vantage spot; so the optimistic mind took precedence. We had experienced a journey of frustrating traffic jams on our way up to Port Isaac and I did not envy Neil having to make the return trip. In contrast, assuming I could row out against the gusty wind funnelling in, I expected minimum boat traffic on my way to Boscastle.

At ten past three I headed out of the little bay. Following a session of strong pulling, I set both sails. Using one or other oar to assist, I battled on for an hour or so. The wind was always blowing from my first target, Tintagel Head, six miles to the north-northeast of Port Isaac. Visually checking my position against islands to the west, off Rumps Point, it was clear I was not making sufficient progress to reach Boscastle in daylight. With full sail it was not possible to make a satisfactory heading, or row with one oar and steer properly. I pulled down the Red Admiral that had been on jib duty, gymnastically securing it with a rubber shock-cord. The Bosun, set against the mast, was a bit of a nuisance, clipping my head with regular monotony. It was easy to haul down in an emergency, so was a fair trade-off. Though heading out to sea a mite too much, I made reasonable progress rowing right-handed.

Reaching my objective in darkness did not worry me much, but it did hasten me on somewhat with the hope of arriving in the near vicinity before total darkness set in. I was confident of rounding the historic headland of Tintagel and finding Boscastle, 'roughly' three miles further on. Passing between towering rugged cliffs to enter the mysterious hidden harbour, at the head of a narrow channel, was my most eagerly awaited moment of the voyage. Over the previous few months I had

191

mentally previewed the occasion – imagined spending a night lost in solitude in that legendary hideaway, having made my way in seclusion along that dramatic coastline.

At six o'clock, I was judging progress against yet another Gull Rock (off Trebarwith Strand). I was a mile or so offshore, with two-thirds the distance towards the headland covered, when I detected a small, engine powered boat heading in my general direction. The craft made good time bouncing over the waves and I found the distraction welcome. At first it seemed so small – perhaps an escaped toy boat – then I noticed three life-sized humans. They were heading towards me. Not until they were fifty yards away did I realise my visitors, dressed alike in yellow oilskins and red lifejackets, were lifeboat-men. As they slowed down I noticed the RNLI on the bow of the rubber boat. It was not until that moment that I realised, with dread, that I was the object of their mission. (It seems odd to me now that I was so slow on the uptake.) As the grey and orange boat bumped into Epic I felt really bad. They came to rescue me, not knowing I did not want to be rescued. The dedicated trio had received a call, launched their boat, travelled four miles and were 'going' to tow me back to Port Isaac.

That conversation off Trebarwith Strand was extremely difficult for me. For the lifesaving crew to allow a 'kamikaze' mission was out of the question. Without causing offence I had to justify my action. My qualification, having come so far was not sufficient justification – perhaps I was a lucky mariner. They did not want me to carry on towards dusk and dangerous headlands. There were several hours of strenuous rowing ahead of me, and of course they could not know if I had the strength for such an undertaking. With constant manipulation of the oars, to counter the motion of the confused seas ahead, progress would not be at all straightforward. In their opinion there was not time for me to row to Boscastle before nightfall. We were in agreement on that point. They did their utmost to dissuade me and I was pretty well convinced by their arguments. About to succumb – advantage against. The lifeboat-men's, "We can't force you", reversed the balance. Match point won, but a close call – just as well no vote was taken.

The 'action-men' did not return to base but roared off, as if let out to play, to find out what conditions were like round the corner. They seemed to be enjoying themselves, making me feel a lot better. Returning fifteen minutes later, they found me on my best behaviour, efficiently plying the oars with gusto. In the meantime there had been communication with Falmouth Coastguard. The lifeboat-men were asked to keep me company till we had passed Tintagel Head.

The hour taken to reach and then round the headland was slightly stressful. Not wishing to keep my escorts waiting, I put extra effort into rowing and wondered how long I could continue in overdrive. It was agreeable to chat with the crew from time to time, and they assured me it was no trouble for them to be out on such a fine evening. Occasionally they zipped off to investigate huge plumes of surf, forced from caves by the swells. The lifeboat was dwarfed by the casual show of nature's effortless power. From my vantage point the display seemed to be in slow motion, and I was too far away to hear more than the faintest of 'boomphs' from the soundtrack. The smallness of the inflatable at the foot of the towering cliffs put the scale of my surroundings in perspective.

Before turning back to Port Isaac, the crew described the markers of the concealed entrance to Boscastle Harbour. Over the previous months I had traced my imaginary track on the map, and it was reassuring to hear that the 'signposts' were in place. On the high promontory, west of the channel, stands a square white lookout resembling a tiny fort, and on the other side there is a tall mast/aerial. Their task complete, the lifeboat-men departed. I had my voyage back.

I pinpointed my exact position on OS 200. A headland named Willapark, a mile from Tintagel Head was on the edge of the map. On the adjoining 190 there is another headland of similar configuration, facing the same direction, also named Willapark. Fortunately, the first Willapark does not have a mini fort/lookout. Even Gull Rocks are not that close together. When three men in a grey and red inflatable raced up from the west, I could have been forgiven for thinking the area possessed a duplication phenomenon – the Tintagel Triangle.

"Falmouth Coastguard have asked us to escort you to Boscastle." The boys had returned. I felt adopted.

Chaperoned, I battled on. With the huge King Arthur's Castle Hotel making frequent appearances between grassy-topped headlands, I pressed slowly onwards towards Boscastle. In total contrast to the hotel, the castle, of which very little remains, blends in well with the landscape – so well in fact, I did not see it.

It was after half past eight when we passed between the two to three hundred yards long, craggy Meachard islet and the second Willapark headland. As we headed into the harbour channel the crew advised me to take a central course, which would have been my option, for backwash created a great deal of motion in the narrows, making for uneasy rowing. The sound of the seas in that awe-inspiring amphitheatre scored a memorable finale to an unusual leg of the voyage. From the steep, ferny, gorsy, heathery hillside that overlooked the channel, a few small groups of holiday-makers observed the end of the show. Without credits, they were not to know that the one in the little white boat would rather have come quietly on his own. As the lifeboat-men powered back to Port Isaac I waved goodbye, wondering what they were saying about their odd evening and strange 'customer'.

In calm water on the south side, alongside the inside of the inner harbour wall, I temporarily tied Epic. It was a quarter to nine. With satisfaction, I laid the oars along the gunwales and climbed onto the steep, narrow stone slip. Oddly, I was not unduly tired after the exertion, but was extremely relieved to be able to relax mentally. No longer did I have to worry about Falmouth Coastguard (I'm sure the feeling was mutual) or three men in a boat worrying about me. Once I upped tempo after 'forming convoy', I seemed to be locked into automatic row mode. Rather self-conscious and ill at ease for much of the time, I now happily remember the unusual episode. Although sometimes it is still better to arrive than to travel.

On warm windless days Boscastle is a cosy little harbour. During winter storms it would be bleak indeed. Even the 'downtown' cluster of cottages nestle safely a couple of hundred yards back alongside the small River Valency (At least I thought so at the time). On the other side of the rushing river I found Fred the Harbourmaster at home and paid him my 'Dinghy Overnight Stay' fee.

The evening was grey, with a touch of dampness in the air. Half an hour after landing I strolled back from the Cobweb Inn, having phoned Julia and the coastguard. All the way back to Epic, I munched a large tasty homemade beef burger, purchased from the pub and cooked to juicy perfection as I celebrated with a swift pint of mild. In case I got caught in the Cobweb later, I felt it prudent to move Epic to an overnight 'parking' position before the tide went out. I moored a little way upstream from the fishing boats, away from possible morning manoeuvrings. There were about a dozen boats, mostly outboard powered, between fifteen and twenty-five feet long. They were moored bow to sturdy wooden bollards set into the quay, and stern to chains on the harbour bed. All would be taken out of the water before the winter storms arrived.

With thoughts of heading out of that crazy sanctuary and completing my journey round the Cornish coastline, I lay down in / on Epic. The temperature eased down as I slipped into my sleeping bag. Later, a light drizzle descended, persuading me to pop into the plastic survival bag; therein, I happily perspired into the night.

The harbour emptied as I steamed in the bag. After grounding for a couple of hours in the drizzly darkness, Epic floated in the new day with a duck enriched dawn. It began just after four o'clock with much frenetic dabbling. The saltwater ducks' energetic lifestyle was due to the racing river rushing over slippery water-worn stones. Despite the sounds of scouring water, and agitated quacks, the idyll remained. I was content to observe and relax for a while. When peeling my breakfast, I perceived the banana skin exactly matching the colour of my oilskin. At a quarter past five, even though the hilltops were shrouded in mist, I optimistically hoisted my royal blue sleeping bag to dry. The modest scale of my enterprise was emphasized by the size of the unzipped bag being larger than the sails. (A reefing sleeping bag is a nice thought, but I feel the market would be limited.)

To check sea conditions, I walked out to the end of Willapark 2. As on the previous evening, the conflict of ocean against cliff produced a great deal of noise in the channel and from the island. As I progressed upwards, the sea's motion appeared less obvious. I imagined rowing out through the ribbons of white. Knowing the cause of that patterning, my eagerness should have been tempered. Patience was required. Two shipping forecasts would be broadcast before I would know if it were safe to set out for Bude.

I brushed on upwards through the ferns. Above the hills, across the valley, the sun's glare faded behind expanding mist that seeped seaward. Reclining on soft grass, the shiny round-stemmed type that formed plump cushions between the heather and ferns, I continued breakfasting. The ham and lettuce sandwiches had become a lump, belonging to the same genus as the 'Cadgwith amalgam'. As before, the battered and compressed presentation did nothing to diminish my appetite. My spirit dipped as dining was disrupted by an unwelcome forecast – 'Veering … three to four; occasional rain or drizzle.' An onshore force four at Bude would be too much for my little boat. There was plenty of time for moderation. While listening to the 'wet Sole' prediction, I noticed low misty cloud out to sea, clearing to reveal soft blue sky. Still munching my distressed sandwich, I wended onwards, up through the bracken.

At half past six I lay on an exposed slab of rock on the cliff edge, close by the lookout, witnessing changing conditions. In the logbook I drew the marker beacon, followed by a drawing of the headlands I was impatient to sail round. While I was sketching the panorama, an ominous bank of cloud developed far out to sea. As I shaded, the formation grew, spreading landward. I shaded some more. *'7:15 Fog from land and sea meet. Sun obscured. Vis. 2 1/2mls.'* The atmospheric view, though inspiring for the painter, was stressful for the small dinghy sailor. I left to explore the locality.

Mooching up to higher Boscastle I poked around, noticing compositions that, if I could have settled and mustered the necessary concentration, I may have painted. I ambled back down the steepest of steep hills. My mind was engaged in running through the forthcoming push towards Devon. I could think of nothing but the possibility of heading back out and turning right for Bude. Waiting increased my worrying. A happy diversion in the form of a second breakfast was taken at the Toby Jug Restaurant. In conversation with the proprietor I mentioned my dilemma. In addition to much tomato and mushroomed rounds of toast, was the suggestion that I have a word with a particular local seaman working out of Boscastle. He was at that moment preparing to go to sea. I made haste to the harbour to catch Ken.

Presently I was engaged in shouted discourse with the obliging skipper who was aboard his boat Pengenna. After introducing myself, stating my proposed destination, mentioning the forecast wind strength and direction, and size of my vessel, the oracle 'advised', without hesitation, "Don't Go".

Until nearing high water, a Bude landing is a beach landing, unsafe even with moderate onshore winds. The sensible course of action had been given loud and clear – an unequivocal, not yet. Rather than being happy with the reprieve, I foolishly decided just to pop out into the Atlantic and, if the lunchtime forecast showed no improvement, just pop back. I know, I know …

Patient Panda
Boscastle to Bude

Bedevilled again by the lure of adventure, I had ignored prudence and chanced my hand with another roulette run. Better judgment lost out to temptation. Self-hypnosis, fed by a lucky streak, made me immortal. At twenty five past eleven, after informing Falmouth Coastguard of my intention, I cast off. Gripping the oars, I tentatively rocked out of the channel. Low water, and the turning tide that would favour me, were still over two hours away. At a lazy pace I made my way between The Meachard and Penhally Point, away from the pounding surf and out to sea. Just a short distance from the cliffs the ocean was almost flat. Though slightly overcast, the clouds were mostly high-ish. The exception was a touch of cloud, way ahead, where change looked possible.

A gentle wind breezed Epic Bude-wards. At noon, with the Bosun raised against the mast and poled out with the boathook, and the Admiral delicately pulling on the forestay, Epic eased to the northeast. It was still a simple matter to row back to Boscastle. Sometime in the next hour or so I was committed to playing my hand, for it would be too dangerous to attempt to beat back. On reaching Cambeak, the largest and first headland, just before Crackington Haven, the latent power of the ocean became apparent. At one thirty I noted, *'Big swells and crashing waves off before Crack'*. Fooled by the sea's lethargic demeanour, I allowed Epic to stray too close to the shore. The dinghy was pushed sideways for a few seconds on a steep onrushing slope. A hundred yards further in, a previous swell thundered against dark jutting cliffs.

A simple line drawing in the logbook reminds me of the uneasy feeling that was to grow over the next few hours. A few minutes after that scary moment, I drew Epic on the steep, landward side of a long swell. Those few simplified lines suggest a more complicated story. Not wishing to be caught out by another sneaky predator, I hurriedly steered further offshore. Captain's log, *'Black sk all across. Bos. Lost. Ominous calm. Ghosting – poled out Bosun. Must get Shp/f.cast'*. The forecast was virtually the same as the early one; the only difference being – rain and drizzle no longer occasional.

At three o'clock, with the breeze almost deserting me, I row/sailed for a while with the sails boomed out on oar and boathook to stop them flapping. A short while later the wind picked up, speeding me over the flat sea for an exhilarating half hour. I stood up for a minute or so, balancing by holding on to the mast. Epic seemed smaller and I imagined the exhilaration windsurfers must feel. Wind strength increased, kicking up little waves that became bigger as my irresponsible journey progressed. Fun and games ceased. I became more and more anxious. Well over half way to Bude, off Dizzard Point and other nearby outcrops, there were breaking seas. A mile further on, with Millook Haven abeam, I was really frightened. The reason was only partly due to threatening conditions, which I seemed to be getting to grips with. My main concern was being propelled at too great a speed towards an inaccessible destination. Dawdling along had suited me fine, but Epic's rapid acceleration ruled out reaching Bude around high water. I dreaded the thought of arriving in bad weather before high tide and not being able to land because of the surf. It would be several hours before Epic could round Bude Breakwater and pass outside the breaking waves into shelter.

Mist shrouded the cliff tops. At times it seemed to brighten, then all would be obscured save for the slightly darker form of a headland. OS 190 showed a sandy beach ahead at Widemouth Bay. There was temptation to head in and take a chance with the surf. From my low viewpoint I may not have seen it. I really wanted to end the ordeal, but had to continue. With the thought playing on my mind, that I may even miss Bude, I spent a desperate hour in the mist. What if I were driven further along the coast, past Hartland Point, on into the Bristol Channel? My mind was in turmoil. I had to locate Bude – there was nowhere else to go. The map showed Hartland Quay, but it was twenty miles on from Bude. It did have a hotel, parking and a 'Mus', that I took to be a museum (of shipwrecks, perhaps). Though there was a suggestion of some sort of bolt hole, it was too far away, particularly as the onshore wind was increasing.

To my good fortune, visibility improved. There was definitely a beach ahead, but was it Widemouth? No, there was a tower on the skyline and a breakwater a few hundred yards ahead. What joy! The relief at finding Bude was most likely the cause of a couple of unforced errors (which I will relate later). An hour earlier I had decided to head straight in if I was lucky enough to arrive off Bude. Even if it were raining, there would be people on the beach. Waves + access = surfers.

My emotions were way beyond the usual. At that stage I was carrying a pack of mini flares. (They should really have been part of the inventory since leaving Plymouth). Though worried, I decided not to fire off a distress flare, for I was sort of safe. Though still pretty scared, I felt a bizarre eagerness to experience what lay ahead. In a supercharged state I rushed through emergency beaching preparations. After the long period of anxiety I felt comparatively composed – quite impressing myself. The increased wind strength had forced me to take in the Admiral half an hour before, so it was just the Bosun to secure, which I hurriedly wrapped and tied round the mast. There was no time to fiddle with the zip on my painting bag into which I had stuffed the map and logbook. Odds and ends, including the polystyrene fender bits, I pushed into the cubbyholes. The lid of the red picnic box fitted tightly, providing a thoroughly seaworthy container for the Walkman and camera. The centreboard and rudder I placed on the stern-seat, having de-shipped them in a frantic trice. Only once before, off Portwrinkle, had I fully inflated my lifejacket. My location was not a mystery this time.

When passing the breakwater, I was perhaps two hundred yards out from the beach. Considering it was not sunbathing weather, the sands were well dotted with people. With Epic already rising to the swells I increased the stroke rate, heading for the breakers. Rowing aggressively I surfed on a pre-breaker wave-face for a couple of seconds. I had never been surfing, but for a beautiful moment I imagined riding a wave right onto the beach. Seconds later, boiling froth piled high above the stern. Epic's blunt bow dipped into the sea, tripping my 'surfboard'. Epic was vertical when a great weight of white water descended. Still gripping the oars, I awaited the engulfing.

Waking, warm and weightless, I became aware of my predicament and, surprisingly, did not panic. A pleasant serenity cradled me. Fear and cold left me. The sea soothed. Though face down in the water, there was no need to breathe. Time stood still. Something round my legs, then it was gone. Forcing mouth to air I gulped. Sudden roaring – I sighted the next avalanche. Inside the green bubbles I wished to breathe. Patience. Desperation. Freed from the second tumbling, I sucked in beautiful oxygen. Riding high on her buoyant side and dragging her mast, the Mirror drifted onto the beach.

Heading towards Bude I ran through imaginary beachings many times. Removing my green wellingtons was a major priority. Bobbing towards the beach I was rather perturbed to find myself encumbered, not only by a large heavy jumper, but also my wellies. Treaded soles had made contact with the sand a couple of times when a bronzed lifeguard on a surfboard paddled up to ask if I was alright.

"Yes thank you", I said.

With Atlantic lapping my waist, I became acutely aware of gravity. In slow motion, I ponderously lumbered towards my natural element. Fantastic fortune favoured me at that auspicious moment. I spotted, close to my port thigh, the grey nylon painting bag. It hovered below the surface in a most surreal manner. The contents, though poking out, seemed present and correct. Again I was fortunate to be reunited with my faithful old cardboard tube and brushes. They were taking water alongside the map and log/notebook. Lifting the bag from the sea, emptying out a couple of pints, then nonchalantly hanging it from my shoulder was quite 'Daliesque'. There was reason aplenty for self-consciousness, but I did not care. Water slurped from my welly tops, and my sagging jumper stretched over the thrusting lifejacket – reminiscent of those ludicrous, throat-inflating, show-off birds you see on wildlife programmes. Relief cast aside any embarrassment. Though strained and draining, it was a mightily thankful mariner who walked from the water onto Bude beach.

At first sight, Epic seemed in a bad way – listing a sad one hundred degrees at the tide-line. I thought the mast was broken, but happily that was not so. An oar had fixed itself between mast and shroud, and the boathook was caught on the forestay. Those items were the basis of a giant cat's cradle, impressively tangled, courtesy of my long green mooring rope. With the help of Minnie, the muscular lifeguard, Epic was righted. The wind pressed her safely against the beach. While pouring Atlantic from my wellingtons, I began to take stock. Lifeguards and others collected together my flotsam. I regret littering Bude with portions of polystyrene which, with cords still attached, had flown away up the beach. It may have been ten or even thirty minutes before the last item was recovered and returned to Epic (I was not making notes). An oar had gone adrift. It had broken away from a rowlock housing, sending a small, galvanized fitting to the bottom of the sea. The bootlaces had kept one oar tethered to the boat. The other, though it escaped, still had the rowlock tied to it. Little had been conceded to Neptune. The rowlock plate joined a few pound coins, a small bucket and a few short lengths of rope. My oilskin must have sunk and drifted off like a big yellow skate, never to be seen again. To this day, off the coast of North Cornwall, a yellow handless sleeve may signal from the deep. ("Don't go".)

Minnie asked if I would like to use their phone in the hut at the top of the beach. My first call was to Falmouth Coastguard, informing them of my arrival. I did not go into details. The second was to Julia, asking for a lift home and some dry clothes. Back down at the landing site I thanked Minnie and set about untangling Epic. While releasing the oar and boathook from the rigging, I noticed a bunch of bungy ties caught at the masthead, and left them there. My 'seaworthy' red box turned out to have a cunning ventilation system. It stood on the beach for at least half an hour, innocently protecting my Walkman, camera, numerous other odds and ends and several gallons of seawater. Fearing possible malfunction from my severely tested, water-resistant camera, I photographed the gleaming, virtually undamaged Epic, hoping for the best.

Feeling a need to record the sorry episode with certainty, I extracted, with numbed fingers, the damp logbook and a pen from the soggy painting bag. I noted the estimated time of turning turtle in large scrawl on the cover, – *'4:45 12 July'*. The next two hours I was kept busy leading Epic up a channel formed by the River Neet. The watercourse, too shallow to float the dinghy, ends at a quay, close to lock gates that hold back the Bude Canal. There is also a slipway leading to a small lifeboat station. Shepherding Epic off the beach seemed to take forever.

With the dinghy safe for a while, tied alongside the quay, I was able to pay attention to the 'captain'. Carrying my plastic clothes bag, I nipped round to the front of the lifeboat shed, out of the chilling wind. The location lacked privacy, leaving me rather exposed as I changed into what dry clothes I had. Fortunately, the heavy-duty plastic bag was tied closed with a cord. The old shirt at the top of the bag was slightly damp, but the rest of my ensemble was perfectly dry. (The shirt, though washed many times, still retained faint oil stains picked up following my lucky landing at Portwrinkle.) To be out of the wind was bliss. To divest myself of heavy sodden wool and cold clinging denim was sublime. Though small, the dry towel taken from my 'goody' bag was a wondrous treasure. After so much discomfort and misery, the fluffy talisman marked my changed circumstance. In dryish shirt, shorts and battered old trainers, the transformation was complete. From the lee of the lifeboat hut, emerged Mirrorman.

In retrospect, the rejuvenated me may not have been fully compos mentis. A wet person, however happy to be alive, should not spend hours chilling on a windy beach. Surely, he would have sought help to carry the dinghy above the high water line. A totally sane person would not have left Boscastle, or even Plymouth Sound.

Neil had again been pressed into taxi service. He duly arrived in his soft-topped motorcar. My intention had been to take Epic home for repairs, but the convertible forced a change of plan. While I had been dismasting Epic, two of the lifeboat crew arrived at the hut. Noticing the front doors open, I entered. It transpired that it would be in order to leave my boat alongside the hut for a day or two, and no trouble to leave the mast, oars and a few other items inside. I was filling in the background that led to my request for storage when one of the crew noticed a large lump on my right temple. My hair had been concealing the disfigurement. Being concerned for the wellbeing of others, the lifeboat men suggested I hang on a moment, for their medic-man would soon arrive. Though I felt fine and wanted to go home (it had been a long day) I agreed to have my head seen to. Neil drove me the short distance to Stratton Hospital. We made our way through the deserted interior and seated ourselves in the waiting room beside a life-sized giant panda. Though I had come to see if the balance of my mind was unimpaired, it was Neil who asked the panda if he had been waiting long. A nurse duly arrived, informing us that there would be a few minutes to wait. She may have wondered if there was any connection between my lump and the man who talked to stuffed animals. My attempt to phone home was thwarted. The photo-chromic glasses that gave restful protection against the sea's reflective glare, and enabled me to read small print on maps and telephone directories, were lost. The whereabouts of the spectacle's came to me, as I knew they would not, for they resided a little way off Bude beach.

The nurse returned and ushered me in to see the doctor. Seeing the evidence, and believing my diagnosis was possibly correct, he seemed happy with my lump. I suggested the possibility of being struck by the heavy copper bound rudderstock, or a Mirror dinghy, as the breaking wave descended. Sometimes I think I should have been a doctor. We took our leave, saying goodbye to the patient panda, and headed home to Mevagissey.

Machere

Toby was seven and Robin five. We must have had a successful season in the gallery, for on the spur of the moment we flew to Crete for what turned out to be a fantastic fortnight of October sunshine. Happy memories of that inspirational holiday remain with us. The boys hunted lizards over boulder-strewn hillsides and snorkelled in the warm sea. Our apartment stood serenely isolated, a couple of kilometres out of Ag. Nicholas. (I don't expect that's still the case.) Exploring the terrain round our pad, we stirred wonderful aromas from yellowed herbs that prospered in the dusty earth. Passing through timeless olive groves, we chanced upon isolated homesteads. A couple of outdoor tables and a scattering of wooden chairs with grass seats 'advertised' feasts of feta salads with fresh crusty bread soaked in salty olive oil. The boys delighted in picking their own puddings from overhead vines. The relaxed interlude nourished body and soul.

For a painter relatively new to battling with watercolour painting, I was most grateful for the presence of those olive trees. The knarry, dark dusted trunks, deep black even in the brightest sunshine, contrasted so delightfully with their delicate, smoky-green canopies. Tone is perhaps the most important element in painting, and those saving touches of dark helped me come to terms with that most elusive medium. I still have the first outdoor watercolour – painted from the villa roof. That sunny souvenir, together with a painting of the boys under an ancient olive tree on the islet of Spinalonga, encouraged me to set off eighteen months later on an Iberian painting trip – to renew my skirmish with high temperature watercolour.

A short while after our Cretan adventure, Dennis was selling Machere, prior to his relocation to Australia. The somewhat reluctant vendor of the solid, beamy, twenty-two-footer, had admirably upgraded from the humble ANT, and to my satisfaction, a transaction was unhesitatingly concluded.

Machere was moored midway along the previously mentioned Pont Pill opposite Fowey. While sorting out a new mooring in Mevagissey Harbour, I left the gunter-rigged Westerly in the idyllic setting off the

Fowey River, protected from the elements (mostly), gently swinging on her mooring. One day I popped over to the waterfront at Fowey to check the wellbeing of our new prize, and was shocked to find her AWOL. After a desperate few minutes searching from a higher view-point, I spied the wilful wanderer, tucked away at the top end of the creek. A hasty return to Fowey, after collecting my little yellow inflatable, was followed by a row over to Machere – to eliminate fears of foul play. The Westerly had been secured to a single fixing from the bow. Every tide she swung round three hundred and sixty degrees, kinking and shortening the chain. One particularly high spring tide, after several weeks of good behaviour, Machere lifted her concrete mooring block and relocated to a pleasant spot well away from other boats. Though I had further to row, she had plenty of swinging room.

Before sailing the self-mooring Machere to Mevagissey, I had cause to visit Pont Pill one last time. A long spell of windy weather kept me away from the boat and I felt it prudent to go over and unwind the chain and check for chafe on the rope attached to the chain. The strong west wind ruled out an approach from the Polruan side, so a brazen frontal attack was called for. As I expended an enormous amount of energy, pumping miniscule puffs of air into my deflated and seemingly dormant heap of yellow rubber, I wondered what would happen when I cast off onto the wind-torn stretch of water. If whisked straight to the top end of the Pill, it would not be the end of the world – it would be the end of the Pill. Other than becoming airborne en route, there was nothing to fear. It all happened so quickly, but I did not fly. With the dab of a paddle now and then to make slight course adjustments, I was soon hurtling towards the high bow of Machere. I managed to grab the chain and remain with the dinghy while making my way to the stern to embark. With all shipshape on board, I continued my whirlwind ride to the top of the creek. On arrival, I casually stepped onto the mud and carried the inflatable above the tide-line. There, I squeezed air out a great deal quicker than putting it in. With the unwieldy bundle of rubber under my arms, on my shoulders or clasped to my front, I made my way round the creek edge and along to the foot ferry at Polruan. So ended a boating adventure; though short, it was sweet – unfolding according to script – most unusual.

It was from Machere, anchored off Portloe, that I rowed my junior crew, Toby and Robin, ashore in that same bright yellow rubber dinghy. After supper in the Ship (pub), we spent a comfortable night afloat, something I had not experienced before (and seldom since). The following night we swung at anchor in Polgwidden Cove off Durgan, on the Helford River. At slack low water, the morning mist gradually lifted, unveiling a beautiful, peaceful setting. In diffused stillness, a brace of adventurers rowed round Machere. It mattered not that the boarding party were capturing their own ship. After breakfasting heartily, we cast off sharply to beat the tide to open sea. It was from the August rock that a large seal, with a sleepy turn of head, bade us goodbye. The following year Julia came too, to explore more of the Helford creeks. We enjoyed the boys, enjoying being boys in that magical protected environment. In Machere they could stand up 'down stairs'. Years later I would be reminded of those happy times. The trigger being the night-time vocals, perpetrated by a far from melodious Gweek seal.

Had Dennis sailed to his new job in the gunter-rigged, tan sailed sloop, we would have missed out on those wonderful voyages. Next time I chat with Toby and Robin I will ask them what they remember of the Helford River trips. I hope they recall some of the adventure. When asked what was the best bit of our French holiday a couple of years later, it seemed gorges, caves, forests, rivers and chateaux were forgotten. The little darlings agreed the highlight was the Big Mac in Bordeaux.

Eighteen months after my outdoor painting appetizer in Crete, I set off for the main course – a five-week painting trip to Southern Spain and Portugal. An uninterrupted period of work in favourable weather conditions would help me become 'fluent' in outdoor, or 'plein-air' work, as we painters say. With great expectation and heavy case (I intended to hire a car) I flew south. Before driving out of Malaga I purchased an A5 spiral bound notebook. It had a blue cover with a picture of a little white bull on the front. Using my mini Hugo's Spanish Phrase Book, I thought I had done well composing the request. The blue book reveals a trip that was not all milk and honey. The passing of time, remembering only the best bits, left me with the idea that I wined and dined through magnificent landscapes, painlessly producing a pile of paintings. That was partly

A Church in Tarifa

14″ x 13″   1984

207

true, for there are many references to half litres of 'vino tinto', but also of 'the rain in Spain'. The initial entry in the 'diary' (which to my surprise contained graph paper – it was my first go with Hugo) reads, *'I should think Malaga an interesting city – can't judge in the rain.'* Two lines on I find, *'Small, scruffy, unshaven man hurried off with my very heavy case.'* I splashed after the surprisingly strong little chap to reclaim my luggage in the foyer (stairwell) of a dingy hostel. Well it was only for one night. *'Cold water – room smelly – bit grubby.'* The next day I departed in haste from my drab 'cupboard' on the sixth floor, hired a small Seat Panda and drove off into the mountains. In Spain, the rain not only falls on the plain. *'Started painting 2:40 – raining 2:50 – ran back to car at 3:00'.* The next day I noted, *'The landscape I just painted has totally disappeared. Rain and mist closing in …'*

Four days on I arrived in Tarifa, a town overlooking Morocco, at the very tip of southern Spain. There I enjoyed a couple of happy productive days in brilliant sunshine, and relaxed evenings in tapas bars. Following a night in the car, between one-night stays in dubious accommodations, I had struck lucky. The reasonably priced, sixteen-roomed Villanueva was well appointed and ultra clean. From the roof terrace, the Atlas Mountains seemed almost touchable in the clear air. From my window I could see the outer harbour wall. Alongside was moored a streamlined, passenger hydrofoil. There was no early sailing to Tangier the following day, so I booked a day trip for the day after. My excitement was unbounded – I was going to Morocco. Meanwhile, a little way out of town I painted a ruined bridge with shipping passing through the Strait of Gibraltar in the background. The whole scene was dwarfed by the Atlas Mountains. I must have felt in good spirits, painting in Southern Spain with the prospect of painting in North Africa the following day.

Early in the morning, before walking down to catch the hydrofoil, I drew a view from my bedroom window. The small sketch, on the top half of a page in the blue book, showed the buildings of Tarifa standing upright (thanks to the little squares) against the giant mountains of another continent. The half hour crossing was exhilarating. I could not wait to explore the mysterious Medina. All good things come to those who wait. I had to wait three years.

view from bedroom. Tarifa –
Hostal Villanueva. looking at Africa — Morocco.

28 · April

Tangier from the
hydrofoil
28 April.

From the 'Blue Book'   1981

Almost last to disembark, I handed over my passport for inspection.

"Passport does not exist in Morocco." I was unceremoniously pushed back into the cabin. Being detained for having an uncanny likeness to an international criminal would have been bad enough, but for only having a temporary passport, a bitter pill. The ticket vendor who checked my passport back in Tarifa must have known the score, and I was sure he would have left his booth and disappeared by the time I returned, dream shattered, back to Europe eight and a half hours later. Surely it could be sorted. After ten minutes or so I went on deck intending at least to set foot in Africa and was shoved back into the cabin again, this time by a guard with a rifle. He spoke no English.

I complained to the blue book, *'I am a prisoner – no passport – no food or drink – no apology – no communication.'* At about two o'clock a deck hand chanced along. I mimed hunger and handed him a many peseta note (equal to the daily tariff at Villanueva). Time passed. Eventually, a cheese roll, a tuna roll and a bottle of Coke were delivered. I was grateful; so too was my 'porter', who took it upon himself to keep the change.

Reprieve seemed rather unlikely, so I searched the cabin for something to read. Lying invitingly on a seat was the Sunday Observer. It was time I had a little luck. That was not the time, for I had thoroughly digested that edition on the flight to Malaga.

I tired of trying to memorise days of the week in Spanish from 'Hugo', and used it instead to help me compose a letter to the Customs – which I duplicated. I now copy the remaining half page from the blue book:

Hydrofoil (Sinbad) pasajero	
DAVID WESTON (DEFECTUOSO PASAPORTE)	
hung Hambriento conj sediento	Hungry and thirsty
(no desayuno)	(no breakfast)
Poder comparar almuerzo?	Can you buy me lunch?

To whom I gave the folded note I cannot remember. The exercise helped to pass the time, but other than that, was a complete waste of time.

Just as I was about to commence a drawing of Tangier, a sudden heavy shower blurred the windows. Would there be a plague of locusts next? I wondered. Visibility eventually returned and I set about 'Tangier from the Hydrofoil', below the earlier 'View from Villanueva'. As well as the drawing, I assumed I had acquired another memento of my stay, very nearly, in Africa. The Coke bottle was adorned with Moroccan script. Later, despite my protests, the deck hand took away the keepsake bottle. Some days are best forgotten.

Weeks of wine and watercolour trickled by. I was pleased with the mounting portfolio. I still have a particular work, 'Villa Roofs and Olive Trees'. It is one of the 'half-litre' paintings. Some architectural details are a bit wonky (should have used the graph paper), but overall, the 'vino tinto' influence adds vigour to the piece. Sitting at my easel under those shady trees in Southern Spain, with bread, olives and a bottle of wine to hand, I was close to heaven.

Three years later I was in Morocco, leading a double life. My plan was to finally paint in the Medina in Tangier. To that end, for reason of economy, I took a half board holiday package. Billeted in a large hotel on the edge of town, I was left to do my own thing. Being part of a package held a useful perk – a guided tour of Tangier on the first morning, first by coach then on foot around part of the Medina. In tight convoy we were begged at most energetically. Having been instructed not to 'pay' attention, we were not entirely relaxed. How would it be for me, a solo target, I wondered.

The following day I walked out of town to paint boats on a beach. Day two: after breakfasting in the hotel, I changed into old jeans, shirt and trainers in an attempt, not to tempt hasslers. With painting equipment in an old army bag slung over my shoulder, I headed for the old Medina – a daunting, swarming tangle of tiny streets and alleyways. Before even reaching that bustling cauldron of humanity, I received *'six offers of dope …'* There were so *'many places to paint in the old city but no peace'*. Eventually I found a quiet-ish spot in the railway sidings. Quiet-ish that is, if you exclude the odd train that clattered by a few inches from my easel. As I was finishing my painting, *'Kids pulled my hair and tried to pinch a brush out of my hand'*. I set off in search of another painting location. *'… young men trying to sell me hash and 3 or 4 would be guides 'just want to be*

sociable' 'learn English' 'no hassle – come this way – my brothers' shop (bazaar) …
you smoke very good, very cheap – young lady very cheap!!!' My resolve was to
paint in the Medina that afternoon; but first some lunch. I was playing
for time.

Earlier I stopped at a quiet bar for a cold beer, and to that refuge I
returned to psyche myself up for the challenge ahead. Again I was given
a small bowl of some kind of shellfish, or so I thought. Perhaps my
shabby clothing was the reason for being offered a glass of "soup". To
the lukewarm, off white liquid, I added pepper to override the *'dishwa-*
tery' nuance. My light lunch of chicken and olives, purchased afterwards,
was just the ticket. I quizzed the barman, whose only English seemed to
be 'soup', regarding the mysterious fish dish. Apparently I had downed
half a pint of gritty water in which mountain snails had been lightly
boiled to death. No wonder the chicken tasted so good. *'3 would be guides*
walked with me and chatted me up. (I must add that I felt most uncomfortable) *Lost the last one when I asked the shopkeeper if I could sit on the high front*
step 2ft. In the Medina / Kasbah; very brave – left to paint – lots talked – v. nice
people. 2 paintings to-day!! I had cracked it. All I had to do was find a painting subject, sit down, start work and I would not be pestered too much.
It was such a relief.

We all have a sense of direction, some better than others; then
there's mine. One time when painting in the Medina I was rained off, or
rather upon. A few days later I was pleasantly surprised to chance across
the same scene, which I duly completed. Built on hills, Tangier has a
great many sets of steps of various configurations – from wide, straight,
long multiple flights, to short, narrow, haphazard sections, often leading
to mysterious, dark covered passageways. Many of my paintings were of
steps. *'Sat 11:00 v windy. Medina. Paint on steps, lot of children as usual – I like*
them – 6 year old angels will pop off to beg "One dirham please" and pop back to
watch painting – much friendly kicking and thumping. I get a little upset sometimes
when a man will hit them on the head with a stick to clear a way for me to see.' After
completing that painting, I took a couple of photographs of my audience. The first shows a group of boys with one beaming little chap
sitting on my painting stool holding the painting bag. The remaining girls
and boys did not want to be left out, so my second picture is crammed
full of smiling Tangerines. Three paintings from the trip I keep. They

9″ x 8″ 1979

'... the boys under an ancient olive tree on the islet of spinalonga.'

The Medina – Tangier

7½″ x 7″ 1984

'... produced while dense crowds passed to and fro,
yet ... the pictures are uninhabited.'

were produced while dense crowds passed to and fro, yet apart from one or two figures, the pictures are uninhabited. Strange – painting scenes that did not exist.

My last day in Morocco was pretty perfect. *'Last painting 2 doorways – simple – quite pleased. Still life for student pencil bulb, pencil sharpener and keys on chain. Seemed pleased. Lunch 2 fish boiled on charcoal fire (earthenware) in L earthenware bowl* (The notes surround a drawing of the short cylindrical fire pot with a wide, shallow bowl on top containing the stew.) *lemon rings chillies tomatoes potatoes etc. v. v. good 9 D.H. …'* Later, in a rather basic Medina café, I relaxed over mint teas. There were a few tables and chairs, a large fridge and little else, except for a couple of advertising posters taped to the walls. With much smiling, pointing and gesticulating mime, I asked if it would be possible to purchase a Coke poster (with Moroccan script). That was not possible, but I was most welcome to take one as a gift. The gift given happily meant a lot to me; certainly more than the 'hydrofoil Coke bottle' that nearly was (even if it had been).

Trailer

Had I taken my unorthodox arrival at Bude as a sign, the journey with Epic would have ended there, on a suitably decisive note. The county border was a mere eight miles away and there was no sensible landing place before Clovelly on the North Devon coast. Common sense had not interfered up to that point, so I decided to try and take Epic right round Cornwall. It would mean an overland trek, which could be interesting.

The day after walking ashore at Bude I returned to collect the dinghy. Brother Michael, bless him, holidaying in Cornwall at the time, accompanied me. The 6′ 6″ oars were attached to the Fiesta's roof rack to support the dinghy on the journey back home, where repairs and modifications would take place. A pity the two lengths of timber, cut to support Epic on the car, were left behind, for the oars were too long.

Leaving the lifeboat hut I drove alongside the canal out of Bude and headed north to check out Welcombe Mouth, a less than sensible landing place eight miles away, just over the county border. We drove down narrow lanes and finally along a half-mile rough track. Due to the projecting oars and unruly foliage, progress was slow as we approached the beach. After parking close to the cliff edge, we walked a few yards to look down on a comprehensive range of pointy rocks. Over aeons (if you can have more than one) the tops of folding strata had been eroded, leaving a series of toothed slabs running out into the ocean. The tide was out, uncovering a few narrow strips of sand between ranks of rock. A landing would be possible at low tide in the quiet conditions that we encountered, but it would have been a 'drag' to manhandle Epic up to, then over the black pebbles that formed a steep-ish slope at the high-water mark close to the cliffs. Remembering the Bude experience, I reckoned a high tide beaching would have many advantages. Epic would sail over the menacing breakwater formations, arriving close to the steep cliff path. (I can't think why I thought the 'drag' a problem – considering we looked down from a cliff.)

The reason for thinking of a circumnavigation: I simply wished the adventure to continue. It would be a tidy way of 'finishing off' Cornwall – taking Epic all the way round the county border. Cornwall not being an island makes the prospect seem a rather odd proposition, I must admit. Looking at the map though, the idea does not appear so crazy; at least to me it did not. The River Tamar, save for four miles, severs Cornwall from Devon. In reality the northern extremity of the river is barely a trickle in summertime. That was of no consequence, for the border does not follow the course of the river exactly. After taking Epic overland, I would re-launch some miles downstream. Above North Tamerton there is a five square mile portion of Cornwall that lies east of the river. Below, the river divides the counties all the way down to tidal waters at Gunnislake. Surely, from North Tamerton, such a modest vessel as mine would be able to drift down the mighty Tamar; I mused. Investigation would have eliminated the element of mystery.

From the beach at Welcombe Mouth, I hoped it would be possible to haul the dinghy up the cliff path. Help would not be sought, for up till then my trip round Cornwall had been unaided. Though assistance had been given in loading and launching, I could trace an unbroken track of solo progress, with Epic of course, from Gunnislake to our separation in the surf off Bude. The road section I reckoned was about twenty-five miles. The distance did not deter me, even though the first mile would include a climb of four hundred and thirty feet. I would build a set of wheels and, given time, push or pull Epic to North Tamerton, then drift down to salt water; I mused on. To make life easier I would dispense with the mast, centreboard and rudder for the final coastal leg, which would be rowed. The wooden mast, designed to hold a gaff, is very weighty, and the rudder, as my multicoloured forehead testified, was deceptively heavy. After an intermission of a week or so, there would be spring tides to cast Epic high up onto Welcombe beach at a sensible time of day.

Two days after my Bude encounter, I attended to Epic on the front lawn. Luckily, the piece of rowlock housing that had broken off still dangled on wood fibres. It was a simple task to relocate, glue and screw it back into place. A long shot, calling at John Moor's small chandlery section on the harbour, to see if they still had the remaining small galvanized rowlock fitting (I fitted two of the last three at Lostwithiel). Success. So apart from creating a transporter, I was set for re-engagement. Epic would soon be ready for battle.

As with glass-fibre mixing, you may not find trailer construction riveting. Feel free to skip a few paragraphs.

Down in my studio at the bottom of the garden, I sorted materials to construct the transporter. The wheels I claimed from Robin's old bike – long outgrown. A pair of wheels with axle would have made construction much easier. A simple framework was assembled utilising lengths of rough 2″ x 1″ timber left over after building stands to display a series of paintings illustrating the first Epic trip. One piece, a little longer than the boat's 4′8″ beam, was laid on the floor. On to that, 6″ in from the ends, I glued and screwed two pairs of 10 1/2″ uprights to hold the 20″ wheels. Holes were drilled down into the centres of the uprights to hold little devices taken from the rear wheel axle. These items consisted of washers welded to threaded shafts, used for tensioning the chain. They looked like miniature, long-handled ping-pong bats with holes in the flat part. (I trust this is not too technical.) The fit of the 'bats', in the timber uprights, was tight – just right in fact to self-tap (self-thread, sort of thing) the bolt ends. With the little bats screwed home and aligned, I inserted the wider cogged rear wheel and 'nutted' tightly. The outer uprights were strengthened with small shelf brackets (taken from a small shelf).

It is unfortunate that bicycles have only one set of 'bats'. A trip to the cycle shop, situated upstairs in the St Austell Market House, was called for. (The belt man's stall had gone. Perhaps he was wholesaling.) The unusual use of bats was easily explained, but the reason for doubling up on reflective stickers, because I was unsure from which end of the inverted boat I would push or pull, was more difficult. From the ironmongers at the other end of the building I bought half a dozen 'small shelf' brackets.

With the second wheel in place, between narrower spaced uprights, the construction looked plausible, but still required pieces of wood at right angles, to line up with the gunwales. (The assemblage was upside-down at this point.) These extensions needed to project from just one side of the ends of the long piece, to ensure stability. The pieces were, to use old nautical parlance, just over a cubit (14″) long (or half that of a small shelf).

From feet and inches, some might think it regressive to return to 'Noah-measurement'. It 'aint' necessarily so. A cubit is exactly a third of a metre – the length of a forearm. Personally I find metres frustrating, not being divisible by three. I strongly recommend the shelf, or 'dozen-imal' system – one to eleven then add a nought. Of course the eleven would be changed to another symbol so it did not look like two ones (a Roman two). A backward 'E' would do, otherwise it might be a bit confusing. It goes without saying that the ten would have a single symbol, possibly an upside-down 'T'.

For some time I deliberated, trying to work out a simple lightweight method of attaching the dinghy to the transporter. The solution – two 10″ lengths of thin red nylon guy rope, scavenged from the remains of the old blue tent, passed through tiny holes drilled just below the gunwale (above, if the boat is inverted). The lines, passing round the gunwales and the ends of the half shelf extensions, would hold the dinghy and wheel assembly firmly together. Small strips of wood were fixed on top of the half shelves to prevent the boat slipping sideways.

With the front end of the inverted Epic propped on a five foot length of 2″ x 1″, I secured the undercarriage to the boat. On removing the prop, I found Epic balanced beautifully. Hand positions, whether pushing or pulling from bow or stern, seemed a perfectly comfortable mid-thigh height. The first test run began well, but after a couple of boat lengths, the one-inch step leading from the front garden gravel to the road proved too great an obstacle. The structure creaked alarmingly and one wheel, quite independently, turned inwards. The mission was temporarily aborted. The fourth and final test, six days later, was a robust success. Five pieces of tent pole, ends beaten flat and drilled for screws, a length of aluminium carpet edge strip, two short lengths of 2″ x 1″ and a batch of small shelf brackets were added by degrees as weaknesses became evident. (The missing sixth section of tent pole cost style marks.)

Captain's log, 20th June. Two hundred yards along from our house, the lane joins a steep hill with precipitous gradients. It is so steep that the lower section has been grooved to facilitate tyre purchase. I heaved Epic thirty or forty yards up the hill, turning round in Ken and Sylvia's driveway. It was a small step in relation to the portage envisaged, but a pretty large leap for me. It was twenty-five years to the day since men first walked on the moon. Ken has met Buzz Aldrin. It's a small world (the moon).

From Bude, I would carry the wheel assembly onboard Epic. The simple system to accommodate them utilised the same fixing points – little hull holes and shelf extension ends. The extensions pointed forward instead of backwards, positioning the wheels further aft, so as not to interfere with the oarsman.

Three days later, my new-look voyager would be transported to Bude. From there I would set out to complete the final sea leg to Devon, and a final beach landing.

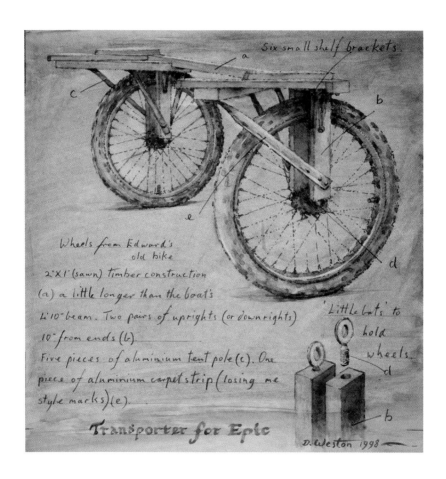

Six small shelf brackets

a

b

c

e

d

Wheels from Edward's
old bike

2"x1" (sawn) timber construction

(a) a little longer than the boat's

4'10" beam. Two pairs of uprights (or downrights)

10" from ends (b).

Five pieces of aluminium tent pole (c). One

piece of aluminium carpet strip (losing me

style marks)(e).

'Little bats' to
hold
wheels.
d

b

Transporter for Epic

D. Weston 1998

(The wheels, in fact, were from Robin's old bike.)

219

Talking Boat
Bude to Darracott

From the roof rack of the Fiesta, parked at the bottom of the slip by the lock gates, Neil and I carried Epic fifty yards or so down the beach, setting her beside the channel to await the incoming tide. Eleven days earlier, I shepherded my wounded dinghy slowly past that same spot. Then I was cold, lonely, and slightly out of touch. I returned in warm sunshine, eager to head off on my own again. Our three o'clock arrival at Bude allowed plenty of time to load Epic with reduced gear and tie on the wheel assembly. Along with weighty items left behind was the red picnic box. I should have brought it, although a little cumbersome, it kept things tidy and weighed very little. Discarding it was perhaps a subliminal decision – blacklisted for poor showing after capsize.

With the camera that earned Brownie points on that same beach, I recorded the scene. While photographing the be-wheeled Epic, I was amazed to witness a red amphibious car driving out of the sea. In one snap I shot both wheeled craft, then the 'boat-car show off' driving off showing twin propellers. Bude for me had been over rich in tide-line incident. I hoped the unusual vehicle was the final surprise.

Minnie was on duty, so I wandered down the beach to thank him for his assistance following my unorthodox arrival. Though little had changed, the scene appeared quite different. It was 'peacetime', a happy relaxed place with holiday-makers having fun. Previously, from offshore, I viewed the 'beachhead' through a weary combatant's eyes. Soon I would be on the other side of the breakers, which happily for me, if not for surfers, were delightfully petite.

As the ocean flooded the narrow channel, I pushed Epic into the deepening stream. During a lull in wave activity, I rowed quickly out over the swells. The Atlantic, dark blue and dappled with wavelets, seemed in gentle mood, reclining under a cobalt heaven brushed misty white. To the north, surf rolled onto a headland. I kept well clear.

Relief and a hint of sadness juggled my emotions. The last sea leg meant an end to masochistic excitement – an end to pushing my luck with the unpredictable Neptune. Happiness reigned; for I was in no apparent danger, knew exactly where I was and the location for the final beaching. Meanwhile, a most exquisite coastline of sun-warmed cliffs was presented for my enjoyment. A continuous geological presentation slipped by. Vast surfaces, decorated with flowing seams of layered, contorted strata, with abrupt changes of angle marking past earthly conflicts, resulted in fascinating, folding compositions. The natural beauty of butterfly wings can be magnified to create powerful paintings. Cliff paintings can be fashioned by reducing areas of interest for transposition to canvas.

The onboard fixing of the chunky BMX wheels and chassis worked well. The position did not hinder my rowing and I soon got used to the odd assemblage dominating the view. Four miles on from Bude, off Lower Sharpnose Point, I noticed a cluster of delicate-looking dish aerials peeping over the cliff top. They were smaller than their famous Goonhilly cousins, left behind at the other end of the county.

Though not intending to venture out to sea at the onset, I was so pleased to have been caught up in the adventure. To circumnavigate – return to the tidal Tamar – now seemed a tidy goal. It was something that could only happen by chance. Who would contemplate such a thing – push off in a simple craft and keep turning right.

Those last idyllic hours afloat on the ocean were without urgency. My Welcombe arrival was planned to coincide with high tide at seven o'clock, so I treated myself to a period of leisurely rowing. There was a little less than three hours to cover a tide assisted seven and a half miles, enabling me to proceed at an economical, effortless row rate. I idled north, wondering what lay in store at Welcombe Mouth. One scenario imagined in darker moments a week or so earlier, saw Epic crash-landing, sustaining enough structural damage to end the 'voyage'. That afternoon I sincerely wanted to continue, and hoped for a trouble free beaching followed by a successful cliff haul. It would have been a shame to waste those wonderful wheels.

Less than a couple of miles beyond Lower Sharpnose Point, is (have a guess) Higher Sharpnose Point. Though projecting just a few hundred yards into the ocean, it is a major landmark, being the last headland before Devon. Appearing very tiny beyond the great cliff was a church tower. From the map, I reckoned it stood in the village of Morwenstow. The distant square of stone and the giant modern mushrooms, were the only signs of man's occupation. The OS also informed that just two miles on lay the 'gateway' to Devon – and, wouldn't you just know, the offshore 'post' was another Gull Rock.

Ahead of schedule, I had plenty of time to study the structure of the islet in detail. Though not much more than a hundred yards long, that particular Gull Rock was mightily impressive. The evening sunshine, filtering through a hint of mist, showed off the powerful formation with dramatic effect. Viewed from the side, the long awaited goal (post) resembled a great whale. The formation angled gently from the water on the seaward side (the tail end) to form a rounded head crowned with layers of strata. The vertical sides had succumbed to relentless sculpting by the ocean, flaking away the flanks.

At high tide, there is a thirty-foot wide passage behind the Rock. While riding cautiously over the swells towards the channel, I was surprised to pass alongside a tall rectangular tunnel where the eye of the whale would be. Through the seemingly, precisely engineered feature was an invitingly bright, tall oblong seascape. Swells rose and fell, sucked and expelled, as if the whale lived. Edging towards the opening I felt a mischievous force stirring. 'Please don't', I pleaded with myself. My copybook did not require further blotting. Had there been a mite more width in which to manipulate the oars, the temptation to thread my way into Devon waters would have been too great. I so nearly entered the whale's eye.

I rowed into the confined channel behind the whale, close to its head that resembled half of a giant swiss roll viewed end on. A couple of dozen concentric fossilised layers were being patiently digested by salty water. (Later I painted the unusual formation, giving it the confusing title, 'Whale Rock'. The genuine article lies just east of The Lizard.)

The regimented structure of the whale reminded me of the time I wore a tutu. Seriously, or should I say, not seriously. Let me explain. The whale possessed grandeur, similar to that portrayed on the sleeve of our LP recording of Mendelssohn's Fingal's Cave overture. With clarity, I recall the crucial compliment of the dramatic accompaniment that 'lifted' a quartet of youth club ballet dancers. The choreographed sequence was synchronized to perfection. A glimpse of leg or flash of organza, enticing from the wings, together with introductory overture bars, led the audience to expect a different experience to that received. The four 'artistes' leaped into view at split second intervals, diagonally crossing the small stage in mid flight. Our athletic nimbleness and neat costumes with half tennis ball enhancements (pretty authentic I would say), contrasted delightfully with outsize footwear. The heavily studded working boots added 'thunder' to the experience. Such was the success, the act was booked to perform at other venues; but I never did think of becoming a ballet dancer.

The constricted, swirling water behind the whale gave way to calm. Off to my right, draining into the south side of the bay was Marsland Water, marking the County border. Feeling pretty chuffed I rocked on. I had taken Epic round the entire coastline of Cornwall. It was not the time or place to go completely overboard though, for I had my final landing to deal with. Expecting a private beaching a few hundred yards across the bay at Welcombe Mouth at the far end of the beach, I felt slightly self-conscious seeing twenty or so persons close to my intended landing place. Minutes later, on hearing the sound of waves crashing against the steep slope of rumbling pebbles, I thought it well to be a little public.

At a quarter to seven I noted the time, then pulled hard for the beach, hoping to catch one of the waves that rapidly formed within yards of the shore before extinction in the pebbles. Wearing shorts and flip-flops for the occasion (not wellies), I hoped to hop nimbly over the side and execute a hurried, though casual looking haul a few feet up to the dry stones. My run in was decisive. About five yards out, I shipped oars and jumped ahead of a folding wave. To my dissatisfaction I sank up to mid-calf in the pebbles. The flat stones, resembling a vast expanse of large, shiny black mussels, some up to six inches across, were rendered relatively weightless following their engulfing. Before I could extricate myself, the following wave lifted the dinghy's stern, slewing the buoyant beast round for the gunwale to strike me aggressively on the thigh. In a moment of panic I avoided being run over and was hastened up the incline by the frisky Epic. Trying to appear nonchalant, I hoped the onlookers thought my arrival standard procedure.

For a moment, emotion cavorting within, I stood somewhat trauma-tized. The cause had nothing to do with the dead-leg landing, just the fact I was actually standing on a Devon beach – the sea voyage over. Epic was in one piece. Countdown for wheeled continuation was go.

The Coast Guard needed to be informed of my safe arrival. A couple leaving the beach kindly agreed to phone on my behalf. I would have liked to make that particular call personally, to sign off, but there was no phone box near that remote spot.

A wave slapped against Epic's transom, dousing socks and jeans foolishly left unprotected on the foredeck. Not wishing the Atlantic a further, final fling, I dragged the dinghy a few feet up the beach to unload. I lay out my wet clothing on a large rock in weakening sunshine. The wheel assembly was removed in a couple of seconds after releasing the little red bows. There seemed an awful lot of gear lying around at the bottom of a very steep slope. Up that daunting incline, Epic, wheels and other clutter had to be manhandled. There was no need for haste. Soon enough I would have the beach to myself.

The sun gradually sank towards the misty blue horizon, dancing a scintillating golden path over the ocean all the way to the beach. Relaxing for a while in peaceful pearly pink stillness I had plenty of time to appre-ciate my situation. A pleasant contrast to the pulse racing relief of safe arrival was a serene inner calm. Matters seemed less urgent. In tune with the surf's slow rhythm, I took time out. In dribs and drabs, unhurried groups departed the scene to climb the steep cliff path. In little over an hour the last 'drab' departed. I was alone. Time to tackle the climb. Epic always appears small on the water, but there, at the bottom of the cliff, she seemed inordinately large, and very, very heavy.

The most difficult task was raising Epic onto a narrow ledge. It was about four feet above the beach level at that time. (A storm can rearrange the giant mussels.) Using the oars as a ramp, I pushed the dinghy up to the ledge, and raising it on its side, joggled it on. The bottom of the path was very narrow. Epic balanced on its gunwale was most unwieldy. Coaxing the dinghy those few yards to where the path widened was an interesting though precarious challenge. After a few minutes delicate balancing, combined with brute force and words of 'encouragement' to my silent partner, I was able to lower her right way up. Five yards completed, twenty-five miles to go.

Had I bitten off too much? I must have wondered. My five-foot boat prop had been left behind, which was a pity. As well as an aid for fitting the wheel assembly, it was to be employed as a lever for dinghy manipulation. The oars filled that role and more crucially, doubled as slides or rollers on which to push the boat. The procedure went as follows – lift bow, place an oar at right angles underneath, heave the dinghy forward a little, lay down the second oar, heave some more till weight comes off rear oar which is placed back under the bow and so on, and on. In half boat-length increments, I edged Epic upwards. More heaving; a couple of yards gained. Repeat the process. After a while I carried the wheels and other gear up past the area of operation. A brass protective strip along the bottom of the boat was reduced in length by degrees as it broke up on rough outcrops. From the beach to the top of the slope, where I attached the wheels, was only sixty yards. (I imagined it to be at least a quarter of a mile until I went back to check). Inching upwards I soon perfected the procedure. When realizing reaching the top was just a matter of time, the task became quite therapeutic.

A couple of lady bathers heading down for a late evening swim, asked, as they inched past what looked the aftermath of an unusual ship-wreck, if I needed help. Assuming they meant physical rather than coun-selling, I explained the single-handed nature of the circumnavigation, which may have added confusion.

Darkness was in the offing as I reached dusty gravel at the top of the rise. Tired but triumphant, I hastily raised Epic's bow on crossed oars. (There's a first time for everything). Aligning the wheel carriage to the gunwales was akin to testing triggering mechanisms on mantraps, whilst being inside. Equilibrium was a swaying uncertainty till the first red bow was tied.

All the gear could be stowed inside the inverted boat, but I had no wish to test the transporter's strength with extra weight. Faith in the four little bats was reserved. When a safe home could be found, I intended leaving the oars behind, they being the heaviest and most awkward items to carry. For use on the river I had taken a pair of plastic paddles – a legacy from the old rubber dinghy. They were in two sections – bright yellow blades and blue handles, giving me four small buoyancy units – useful safety equipment at sea, and better than a life belt for rowing down rivers.

Most of my equipment fitted into the tatty off-white sail-bag. Accommodation would be the sleeping bag and a six by six feet, heavy-duty, semi-transparent polythene sheet. This time my minimal tool kit comprised a few brass screws, tacks, a roll of two inch black fabric rein-forced adhesive tape and my trusty Swiss Army knife. A few sandwiches remained, and together with two Crunchie bars, a packet of glucose tablets and three half litre, plastic bottles of water, that was my fuel reserve. In addition I carried a lightweight change of clothes and flip-flops, a small towel, mini-soap and mini-toothpaste and brush. The Bude encounter deprived me of Walkman escapism; but no longer needing the shipping forecast, it was not replaced.

Having left the sail-bag and oars at the side of the rough track, I shouldered the painting bag and set off eastward, pushing Epic into the fading light. Even over potholed terrain, dinghy pushing was quite easy, though I did worry about undercarriage durability. After timidly pushing for a hundred yards or so I left Epic parked as off track as possible, col-lected the sail-bag and oars and carried them on past the boat. With pushing, parking and porterage, my progress was about a quarter as quick as would have been a single loaded push. In half an hour I passed from track to leafy lane, having avoided contact by millimetres, two vehi-cles loaded with persons and branches. The mini-convoy was on barbe-cue business, I presumed.

The OS showed a PH (pub) one and a half miles inland at Darracott. An hour or so into the trek, at a lane junction, I came upon a heavenly sign – a slim oblong of white painted hardboard nailed to a fence. Roughly lettered in felt-tip, it informed – 'OLD SMITHY INN 1/2 MILE'. My rate of progress was not sufficient to lift me immediately onto cloud nine. The half-mile times three, the late hour and a double chevron symbol on the map indicating an imminent steep hill, accelerated my mind into 'cunning plan mode'. Abandoning Epic at the lane-side on rough grassy ground beneath overhanging branches, I gathered together the oars and a plastic bag containing rowlocks, distress flares and life-jacket. I headed speedily up the hill, arriving in good time to order a pint and beg storage for the redundant inventory. The helpful young barman named Chris (for a moment I sensed a limerick coming on) directed me round the back to a stable where I could leave my stuff – there being no room at the inn.

Later, back down the lane, I cleared away a quantity of stones, spread out my plastic sheet and crawled under Epic. For the first time I lacked my 'swiss-roll' – the non-absorbent, thin foam sheet you see tied on top of backpackers' backpacks. The luxury of sleeping under plywood was diminished somewhat, owing to fiendish sticks and stones that interspersed the lumpy, cloddy soil.

The sound of footsteps and jolly banter from young folk turfed out of the Old Smithy reached me as my head nestled into the old sail-bag. If a boat appeared beside your lane where one had not been when you walked by a few hours earlier, you might be inclined to tap it. Fresh from the pub, the lively youngsters made contact. After silently receiving a few playful, amplified pats, I thought it advisable to advertise my occupation.

"Good night", seemed a reasonable gambit; enough I hoped to dis-suade high-spirited relocation of my quarters.

"Hey, this boat talks." Further light-hearted boat communication broke out; then faded. All but one weaved merrily on. Despite the improbable situation, the ensuing conversation was unexpectedly rational. Who felt most ridiculous, I do not know. The voice from without inquired of my quest. A serious response came from the dark-ness within. Was I being humoured? I will never know.

A Good Morning's Work

Darracott to North Tamerton

Just before four o'clock I emerged from my lair into night, extra darkened by tree cover. It was not unsympathetic ground that caused early rising, but would you believe it, sheer excitement. You will think me easily pleased if setting out, pre-dawn, to test the feasibility of an arduous boat-push excited me. Chilly remains of the cheese and chutney sandwiches went down well, helped with a little of the second bottle of water. The plastic sheet was soon folded and cubby-holed. The sail and painting bags were wedged on top (of the underside) of the thwart. My ship and I were ready for the big push.

Gripping my finely balanced charge by the stern, I set off to immediately confront my, or rather the transporter's first challenge. There was no way up to higher ground without negotiating one of the steep hills classified on the OS with at least one chevron (gradient 1 in 5 or steeper). I chose a route where, in a two hundred yards climb, one hundred feet's worth of contours would be crossed. Ten steps, rest against the boat, ten more, rest; repeat. Into that gloomy tunnel of trees the 'mind game' advanced. Nothing else mattered. My world was reduced to a small area of toil. Once at the top it would be 'all downhill', so to speak. Meanwhile – six inch steps into two hundred yards; two steps, one foot; three feet one yard (where did that extra foot come from?) One foot after the other.

How long it took to emerge from the tree-enclosed climb into the aptly named village of Welcombe, I have no idea. After two miles trekking I crossed the main road (A39), two and a half miles into the journey. Five o'clock heralded daylight, along with a very big, perfectly round moon. For a while, from the other side of a hedge, I heard munching from unseen cows as I continued down the deserted lane. Apart from the 'herd' unseen and left behind, there was no other sound from the landscape. I rolled along over undulating Devonshire countryside.

By degrees, Epic became a moving table. When I had finished with an item from inside the hull, I did not return it – there was no one to tell me to tidy up. My food and painting bags, notebook, map, sponge and an assortment of garments decorated the helpless craft. To facilitate my slovenly practise, I tied a thin cord right over the boat to stop things falling off. Inspecting photographs of 'Epic the overlander', I am reminded of similarly festooned carts that acquired stock through gold-fish dispensing.

The names of villages passed through seemed like a character list for a Dickens' novel. Allow me to introduce: Ugworthy Barrows, Derril and Pyworthy. All were left in my wake more swiftly, and with greater ease, than I could have possibly imagined when examining the Ordnance Surveys before setting out.

Sometimes pulling, I pushed on. If sections were not too downhill I was inclined to jog. On one occasion, my mind engaged elsewhere, I found myself carried away by weighty momentum. Epic was as near destruction as at any time at sea. Wide-eyed, and utilizing maximum reverse leg thrust, I narrowly avoided a five hundred feet above sea level shipwreck. '8:21 Soldon Cross.' '9:45 cross main Bude / Holsworthy Rd.' I was fifteen miles on from the beach landing, well into my encumbered marathon – just ten miles to go.

Twelve years previously I thought, 'only eight miles to go'. I was running a marathon. It sort of happened, rather like the circumnavigating. A year and a half before the event, I had the urge to run up a hill out of Mevagissey. Wearing shoes and jeans I was ill prepared for the sponta-neous, self-set assignment, but thought I would keep turning right till I ended up back at base. Six point two miles later, a rather knackered, slightly sore of foot person arrived home. A short while later, the staging of the first London Marathon was announced. As I had just run the first six point two, of the twenty-six point two mile distance, I thought, 'how hard can it be? Unfortunately, though I had started training (wearing shorts and trainers), I was unaware of the entry procedure. So it was the second London Marathon for me. The previous year I had watched on television as some of the participants crawled to the finishing line after hitting 'the wall'. Having completed a fifteen-mile training run two weeks before the 'big one' (how hard can it be?) I was not wholly con-vinced regarding 'wall encounters'. Something strange occurred at the eighteen-mile mark. It was nothing to do with me, or rather there was nothing I could do with that part of me. My legs stopped working. They suddenly, quite out of the blue, became free agents. It was a physical impossibility for me to run one more step. My abused lower limbs knew best, and disengaged. After an involuntary pause and a little staggering, followed by a few minutes walking, my sensible legs permitted a light jogging session. The jog/walk pattern was repeated till merciful relief, and a medal, at Westminster Bridge.

As well as remembering that magical day, attempting to 'run' the marathon, I recall the less than wonderful night before. Arriving late in London on pre-race day, I thought myself lucky to find a vacancy at a small hotel in which I could relax. The accommodation at first looked rather seedy, but considering the circumstances was acceptable. Later I realised my assessment had been over generous. As beauty, seediness is in the eye of the beholder. After cursory inspection, I found the establishment exuded more than a shabby aura – it was downright filthy. With a forgiving, 'it could be worse' acceptance, I sat on the bed and the bottom nearside corner collapsed onto the threadbare carpet, dislodging a large empty coffee tin and two bibles. Retiring to the TV lounge I found a smoke-filled chamber. Wishing to preserve my lungs, unsmoked, for they needed to be in fully working order the next day, I withdrew immediately. I sought the management to request an early breakfast. 'No trouble at all sir; might I suggest a Lucozade set-you-up?' was not the reply. Marathon participation held no sway. "Fraid not, breakfast's eight t' nine" was the response. After some pleading, I negotiated my taking a bowl of cornflakes to the bedroom, with the promise of a pint of milk in the morning. The dining room was out of bounds. I was obviously too great a risk, alone with the cruets.

With the support of the good books I slept well and an early milkman ensured an adequate breakfast. With A to Z in hand, I stepped onto the quiet streets of London to navigate my way to King's Cross. As I progressed, other persons, mostly lone males wearing new large white trainers joined the flow. The trickle became a stream. By and by, an orderly torrent escalated down to the Marathon specials to be rattled, with other soon-to-be also-rans, to Greenwich.

To participate in such an orgy of extreme camaraderie was an uplifting experience. Goodwill was rife. All soaked up a contagious saintliness. Vocal bonding was unbounded. "Greased your nipples yet? I have Vaseline to spare". Hands delved into shorts, lubricating with unselfconscious abandon. The starting gun fired and … we all stood stock still for a while. I suppose it was as well that most of us were prevented from racing off too quickly, particularly me. Slowly we shuffled along, thinking the greyhounds at the front would be at Tower Bridge before we even started. Discarded black bin-bags filled the air, for no one would become overheated in that acreage of fired-up muscle and vaporizing liniment. Personal best times and targets became secondary. Assisting fallers, sharing drinks and encouraging fellow sufferers was the order of the day. For most of us, alas, I fear our newly found angelic standing was but a temporary affair. It was most agreeable though, to be part of that caring throng of masochists. How wonderful to go jogging with fictitious rodents – Wombles and Mickey Mouses – and, if only for the day, escape the rat race.

We will leave the congested streets of the capital and return to a peaceful Devonshire lane. Approximately five miles from my proposed river entry point, instead of turning left and keeping to the roadway, I carried on to within a few yards of the county border. The OS showed an 'other road, drive or track' that led to a lane that crossed the little River Deer. I was lucky to notice a dirt track the other side of a metal gate, for there was no signpost. Tied to the gate was a rough plank on which faded letters read ' EASE SHUT CAT '. Entrance to the field was hampered by a herd of inquisitive Friesians wishing to greet the strange, luggage carrying 'headless white'.

The track across rolling Affaland Moor was interspersed with gorsy, scrubby areas and occasional groups of trees under which cows and sheep sheltered from the hot sun. After a mile, I came upon a boggy patch. To make a detour would have meant crossing much 'moor' uncertain terrain. I slipped on my flip-flops and squelched, with the lurching Epic, across a testing obstruction of rocks and bricks tossed into the mire. The undercarriage came through with distinction, and I, with smelly feet and growing confidence in my off road vehicle.

After easing Epic down the track to a little bridge at Forda Mill, I crossed the river (which surely is a stream) and began a long push up to the road. Once at the top there would be just three, mainly downhill miles to North Tamerton. That very steep climb, rising two hundred feet between high grassy banks, was strenuous and time consuming; but what did that matter, I was a hardened pusher, unlike the 'novice pioneer' who tackled the ascent nine hours earlier. It is not that I am masochist, well maybe just a little bit, but the closeness of my goal rendered the physical effort quite pleasurable.

'12:14pm North Tamerton 2 miles.' There was little motor traffic, and pedestrians were few. One bright spark could not resist telling me I was a long way of course. There was no time to explain the joys of altitude boating, for stimulated by squadrons of voracious, venomous horseflies, I cantered by at a rapid rate of knots. The scent of my exertion was irresistible to the midget, sweat-seeking missiles, but that was the price to pay for being in cow country.

At one o'clock precisely, I stopped on a small, single arch bridge above a pool of dark River Deer that lurked between steep banks. Trees overhung the barely flowing tributary that would join the Tamar two hundred yards downstream. Down the road, just a two-minute walk away, was my river rendezvous point. It had all happened so quickly. Far from being the most difficult part of the endeavour, the wheeled trek had been the easiest. Without doubt, it was a good morning's work. I rested Epic's stern on the tarmac and sat down on the parapet.

Studying the map in detail, I found the field, bounded by the lane and the two rivers, was part of Cornwall. Had I launched Epic directly into the Tamar, a circumnavigation would have been incomplete. I had to round those few acres of grazing land. Pondering the predicament, I was joined on the bridge by an old boy and his dog. After reciprocal compliments, regarding dog and boat, I asked the gentleman if he knew to whom that particular piece of Cornwall belonged. "Mr Hobbs wouldn't mind if you used his field."

Not dwelling on the legality of a generous invitation from one to whom the parcel of land did not belong, I wheeled Epic on down the lane. Feeling rather guilty, I opened the gate and entered the field. A few steps away stood a graceful stone arched bridge spanning the youthful Tamar. My first view of the upper reaches was quite sobering. Epic could have floated happily on the bridge pool, but distressingly, the outward flow, though five or six feet wide, was very, very shallow. At the downstream end of the field, the Tamar would be joined by the Deer, and not too far on, the Claw. The combination of all that water would surely be sufficient to carry my miniscule craft down to Morwellham. I trundled Epic the remaining few yards over deep grass back up to the little Deer Bridge. There I prepared to launch. The whole story was unfolding beautifully. 'Hark, a merry tinkling of pixie bells.' In blissful ignorance, believing I was virtually home and dry, I stepped from dairy-land to fairyland.

Kind Bulgars

So all that was needed to complete the circumnavigation was a spot of floating down the Tamar; after all, I would soon be reaching deeper water. No more drama; no more rushing. That same feeling of expectancy, of relaxed meanderings to new locations, I carried to Turkey on my painting excursion the year before the Tamar trip. The adventure became a magic carpet ride – an expedition that ran on silken, oiled wheels till a spoilsport genie cast his black magic. A sojourn of mostly ups included an odd down too many.

Having worked my way round the coast from Izmir to Canakkale, on the south side of the Dardanelles, I faced painting subject number four – a castellated tower standing before a minaret. Trees, along with relics from the Gallipoli campaign, in the form of tanks and guns, stood in the fore-ground. The composition was quite tonal with sunlight striking rough stonework on the fortification and on odd bits of military hardware. The site was garrisoned. Groups of armed conscripts stopped to inspect progress as I worked. A soldier on top of the fort kept very still while I painted. When it dawned on me that he thought I was including him in the picture, it was too late. When viewing the finished watercolour he looked very disappointed, pointing out the empty sentry position. I felt sorry too.

The half-mile stroll to the waterfront the following day was a bit of a strain due to the heavy backpack. I had developed an ache in the left hip/leg area. A recuperative, unhurried meander north of the Mamara Sea to Istanbul was my plan. I took the ferry to Ecebat, three miles across the straights.

Marmaraereglisi was eighty miles away – well over half way to Istanbul. No sooner had I booked a ride out of Ecebat than the coach arrived. In the rush to board I left my easel leaning against a counter. A quarter of an hour or so later, hat-less, for my sombrero hung on the easel, I stepped down onto a shade-less stretch of road running in wet tar. The intense forty-degree (centigrade) heat was almost unbearable. The sun was directly overhead. My water bottle was with my bag of cherries on the previously mentioned counter. Half a mile away, a shady wooded headland tumbled down to a long golden beach caressed by turquoise sea. Should I walk or should I roast? Caught between the devil and inviting blue sea, I feared more discomfort, but luck was on my side. Within ten minutes, a dusty old lorry stopped. Two rough looking Bulgarians made room for me in their cramped cab. On the way back to my left property, an incomprehensible conversation ensued above the din of the engine. Finally, with many 'thank yous', and a 'no thank you', conveyed with shakes of my head, I declined a lift back across the Dardanelles with the kind Bulgars. My attempt to explain heading the wrong way to Istanbul without a sombrero certainly confused them.

A couple of hard won paintings and a night of increased pain later, I was close to calling it a day and returning home. As I was hardly able to hobble, my kind pension proprietor arranged a lift to the main road. As we set off, the driver, who spoke not a word of English, toppled with his seat into the back of the car. After securing the seat with a piece of string he drove exceedingly slowly, in silence, for half a mile, arriving with impeccable timing as the coach pulled up. Happy to give a generous tip for a very unusual taxi ride, I hoped the fare would contribute towards seat fixing, or at least stronger string.

Twenty-four hours after my lift with the Bulgars I was hurtling into Istanbul in a Mercedes driven by a crazy Turk. Topkapi coach terminal at the outer walls was three miles from the city centre. There were thousands of coaches all over the place (there really could have been that many). The excruciating din from diesel engines, and shouted negotiations of traders loading and unloading all kinds of merchandise from gigantic bundles of wool and cotton to crates of chickens, fruits and vegetables, made my head reel. I was in no condition to haggle with taxi touts. The backpack was taken from me before my foot touched the ground. In no time I was shovelled into the back of the Mercedes. The ride to Hotel Emrah took my mind off the pain. Soon after 'take off", my man made a U-turn at speed across a three-lane highway. Oncoming drivers did not flinch. Red lights were no deterrent. The horn ceased blaring only when the driver casually lit a cigarette. Acrid blue fumes; roaring traffic; modern buildings; flyovers. My first impressions of Istanbul were emphatically anti.

With the taxi shake-up compounding my delicate condition, I could hardly stand by the time we reached the hotel. There, the tariff nearly knocked me over. Eighty thousand Turkish lira – had I inadvertently made an offer to buy the place? Though much more than I wished to pay, the tariff was not outrageous really – I was undergoing mental [arithmetic] problems. It was still twenty times my usual outlay. My inquiry into 'anything cheaper locally?' was taken as haggle. We struck a deal at thirty 'thou'. The ensuite room was well appointed. I lay on the bed and stared through the window at 'misty minarets and majestic mosques …' in my dreams. I beheld a close-up view of a concrete wall.

Worrying that room service charges would rapidly eat into my dwindling reserve, I communed with my diary. '… *Pain very bad. Hope I can go out.' '7.45 can't lie down – don't know what to do. If I go out to eat and drink it won't heal.'* Later I took the lift down to reception, and from there I painstakingly made my way over the road to a restaurant. The place was rather plush and totally empty. I limped on a hundred yards to an outdoor makeshift café, furnished with one rickety table and a charcoal grill housed on a handcart. Having lowered myself onto an empty crate, I ordered a fizzy drink and two skewers of strong peppery flavoured meats with salad, encapsulated in half a French stick-type of crusty loaf. I thanked the proprietor in Turkish and mimed with much wincing and shrugging that I did not know what was wrong with my leg. The small group of patrons seemed concerned, making me feel as at home as was possible on that pavement in Istanbul. Food never tasted better, and the kind friendly nature of the gathering was a welcome tonic. Though hardly able to walk, I was not inclined at that moment to phone 'the insurance'. Slowly and gingerly I made my way back to the hotel, had a beer in the lounge, and returned to my room. A second torrid night ensued. At times the pain was so acute I had to roll off the bed and kneel down for relief.

The following morning, in physical and 'wallet' pain, I paid for another night at Emrah – to move on was just too much to contemplate. Feeling my time in Turkey drawing to a close, I decided to make an effort to produce a painting in Istanbul. Though not my usual style, I booked a taxi ride down to the Golden Horn. Along with my equipment, I was set down alongside the ferry terminal on the Resadiye Cadesi in the heart of the thronging, ancient city. Amid the flow of pedestrians, I tentatively climbed a few steps up a nearby footbridge that led over the congested highway. I gazed out across the Golden Horn, down the Bosphorus to the first suspension bridge and back to the Galata Bridge. So emotional was I that tears fell – tears of happiness. The Galata Bridge (replaced now) was a floating two-tiered structure, carrying the main road on the upper deck and a collection of restaurants, cafés, bars and eating stalls on the lower. Both outside levels were crowded with boys and men fishing. I felt I must journey through the amazing labyrinthine structure. Though the bridge was less than two hundred yards away, it took quite a while to reach it.

At the waterfront, large ferries disgorged and consumed vast numbers of passengers. The sight of a four foot diameter, saucer-shaped pan, set over a huge log fire on a wooden boat, held my attention for a while. From the twenty feet or so long vessel tied alongside the quay, the two-man crew dispensed tempting snacks. The (captain) cook was frying dozens of five to six inch long fish in the giant pan. His 'mate' cut large chunks of bread, inserted the sizzling sardines and handed the mouth-watering lunches to eager customers to self-season from salt tins tied to the quay rail.

Vendors, dispensing cups of iced water, were kept busy on the wide crowded pavement. From a stallholder I purchased a couple of savoury 'pitsu' pancakes wrapped round a chopped salad sprinkled with a good pinch of reddish-brown spice. Washed down with a yoghurt drink, my delicious lunch was filling and refreshing, setting me up for the 'voyage'

Galata Tower

10″ x 9″   1990

'... despite the odds, I had fallen in love with that beautiful brute of a city.'

over the floating bridge. During my two-hour investigation, interspersed with many rests, I lingered over a beer in one of the rough and ready cafes in the bowels of that aged, creaking structure. My mind was set to capture the atmosphere. I insisted my body came too.

Leaning against one of a few trees on a grassy traffic island close to where the taxi dropped me, I was impressed by a view incorporating the Galata Tower, standing out above other buildings in an architectural muddle on the hillside. It stood the other side of the Golden Horn (which, by the way, is a waterway inlet). The island location must have been the only area free from vehicular and pedestrian traffic in that cauldron of activity. From there I painted a watercolour featuring the tower. After setting up my equipment, I realized the water bottle was empty. Following a hazardous limp through the traffic, relying on the goodwill of motorists, I returned safely to my easel, bottle filled courtesy of a water vender. Although I had to squat down repeatedly to relieve the ache, I had in one hour finished a painting in Istanbul. In a magical three hours, despite the odds, I had fallen in love with that beautiful brute of a city.

By five o'clock I was back, looking out at the concrete wall. '*8.00 pm Bad, can't lie peacefully … ache builds up. I don't know what to do.*' Dripping with sweat, I read the small print on my insurance document. With the thought of leaving for home the next day, I hobbled to the site of the cart-grill. It was not there. A hundred yards further on I found a three-wheeled bike-grill and was pleased to received similar fare to that enjoyed the night before.

Next day, with hip feeling easier (hooray), I was dropped off adjacent the majestic St Sophia mosque outside a reasonably priced pension. The entrance to a youth hostel was a mite closer, so I entered to ask if there were vacancies, and if I was considered a youth. That night, after sorting out my three by eight feet sleeping/storage area alongside two Australians, Andrew and Andrew, I dragged myself up to the television viewing area on the roof. There I watched the World Cup match between England and Ireland. It was a memorable draw enjoyed by a cosmopolitan crowd including a trio of English lads, faces painted with Union Jacks, performing the smallest of Mexican waves.

During my five days at the Yuclet Interyouth Hostel I produced five paintings, never having to go far for subject matter. For the second painting, 'Bosphorus Bridge', I positioned myself on a low wall in a small patch of shade cast by a sign about twenty feet up a lamppost. I calculated that the area of shadow would move slowly along the wall. My assumption was correct, so every ten minutes or so I moved a couple of feet along, greatly amusing the little band that stayed with me till the picture was complete. Not long after I started work, a corn roaster set up his cart close by. After lighting his charcoal fire, it was not long before he joined me in frequent relocations. I proffered many "teshekkewr edereems" (phonetic 'thank yous') and purchased a couple of hot cobs. (You've heard the expression – I could eat a horse.)

On that rather silly note, we will return to the Tamar.

Tethered Pudding
North Tamerton to Boyton Bridge

Without the slightest inkling that all would not be plain sailing I depleted my sparse food and drink reserve, devouring two bananas and an extravagant amount of water. Refuelling would be from waterside establishments, I assumed. What waterside establishments? Between riverside shops and pubs, I may have had in mind to pluck the occasional peach from overhanging boughs as I drifted by.

Although in a field, Epic looked much happier the right way up. I fixed the wheels further back, as on the sea leg; then tied loops of cord through the rowlock holes as rowlock substitutes, to hold the little paddles. Between clumps of thistles and wands of foxgloves I launched Epic, vertically down an eight foot bank, taking on board over the stern a quantity of non-drinkable water. After dropping my luggage down onto the foredeck, I followed, precariously lowering myself from tus-socks. Epic floated in the shade of overhanging trees on brown water (cows disturbing mud upstream the most likely cause). After sponging out the dinghy, I positioned the ridiculous midget oars, thinking it of no consequence that the proper ones were stabled at Darracott. Had they been available and employed in the usual manner, they would have been too long to fit between the banks. Progressing at a rate that would barely have seen off a tethered pudding, I thrashed my way the few yards upstream to the little bridge. Had I not gone back to the Deer Bridge, there would still be a thin strip of Cornwall left un-circumnavigated.

The 'loop of cord for rowlock' idea was a total failure. Undeterred, with a paddle in each hand, used butterfly-stroke fashion, I headed the short distance towards the Tamar. Before reaching the mighty river, I passed from the shade, rounded a bend and came up against foliage in shallow water. Wearing flip-flops, I stepped into the cool unknown. My feet became intimate with mud and weed and I sensed the presence of piranhas and electric eels. Back on board I drifted a few more yards. The sun warmed my sunhat and glinted on broken water ahead. Silent flitterings of electric-bluey-green damselflies entertained as I recorded that joyous moment in the logbook. '… *peace beautiful. Quietly drift – cover legs – sun. V hot – nice breeze sometimes 2:36 just paddled – off now drift perfection!'* and on that note of great expectation, I exited fairyland.

Epic entered the Tamar, beginning a journey to tidal waters, a journey unlikely to be repeated for reasons about to be revealed. A serious problem was lack of river water – not enough to facilitate passage for a small canoe, or even a large washing-up bowl. It soon became apparent that there would be very little floating for me in the early stages. The oars would have been useful, for although rowing more than the odd stroke was off the agenda, 'till at least round the next bend', they would have served again as rollers, slides and levers.

One of the first pools on which Epic could float was a twenty-five to thirty feet wide, leafy, canopied affair, providing cool shade for the occupying cows. The herd, in palomino, russet and white livery, remained fairly docile as I paddled towards them. There was a little inquisitiveness on their part as I wove within hoof-stepping range of two mid-brown ones. To the rest, my intrusion could have been an everyday occurrence. To prevent cattle wandering, barriers of single or double lengths of barbed wire were stretched across the river. The wheels were a problem on occasions, but fortunately, no puncturing of tyres or crew occurred. I thought the transporter might have been useful later, so it was not abandoned.

Between the few pools where boat floating was possible, I splashed

Paddling Cows

7½" x 9"

'There was a little inquisitiveness on their part as I wove within hoof-stepping range
of two mid-brown ones.'

alongside or walked on exposed gravel, guiding the dinghy along narrow rushing channels, no wider than Epic. Where the river widened, the dinghy needed careful coaxing as the hull grazed the stony bed. The flimsy ply construction ruled out rushing. Even smallish stones could deliver a nasty nick. When not immediately downstream from wading cows, the water was reasonably clear and flip-flops seemed ideal footwear, at first. Shirt and quick-drying shorts completed my wardrobe.

Before clocking up the first mile I encountered an obstruction resembling a beaver's lodge. The huge dam of branches and twigs had been caught in a riverside tree at the height of a winter's flood. The impenetrable barrier stood five feet high, forcing me to make a detour through long grass. What at first seemed a tortuous route turned out a doddle to circumvent. As I was travelling light, Epic slipped over the long grass with comparative ease, without the need for me to unload.

Those first obstructions I should have realized would not be the last. The River Claw flowed in from the left, boosting the flow considerably, but making no apparent difference. The OS showed many more little streams adding to the volume in the next few miles. Surely then, Epic would be whisked effortlessly down to Gunnislake. By the time I had travelled south half a mile, the writing was on the wall (I had learned to take walls seriously). The half-mile was 'crow measurement' – Tamar twists and turns at least doubled the distance. Deep water seemed as far away as ever.

Excruciatingly slowly at times, I progressed through a tranquil land-scape. Apart from an odd break in the canopy, allowing a glimpse of sky, a full spectrum of lush greens pervaded. The Tamar slipped on quietly, past spits of gravelly riverbed, gently scouring and chuckling down to dark shallow pools.

Two and a half hours or so into the trek, with a little over a crow-mile travelled, I sighted in the distance a fine stone, shallow-arched bridge, similar in appearance to the one at North Tamerton. A chance to replenish supplies and find out where and when deeper water could be expected, I must have thought. I dragged Epic's bow onto a shallow bank of small angular, pale pinky-purple stones, the same colour as the bridge. With great anticipation I sauntered up to the absolutely deserted, little-trodden grass track that so gracefully spanned the river. The location was really most peaceful and picturesque, but I was in need of more – drinking water primarily; and I could have murdered a cream tea with extra scones, extra jam and cream and a large pot of tea.

Thwarted, I paddled off downstream with Epic in tow. Pools on which I could float for a few yards were still rare, often ending with obstructions, resulting in more portage. Every fifty to a hundred yards there was a drag down mini rapids. Difficulties with shallows and overland hauling necessitated the rapid understanding of driftwood manipulation. Slippery timbers placed crossways under the dinghy, allowed energy-efficient, onward dragging. Two or three pieces of tree, arm thickness and length (two cubits), were ideal for the job. A pity that sections of brass keel strip lay on the cliff slope at Welcombe Mouth, for if still attached to the dinghy, it would have slid more easily. One major obstruction demanded a thirty yard or so detour across a sloping, undulating sandy bank. Contorted branches extricated from a dam were employed to prevent sideways slip. As a user of logs in boating, I have few equals.

Early into the haul I was perturbed to find a leech fastened to my right calf. Being a non-smoker, I resorted to finger-flicking the beast away. If it was a member of the bloodsucking variety – those that inflate to sausage size in seconds – I was not prepared to research the matter. Many of the visual pleasures experienced while negotiating the river, reside in my memory files (photographs). Fortunately, most of the unpleasant trials are forgotten. Those early hours of toil were expressed in the logbook with one telling word – *'Hell'*.

Pretty tired and very thirsty, I laboured on. At every turn I expected to see another bridge that, on the 'law of averages', would indicate provisions available nearby. Hours passed. Not knowing my speed (quite an optimistic word, considering …) or exactly where I was, my arrival time at Boyton Bridge, my next objective, was uncertain. It had been six hours since communication with the man who knew Mr Hobbs when I detected a movement in the trees. Some yards downstream a fisherman was working his way up to my location of toil. He was casting a fly between the stones, seeking a trout that might be lurking in one of the deeper puddles. I was not too surprised to see an angler, for in the past I had taken a fly rod to such tiny streams. Sometime before my shouted apology for spoiling his fishing, the laid-back fisherman (later recounted) "… could hear occasional rumbling, then quiet for a few minutes … sounded like some prehistoric monster". Bill Dinner glimpsed the white triangle of Epic's flat bow between the trees and wandered up to take a closer look. For one whose peaceful recreation had been curtailed, he greeted me kindly, "… I was about to stop fishing anyway … never seen anything like it in my life".

Bill, a Boyton man, was as surprised as I was relieved at our meeting. Boats had not been seen in the vicinity since the Bude Canal had closed. The man, whose great, great grandfather had been a wharfinger at Boyton, brought good tidings. Shortly I would arrive at a pool that would lead to Boyton Bridge, just a few hundred yards away. Then even better tidings; shortly he would be driving to The Countryman, a hostelry a mere three and a bit miles away where evening meals were available. He would give me a lift if I wished. Deliriously, I wished. Fortunately, the car would travel a great deal quicker than the half mile an hour I had managed on the river, which was as well, for there were just forty-five minutes before 'last food orders' would be called.

Half an hour later, spurred on by imagined goings-on in The Countryman's kitchen, I had pulled Epic up onto the bank in a field to the left and downstream from a flat, mundane iron bridge. Though there was no comparison in the beauty stakes with the stone creations passed earlier, that rather insignificant structure was most welcome at the time. The sandwiches consumed at North Tamerton were a distant memory. In no time I was being whisked foodwards. Major refuelling was required. A large thick juicy steak played the leading roll in my gastronomic fantasy.

After freshening up (I had taken towel and toothbrush to the pub), I pulled my tatty Norwegian jumper over a far from pristine shirt and settled expectantly on a barstool. Perched, pint in hand, with the knowledge that my medium rump, claimed at the nick of nine, was on the griddle, I was in paradise. Phil, the barman, filled my three half litre water bottles (with water). A more than satisfied customer was later delivered back to Boyton Bridge. Perhaps Bill Dinner is an angel. A lone fisherman would be a plausible front for the instigator of such a heavenly interlude.

Still on cloud nine, extremely tired but free from cares, I climbed over the gate and returned to camp. Epic was hidden in a hollow behind a grassy hump. There, in my sleeping bag placed on top of the orange bag for protection against dew, I also lay. The grass was soft. I slept soundly.

Punctured Plywood
Boyton Bridge to Netherbridge

Bats fluttered in the stillness. Fish rose – imagined rings in the darkness. Up at five and back to bag, waiting for first light. The river unseen: only blackness. Soon my private night-space would expand, allowing visual delving down the upper Tamar. '… *can see the bridge birds singing – after crickets chirp. Soon be light enough to start. Dark under trees on river*'. The pool had no end. It could be miles long. I would soon be drifting and paddling south. Resisting the urge to polish off my remaining rations – two crushed Crunchie bars and a packet of glucose tablets – I drank half a bottle of chilled water with a refreshing hint of Colgate. There was great incentive to reach a substitute Countryman, for I could not expect another divine encounter with the 'Dinner-man'.

At ten to six I slipped Epic stern first into the river. It took little time to decamp, load and leave. Other than a small area of flattened grass there was no trace of occupation. It may have been on that first pool that I encountered a fallen tree obstruction. Lying across the river at water level was a large trunk. Positioned a little above, as if on purpose, a hefty bough seemed to suggest a detour. It was a shame that a rare drift on such a lovely deep pool should be halted. Before heading back upstream to find an exit point, I ran Epic onto the half submerged lower trunk. There was just a possibility I could juggle under the shallow curve formed by the upper branch. It was the wrong option. Squatting on the lower bough, with an arm over the upper, I heaved and squeezed Epic through the gap. Hot and bothered and showered with debris that puthered into my hair and eyes, courtesy of fine silt filtered from the river in spate, I eventually pulled through. I picture the scene now – the Mirror dinghy above a dark, still pool, gripped firmly in 'giant tweezers'.

There is more than meets the eye/s when circumnavigating.

Soon I was back to paddling, pushing and pulling. Lack of water was still a major annoyance, except on one occasion when there was too much. *'I lost Epic …'* I am reminded of the situation. My charge had not disappeared but was beyond reach for a while. Deep, sticky red mud at the side of a pool prevented me from reaching the pesky dinghy. Epic had been blown to the Cornish side where it bobbed mischievously back and forth against a six foot high earthen cliff. There were no long sticks handy (to coax, not thrash) so I made my way round to the field opposite. There I dangled from the bank for a while till I was able to capture the absconder's gunwale with my foot. Gymnastic physics then became tricky. A sideways push, resulting in tipping and ejection of captain was avoided with an undignified flop-come-sprawl boarding.

The still water attracted swarms of flies, or was it one big one (swarm that is), so breakfast was taken a few hundred yards downstream where I devoured one of the crushed Crunchie bars. Boughs of peaches were yet to materialise. It was only seven o'clock in the morning and I had nearly halved my food ration. Two hours later, with Epic parked beneath lush greenery on an expanse of exposed red rocky riverbed, I polished off the last Crunchie.

Investigating among little shale pieces I chanced upon a small frog (that is how hungry I was – only joking). Though not an expert 'frogologist', I had reared shoals of the tiny 'transformers' when a child. I am sure they were many times larger than the Tamar specimen when they hopped off. As it was minute in the extreme, I decided to photograph the froglet for future reference. The wind was getting up which accounts for the stone placed three nautical miles south of the tiny frog on the light blue ocean of OS 190. Bearing in mind my rather basic camera has no other function than making objects appear far away, the midget was an unfortunate choice for wildlife study. Even though the portrait is blurry, I can calculate its length overall from lettering on the map. The picture also reveals a smaller object about a mile and a half south west of Hartland Quay. No small island exists in that area (spooky), so I rather think it was a bit of twig. However, a slight stain remains, confirming where the frog posed. The mark could be of great value if frogs and tadpoles become extinct (I fear for both). DNA may be present; so it is just possible that a scientist may trace the trace, and recreate the tiny amphibian. (Film rights reserved.) I feel Atlantis would be a fitting name for the new mini-frog. ('My Newt' would have been a contender; except it was a frog.)

On a few hastily written lines in the logbook there is evidence of waterproof ink running. *'Writing on Raindrops … rain blowing up the valley Quite wet   10.30 shelter under trees – watch rain driving in front of trees across fields opposite. I'm getting damp now. Ugh!! Wonder where I am. Feet sore.'* What I was doing, I must admit, was decidedly odd, but for me it was a good thing – spicing the variety of life. 'A good thing' though, is what 'you can have too much of', and I was beginning to reach that stage.

The rain ceased. A further hard fought half-mile on, a sort of splitting noise, not really very loud, came from the front end of Epic. Foolishly attempting to be afloat, perhaps for novelty value, I knelt on the foredeck whilst easing the boat into a pool. A similar sound a few seconds later I assumed to be a further, flimsy deck fracture, which was of no consequence at that juncture. Later I realized a lurking rock had punctured the hull. With so little water in the river it was not surprising that several minutes passed before the holed area was submerged long enough to flood the front cubbyholes and the problem be manifest. I sought a location clear of tree cover, light enough to inspect the damage. Lo, beyond a lengthy straight stretch of river, light at the end of the tunnel. Double lo, a barely discernible arched bridge in the distance. Towing wounded Epic on, I wondered what services would be available. A boat repair workshop was out of the question, but I would have settled for a shop selling bottles of pop and pies.

At noon I reached Druxton Bridge – a beautiful four arched structure similar to, but larger than, the previous narrow tracked example. A few yards before the bleached pink stone bridge, I lifted Epic's bow clear of the river onto a slight gradient that led up to the roadway. No grass track this time. Expectantly, I sauntered up to the metalled highway. A lonesome signpost informed – 'Launceston 4 miles'. I had arrived at an extremely quiet part of Devon. Across the bridge was an equally quiet part of Cornwall. For a while I enjoyed the rare silence – free from the splashing and the hollow tortured sounds of the Mirror's hull in conflict with lumpy terrain. Had I ventured along the lanes seeking a grocer's shop, I feared foraging would have been fruitless. The peaches would have to wait.

Before continuing the rocky, watery grind, I had to patch poor Epic. A few large stones were required to prop up the bow. Though I had been battling through a stone based landscape, I could not find a single large pebble. There was no suitable material, despite recently slithering over tons of the stuff. I wandered upstream hunting for large rocks to form a mound – red picnic box height. Having located a few lumps, I staggered back over the slippery riverbed. Fortunately, the hull damage was slight and easily repaired. A piece of plywood about the size of a fifty pence piece had been pushed in. It was a clean wound, forward and above the multi-scarred lower section. I cleaned and dried the area of operation with my shirtsleeve, then friction-warmed it with dry, grubby cuff. With my Swiss penknife, I cut a square from the two-and-a-half-inch-wide, fabric reinforced, black sticky tape. The patch still holds, limpet-like, to this day.

Lunch at a pub would have been nice, but I settled for Countryman water. (I was actually closer to said public house at the time than at my overnight camp.) Severe rationing was enforced. To supplement a glucose tablet, crumbs from the Crunchie bars were fastidiously reclaimed from the bottom of the food bag. ('Glucose tablet! In my day we made do licking the wrapper.') The exercise merely served to torture my taste buds. I really needed someone to moan to. A note in the logbook suggests that next time I take the red picnic box. Foodstuffs would remain cool and intact (especially peaches), and more to the point, I would be inclined to be more generous when victualling.

'… *leave 12:25. More barbed-wire – 4th lot?'* There are people who collect short lengths of various types of barbed wire. I have never been fond of it; and even if there had been a latent interest, it has now been expelled. A sketchy drawing of three frayed strands of the vicious, spiky stuff adorns the logbook page (I was at 'the crown of thorns' stage). It seemed the wheels were unlikely to earn their ride, but there was nowhere to store my valued creation. I bet the man with a dog, who knew Mr Hobbs, would have known someone who would not mind …

By degrees, I seemed to loose efficiency. I began to talk to the boat. As if the painter were a lead, I led and coaxed, "… come on Epic". Flip-

Cowboys

9" x 11"

flopped feet slipped on downstream. Pulling and pushing, and hanging on to the dinghy when in danger of falling, I continued the struggle. Shallows were almost continuous. Deeps, over a foot (both feet), were few and of nuisance value.

A row of cows stared blankly down from the bank, my arrival exciting them to a few moments standing still. Half hidden by foliage, the silhouettes looked uncannily like cowboys – their ears sticking out like stetson brims.

That wonderful, verdant mono-colour world was suddenly stabbed with a bolt of 'non green', delighting my senses and prompting future paintings.

> An exception to the rule of green,
> a microsecond pleases –
> kingfisher against white hull,
> as different from chalk as cheese is.

I continued my daily toil with a deep down feeling, reinforced by map inspection, suggesting the end of the trial was someway off. Funnily enough, despite the difficulty, I never once thought of calling it a day. As if programmed, I was drawn to the next bend – ever closer to tidal water. Every detail of the abused boat, from rotten bow to bent pintles, became very familiar. Each item of my motley equipment had its place and what a comic collection it was. Fortunately, human eyes were not upon me and the cows were non-judgemental; though you never knew what they were thinking. The ludicrous little blue and yellow paddles and the bicycle wheels would have provided much amusement. Three useful mini-logs joined the permanent inventory. They rested on the stern seat when not assisting Epic downstream. A fine specimen, the most useful member, had a protuberance at one end. (Just a matter of time before I started talking to trees.)

After threading my way between branches of another downed tree, and selecting a course down a series of rapids, joy of joys, I sighted a long awaited road bridge. The wide, slightly curved concrete span had to be the carrier of the A338. The water deepened; joy unbounded. I boarded Epic and battled with the toy paddles. A gusty wind wasted no time in rushing up that wide expanse of exposed river. I minded not those few minutes of extra exertion, for the bridge was just a two-mile, unencumbered walk away from Launceston – two miles from a wad of restaurants.

Fifty yards or so beyond that mighty span stood an old stone multi-arched bridge. The main highway bypassed the ancient bridge and a stretch of narrow lane, leaving them relatively private. Having stepped out of Epic at the upstream, Devon-side arch, I could see there was access from the other side to a pool underneath the bridge. Before paddling round, I decided to remove a few large stones (where are they when you want them?) to allow Epic to lie against the bank. While de-stoning, a sneaky fierce gust blew the dinghy back upstream. My pursuit was always slightly less than the advancement of the dinghy as she floated skittishly out of reach. After two steps the river lapped my knees, in four it was mid thigh; soon I was struggling, river to my waist and flip-flops adrift. Such irony – battling for hours down a ditch-like water-course, grandly designated a river; then finally reaching deep water and suffering the ignominy of wading. Collecting Epic and retrieving flip-flops, I returned to the bridge and skulked into my lair, hoping my farcical arrival had gone unnoticed. If that were so, my time on the river had been witnessed solely, that day, by the great-great-grandson of a wharfinger (and the cows of course). I was thankful for that mercy.

Though clouds were still growing and greying, there were still sunny periods, so I hung my shorts on a twig to dry. Damp legs were coaxed into jeans, and sore puffy feet into unyielding socks. It was about half-past three and I was about to hit Launceston to recharge ready for the final push. In a couple of days, all being well, the circumnavigation would be complete.

Before heading into town I ensured my drying shorts were securely anchored, for the wind was increasing. The river surface was dashed with ranks of small sharp waves marching upstream. A few heavy raindrops found their way through the trees. A little wind and rain would do no harm. It was July after all, and I was no longer at the sea's mercy. Was I counting chickens? Should I have taken heed of the 'flapping shorts' portent?

A Bridge Too Far

(Near Launceston)

Before heading into town, I took a photograph from under the bridge of the increasingly depressing scene. The trees, set back a bit on the other side of the river, were losing definition in descending, misty dampness. Epic stripped bare, save for the wheel assembly, was being thoroughly cleansed. Still optimistically in the best of spirits, I placed my belongings against the upstream side of the bridge, out of sight and the prevailing wind. Showers were few and light, which was as well, for my oilskin was still, I presumed, in the Atlantic. Speculating that it might be the last night before journey's end, I set out for Launceston. It was not long before a picturesque castle, perched on top of a steep hill, became my guiding beacon. The uncomplicated fortification sat atop a most unlikely, exaggerated mound – reminiscent of a child's painting, lacking only the requisite oversized flag. Had it not been for the tarmac, I could have imagined myself back in time, expectantly wending towards markets and merrymaking. I was not totally transported though, for there were no hay-carts, knights on horseback, or folk trussed up in thonged sacking.

At half past five I reached the old town. Alehouse temptations were resisted, not only because my sleeping quarters were two miles away, beside a river of deceptive depths and malicious humour, but because it was early Monday evening and the place was not exactly buzzing. Happily, I chanced upon the Launceston Fryers and was soon Tucking in to fish'n'chips, mushy peas, faggots'n'gravy, bread and butter and a large pot of tea. Even the most adventurous cuisines would hardly allow fish and faggots to share a plate. However, twelve hours of hard labour, fuelled solely by Crunchie bars and a few glucose tablets, changes one's parameters. Neither convention nor presentation was considered: bulk was all that mattered.

A period of great misery was about to unfold. As I strolled away from Launceston, heading back down a steep hill away from the castle, I sensed a more direct route off to my right. The 'short cut', unfortunately, added some distance to the return journey. Depressing drizzle began as I set out, intensifying my desire to rejoin Epic at the soonest. A spasmodic, irritating tingle in the region of my left shoulder blade became quite uncomfortable. It was due to excessive pushing and pulling, I imagined. The problem had previously occurred during the Boscastle to Bude leg. Dangling my arms did not ease discomfort. To lessen the strain I walked along with hands on head, but relief was short lived. At some stage, drizzle became rain that trickled down inside my sleeves.

How I wished to be back under my bridge, lying down in my polythene sheet. To fulfil my wish, I decided to phone for a taxi. The decision made was way ahead of possible realization – a phone box, in all probability, being a taxi ride away. While trudging gloomily through the gloom, a large car stopped beside me. It was about to turn from a driveway onto the roadway. What luck; I must have thought. Standing in the rain I grovellingly explained my situation, and desire to make a phone call. 'If I carried on there was a chance I would come to a phone box', I was informed, without a hint of helpfulness. I can understand reluctance in allowing damp unknowns into one's car. All was not lost though, for a second car followed. Benignly I bent towards the driver's window. Without stopping, it followed the first Pharisee. All was lost. Half an hour later I arrived back in Launceston, vowing never again, knowing my innate sense of non-direction, to take shortcuts.

Back at my bridge, a wearisome while later, I took stock. Proper rain was driving in at an increasing angle. The mini-logs, that prevented me getting bogged down when unloading Epic, were squashed into the mire. With the odds stacked against restful sleep, I contemplated how best to utilize my equipment. Though I did not expect to be bushy-tailed the following morning, I hoped to be operational. The rain became heavy and horizontal. Trees thrashed wildly as darkness rapidly advanced. With my bivouac items (I use the term loosely) I retreated to a mossy ledge at the downstream side of the arch, just a couple of yards from where Epic also strained at the end of her tether. The sloping ledge was two and a half feet wide and a foot or two above ground level. Looking on the bright side called for a degree of imagination. I could manage only a pessimistic glimmer. Daylight fizzled out with 'the end in sight' feeling fading fast.

Strangely enough, I occupied the downstream, windward ledge. The close proximity of large trees and a peculiar wind-tunnel effect, caused the seemingly more sheltered side to receive a severe lashing. My seat was reasonably dry at the onset. One major 'bivouacal' item, the portion of heavy-duty polythene was in an Epic cubbyhole; darkness, driving rain and squidgy mud ensured it remained there. I unzipped the sleeping bag, folding the square about myself. I held the top corners, trapping the other end under my 'trainered' feet. Holding one end of the plastic survival bag against the vertical stonework with my head, I clutched the other end along with the sleeping bag. The large plastic 'hood' saved my upper body from drips from the bridge and intermittent wayward drifts of rain. Thus it was, my awful night began.

The pressure required to trap the orange bag against the wall, caused my neck and shoulders to ache. To alleviate the problem, the plastic bag had to be coaxed down behind my back – not easy in a wind tunnel. With less plastic for frontal protection, my grip had to be higher. Clawing together the covering became more difficult as my fingers weakened. The bags escaped from time to time, further cooling the 'ledge squatter'. Resting elbows on knees was an option, bringing relief for a while, till I had to adjust position to stop seizing up. The wind increased, probing ever more searchingly, funnelling in more rain.

Gravity had its way. I had to counteract the slippery slope as the squashed moss lost traction. Accidentally lifting a foot, whilst edging back, would sometimes release the bags, causing them to flap wildly until recaptured. The lower part of the sleeping bag became more and more waterlogged, eventually soaking up to my knees. Jeans acted as secondary wicks, insidiously absorbing iced water, ensuring thorough numbing. Eventually, before it became too heavy, I drew the sleeping bag over my head, holding it in place with the orange survival bag. From time to time, in the quieter darkness, I contorted and squirmed into position to operate my watch. The illuminated information was always disappointing. Time itself had slowed. Checking after 'half' an hour would indicate ten minutes advancement. The Casio boasted an illumination function, but no fast forward button. The night was long, and I, excruciatingly achy. ('Beep beep.' The processor didn't think much of achy – there it goes again. At times it seems to think it knows best. Correcting a misspelt sausage, I overlooked a bleep-less assuage.)

Misery built up. Finally I could take no more. The vestige of spark was extinguished. At that time of unhappiness and deep despair, I decided to give up. I would seek help from the police. Relocating to a dry cell would be heaven. The nightmare would cease. (Unhappiness, despair and now bonkers.)

Alas, relief from mental torture was all too brief. Reality dawned. Although I was only a hundred yards from the main road as the crow flies, there was no easy escape. (To proper bivouac people this must seem a pathetic whinge.) After clambering up a muddy bank in a howling rainstorm, in the pitch dark, I would make my way to the, infrequently used at night, roadway and … What would I be wearing? My square of heavy duty polythene, a soaking sleeping bag, weighing at least half a hundredweight, or perhaps an orange survival bag with holes cut for head and arms. I would wait for headlights to appear, flag down the vehicle and ask to be taken to the nearest police station: hardly foolproof so far. If the first few motorists drove by, I must not be dispirited. Would you stop for a large piece of litter, or something resembling a giant sausage?

During the course of the night the wind and rain moderated. I sensed the change from inside my miserable cocoon. Many times I peeped out, but for no reward – it was so dark, it was difficult to know if my eyes were still working. Dawn was late; it seemed like lunchtime. I had been a pupa far too long. A routine lifting of the damp bag shocked me from darkness. It was six in the morning and I was greeted with blinding daylight. I almost fell off my perch. A world promising no immediate pleasure unfolded. Unhurried, in the manner of a two or three-toed sloth, I unfurled my numb body and stepped down into the mud. I wished to be home.

A phone call and an hour or so waiting, would see an end to the misery. It was too early to ring for a lift, so I set to sorting out Epic, ready for departure. Man is a complex animal. Even at that low ebb, I seemed to be contemplating 'voyage' continuation. If the dinghy could be left nearby, perhaps tucked away under the trees close to my bridge, I could return for the final, final push. I would wait a while longer, then walk up the hill. A quarter of a mile away, there was a handy Devonshire farm. I would ask for Epic to be allowed to squat for a few days beside the river. Seven o'clock was the earliest I dared seek such a favour. Farmers are early risers.

How was I supposed to know the farmer did not live in the farmhouse? Though I had been patient, it was still a very early hour for regular households to receive a visitor. It would not have been so bad if I were the bearer of gifts or good news. After ringing the bell it seemed an awfully long time before a light came on. The bell could not be unrung. How I wished to be back under the bridge. The door eventually opened. I rushed into apologetic explanation for my outrageous behaviour. There was no reprimand. My wish was granted, again by proxy, as the farmer lived next door. That sympathetic treatment from the Devon gentleman buoyed me up considerably.

Before setting off to the farm I had studied OS 201 in some detail, the choice of other recreational activities being limited. A phone symbol is shown at the Devonshire village of Liftondown, two hilly miles from my bridge. Having had the pleasure of walking to the old county town (of Cornwall) and not being in the mood for further merrymaking, I opted to head the other way, along a peaceful country lane. The weather remained miserable – drizzle interspersed with heavy showers. Sheep are fortunate creatures, wearing wool not denim. My jumper, being synthetic, provided little protection, while my jeans became more saturated.

Following my torrid night, the early morning walk was relatively soothing – a major factor being the warmth generated. Still not wishing to disturb the family at that hour, I made the excursion into the lanes a leisurely affair. In the shelter of a large roadside tree, during a sharp deluge, I pondered my situation. There were few real downs and the event of the previous night was almost history. The 'ups' outweighed overwhelmingly. Simple everyday pleasures lurked round many a corner – or the one after that. A long awaited pint; rain ceasing; feet drying; even mushy peas pleased.

Before nine o'clock I was down by the bridge, set for strategic withdrawal. My phone call caused no inconvenience. In fact, Robin seemed eager to drive over and collect me. The family unit is a wonderful thing. When in need, willing help is on hand – so uplifting. My plight location, en route to an extremely heavy amplifier also requiring urgent collection, was an uncanny coincidence. The rocking chauffeur would arrive around ten o'clock.

Meanwhile, I removed the wheel assembly, bailed out and sponged down Epic. I stacked items for collection at the roadside. Remembering that pile, words such as 'refuse', as in rubbish, and 'sloth' came to mind. It seemed a fly-tipper had just left the scene. With time to kill I brought my logbook up to date with a moan about my body. It required a 'painstaking' service. *'Feet worn raw by flip-flops. Bites itch. Thigh stiff. Back above shoulder-blades – torn muscles? – like electric current dancing …'*

Robin arrived bearing wondrous gifts: dry jeans, shirt and deliciously dry socks. Before changing, I stepped once more into the river. With Robin assisting from a grassy mid-bank position, overhung with low leafy branches, we raised the waterlogged dinghy and placed it, scarred bottom up, in that delightful spot. Had the weather been kinder, I could have spent a blissful night there and been off down the Tamar. With 'the heap' and wheels loaded, the Fiesta headed eastward, towards narrow country lanes and a large amp.

Rizla Knows Best

While suffering on that sloping ledge, under the bridge near Launceston, had I been offered a magical change of location, it would be to a level slab in a Turkish Bath of my acquaintance.

Meanwhile, back in Istanbul.

On the third (Bosphorus Bridge painting) day, still finding it impossible to stand up straight, I shuffled down to the Gagaloglu Turkish Bath, looking forward to a therapeutic soak. Passing beneath a brash twentieth century, plastic day-glow sign, I descended a flight of steps, passed along a long passageway and entered a different world. The three hundred years old interior of marble and tranquillity was a suitable setting for the minor miracle I wished for. Just inside the domed entrance hall was a great scroll-topped marble desk. A raised decorative pool stood under the dome, water pouring from a carved marble centre-piece. Oranges floated in the pool and there was a great pile by the side, further enhancing the splash of colour. A dozen or so changing-cubicles bordered three sides of the room with the same number above on an iron balcony. They were timber lined, each with a bed on which lay a number of large, folded, white fluffy towels. Supplied with wooden-soled sandals, I retired to a lower cubicle where I changed into my swimming shorts. Stepping forth, to I knew not what, I noticed the other customers and masseurs were sporting a house towel. I felt a right cough drop.

The next chamber, also marble and domed, contained several half-domed recesses graced with marble pools and seats. In the centre was a large slab/table. The floor, worn into soft contours through centuries of use, was pleasantly warm. Deeper depressions through doorways and on steps had been foot sculpted over the years, creating an ergonomic delight. The third chamber into which I clopped was smaller, domed again, with stone seats round the outside. The floor and walls were too hot to stand on or lean against. Sitting down, breathing hot, humid air, I began to sweat profusely. After a quarter of an hour or so, I was ushered to the slab.

Making it known that my poorly part was out of bounds, and I required handling with care, I clambered with great difficulty onto the altar (I mean slab). I lay on my front at the mercy and in the hands of Rizla, a muscular, bearded Turk with an anchor tattoo on one shoulder. My request for kid glove treatment could not have been taken on board, even though my earnest grimacing and beseeching mime seemed totally unambiguous to me. Rizla knew better however, immediately setting about me. Feeling vulnerable and fearful I expected the worst; but then, 'no pain, no gain'.

The manipulator started gently enough, but was soon into rearrangement, getting quite worked up over my defective part. The redistribution of muscle and bones ensured nothing could remain trapped. To make doubly sure he almost pulled my legs off. After a thorough mangling I was led to a warm bit of marble floor in one of the recesses. There I was massaged all over (almost), shampooed and vigorously rubbed with a coconut fibre type of material. My face, head and even my eyes received attention. Finally I was sluiced down with gallons and gallons of very hot water.

Departure from Istanbul was in complete contrast to my arrival. Happy to avoid the crazy road traffic I left from the Galata Bridge area, heading up the Bosphorus. Richer in experience, and body on the mend, I sailed away with my growing pack of paintings. Leaving the ferry at Sariyer, on the left, well on the way to the Black Sea, I looked for accommodation (unsuccessfully). I did little more than lose my easel before taking a twenty-minute ride on a fourteen-seat dolmush. The journey over a winding, hilly, narrow coast road was decidedly tortuous for this particular passenger. The little bus, despite not having standing headroom, was tightly packed. Seats were fully crammed and eight of us were standing, huddled with heads and shoulders pressed against the roof, filling the remaining space. How, or more to the point why, did four or five of the crushed complement manage to smoke? It beats me.

The pension in Kilyos where I stayed for one night (too many) was a great disappointment following many pleasant experiences. There was a plus to my stay though. My vast room had a balcony from where I produced a watercolour painting, substituting a table for the lost easel. Most of the subject, a fiery sunrise over the Black Sea (turquoise blue), had to be painted on a flat surface to allow liquid colours to flow together.

Attempting to freshen up after my arrival, I was surprised by water running down the plughole onto my feet. The washbasin outlet lacked a trap. Not being one to make a fuss, I retired to the shower room along the hallway. There I found the wc cistern spraying the room with a fine mist and the washbasin and shower tray blocked. I became one to make a fuss, bringing the reception chap up to inspect the defective plumbing. He surveyed the shower-room shambles for a while; then, with an exceptionally large screwdriver, proceeded to poke the cistern. Spraying ceased, replaced by an internal, running overflow – apparently an acceptable trade-off. The blockages were of no immediate concern. We moved on to my room where he poked the holey trap for a bewildering period, then proceeded to wedge a whole bar of soap in and around the trap gap. The receptionist with large screwdriver seemed overjoyed with the result. I was speechless.

Before joining the ferry I underwent a return dolmush ride. The inside of the cab was decorated 'gypsy caravan style', with frilly pompon'd lampshades and friezes. A collection of lucky charms, including a few of the mandatory blue eyes, filled all available surfaces. Attached to the windscreen, right in front of the driver, a large hand waved cheerily. To cap it all, wedged above a comprehensive array of photographs of the driver's large extended family, a giant inflatable Boeing 747 – not quite life-size.

Returning down the Bosphorus, I bypassed Istanbul and boarded a large ferry to sail across the Sea of Marmara. Painting my way through the countryside I reached Gelembe – a small town well over half way to Izmir. In dusty heat I stepped down from the coach. The mid-day temperature was climbing towards forty degrees. Sorely missing my sombrero, lost the previous day (the second of three hats mislaid), I trudged to the centre feeling like Clint Eastwood. I leant my pack outside a small general store, alongside a cart on which rolls with meat fillings were being toasted. With mouth-watering eagerness, Clint entered the somewhat dishevelled shop exercising a fair proportion of his Turkish repertoire. "Bir bira dahalewtfen?" ('One beer please?' which had taken a little getting used to – for 'one' (1) in Turkish is 'bir', pronounced 'beer'). Unhappily, the Pilsen sign outside was just a bluff. I opted for chilled cola. Seated outside on a chair provided by the sixteen years old hand, who was running the joint, I completed my late breakfast with a hot succulent sandwich from the cart. I then fashioned a 'sapka' (hat) from a street map of Istanbul printed in German.

Following an impromptu English lesson given to young Eylem, the store boss, I set out to paint a picture of rickety pantile roofed buildings that I noticed on arrival. Leaving the backpack behind, I retraced my steps and settled down in limited shade alongside a low stable-like structure. A middle-aged lady entered the next-door building, so I popped round to see if I could borrow a seat or box. Adjusting to the dark interior, I gazed upon a humble but dramatic subject. Three ladies sat on the floor leaning against a rough wall. A wide uneven wooden ladder gave access to a gallery supported on hewn beams. I beheld a 'Flint' interior. (Sir William Russell Flint, 1880-1969, a fine watercolour painter. The scene typical of his work.) It was one of those, 'I wish I hadn't rung the bell' moments'. Embarrassed, I sort of pathetically mimed that I did not really need anything and left. After a few minutes one of the ladies walked off down the street, soon to return with a chair, for me. Two cups of tea were brought out for me as I worked – such kindness. The shaded area was reduced until my head was being gently roasted. I should not have discarded the map-hat, but it was inclined to obstruct my vision. After completing the painting I returned the chair and showed the picture to the ladies, for they had reservedly inspected progress from time to time. Painting the interior scene would have spared me from troublesome times ahead; but I could not intrude.

A battered bus was undergoing repair in the street opposite the store. While topping up on cool cola I showed my painting to Eylem, the toasting Turk and the bus driver with time on his hands. I explained that I was a travelling 'sanatcha' (artist) and with the aid of my unfolded hat indicated my roundabout route and ultimate destination. I was informed that the bus, when mended, would be heading in that general direction. A short while later I was undertaking a bouncing, winding, thirty kilometre mystery tour in an 'oven' on an unhurried ride to nowhere in particular.

As luck would have it, immediately following the bus ride I was able to step straight onto a coach for another trip of similar distance that joined the main route to Ismir. Such hasty journeying would have been a waste of Turkey without just cause. What I thought to be itchy insect bites developed into a severe rash. By the time I embarked, 'in a severe rush', on a third coach for a traumatic three-hour ride to Izmir to seek medical help, I was desperate. The journey was a nightmare for my condition was quite worrying. It was again incredibly hot and the itch progressed to burning pain. My body, including the soles of my feet, was almost covered by a raised swelling like an inflated nettle rash. For losing a 'sapka', I suffered that most unwelcome experience.

It was about seven o'clock when I put myself in the hands of the first taxi driver at the coach station. The all telling opening of my shirt, revealing the distressing mutation, was enough for the driver to rush me me off to a pharmacy. The staff could not help. There followed a further hurried trip in a mobile furnace through the crowded outskirts to a medical practice a few kilometres away. Within minutes I had been examined and questioned by two doctors, received two injections, and felt almost instant relief.

That's enough of suffering for one's art. There were many happy, memorable times. A few days before travelling home I took a slow train ride to Selcuk. I wondered if I was doing the right thing when stepping into a rather hot and crowded coach. Once we rattled up to twenty miles per hour, the draught created turned the forty-mile ride into a most pleasant and interesting experience.

Midway through the journey, a teenage Turk named Mured engaged me in conversation. It transpired he was a pension tout. Amid laid-back banter he extolled the virtues of Cheerful Pension. One was unlikely to chance upon the accommodation that lay on the 'other side' of the railway track. My gamble to walk out to check out Cheerful paid off. Though en suite showers and fishpond were fictitious, Mured was forgiven his exaggerations, for it turned out to be the quiet retreat, away from noise and fumes that I longed for. It was a friendly place where one could relax. A vine-shaded courtyard with plums and apricots for the picking was at my disposal.

The historic site of Ephesus was just three kilometres away. There, in high temperature, after buying a third hat, I painted three watercolours on the first day. Until then I had not thought myself a lover of ancient ruins. Ephesus retained a human element that time and depletion had not erased. Enough remained, or had been reconstructed, for one to imagine streets lined with stunning stone buildings adorned with beautiful, sculptural works. Seated in a carved stone chair, my hands rested on smoothed scrolls. I became part of the story, infinitesimally eroding the surface as others had done over the centuries. Walking barefoot on the white worn marble, in channels formed by Roman carts, it was easy to relate to previous inhabitants.

I stayed at Cheerful for four fruitful, restful days – time spent painting and mooching. The production of a picture of simple dwellings, with an aqueduct behind, I remember well. Shortly after setting out my painting equipment and clearing away debris from the kerbside, a lady from a small building that I thought was a shed, brought out a chair for me. It seemed like a replay. Not long after, she reappeared with a large handful of wet corn. I accepted the substantial snack, eating it immediately, for without an easel I needed both hands for painting. Children playing in the street checked my work from time to time as they handed me the odd biscuit. Selcuk and district, along with its kind people, pro-

Ephesus

9½″ x 8½″

'There, in high temperature, after buying a third hat, I painted three watercolours on the first day.'

vided an inspirational and delightful atmosphere in which to complete my Turkish collection.

Two days before heading to the airport I took another train ride – one hundred and eighty six kilometres east. Destination Denizli, sixteen kilometres from Pamukkale where I intended to paint a Roman spa interior. Early the next day, a Sunday, I headed up to the site with a great many local people. Their mission was to paddle and splash in shallow, pale turquoise pools, half way up a mountain. The whole area was pure white, formed by hot springs depositing calcium. With the sun reflecting off so much bright white water, it seemed you were in a furnace. (I was as drawn to excessive heat, as to ladies who would bring me chairs.) Small groups of figures, mirage-like, hovered on different levels. The bathers in the sky were as extras in a heavenly dream sequence, ascending a giant water-lily staircase. A shimmering fair-haired sun maiden, draped in white, floated above warm translucent milk – a perfect subject for painting. (Perhaps I should contact the Milk Marketing Board.)

The sun descended, shadowing areas opalescent blue – a darkening moonscape; liquid craters calmed. I followed others down the mountainside. Spa architecture had been overlooked; but nature compensated handsomely.

A Pub Too Far

Netherbridge to Greystone Bridge

Two days after returning home from the river, I was at the back of the house washing my muddy sleeping bag. The white plastic container, half dustbin size, was ideal for the job. Though purchased for home brewing, it holds no sentimental value. The cloudy liquid covering the soaking bag had similarities to our failed beer productions – taste being one of them. On account of much water splashing about I was barefoot, airing raw patches on my feet where the flip-flop straps had rubbed. Hoisting the dripping bag onto the line reminded me of the awful time under a certain bridge. The sound of another Launceston legacy issued from an upstairs window. Tortured reverberations were making the guitar soloist blissfully happy, while I, on the other hand, thought the depths of Devonshire was the best place for the large amplifier.

To minimize future 'Tamar foot' problems, I journeyed to Truro to buy some 'super sandals' – the type with adjustable webbing attached to off-road soles.

Captain's log, Saturday 30th July: *'Feet healing – continue, or perhaps finish – (dare I think it) the voyage, in a few days. Must collect oars etc. Will use red box no crumbs in bottom of damp plastic bag with paraphernalia. Remember 'swiss roll' for I may find myself on stony ground, again. Take some exciting foodstuffs …'*

That evening I sat in my gallery with a pint of HSD (known affectionately as High Speed Diesel – proper name: Hicks Special Draught, St Austell Brewery). I was pouring over Landranger 201 (ho ho), a little peeved to find just one pub close to the river on the twenty-three mile stretch (thirteen crow miles) still to be travelled. You would be mistaken thinking the venture was fuelled by alcohol; it was purely an after 'work' reward – no booze on board during excursions, honest.

Monday: a day of misty rain; Tuesday *'Through rain and mist to Darracott to collect oars* (I checked Epic was alright on the way.) *looked not too bad from the bridge – lounging casually by the river under the green* (leafy) *canopy.'* Closer inspection showed the hull around the centreboard slot had been stripped of paint and the ply deeply gouged after miles of dragging. Where the blue and white paintwork had worn away there was evidence of previous yolk yellow and dark red livery (sounds like lunch). Wednesday afternoon: heavy rain. Thursday: change 'super sandals' for cut-price pair from the market. The expensive pair had wicked little pointy bits under the straps where nylon threads had been hot-cut off. I could imagine the damage such defects might cause to delicate, soused white feet.

'12:44 P.M. Aug 5th. Robin chauffeur. Quite nervous (me) *this A.M.'* On the way back to Netherbridge, village of two bridges, we stopped at St Austell to purchase a fibreglass repair kit. We stopped again at Bugle for a pair of scissors to cut the glass fibre material. Robin dropped me off at Netherbridge where I set about repairing Epic. The bargain priced scissors, a Far Eastern product, were sealed behind transparent plastic on a printed card. A cunning sales ploy, for when unpacked they showed signs of non-suitability for my purpose, or indeed any involving cutting.

An unhealthy rattle was a give-away to flimsy engineering. Despite having to tear apart the rather coarse matt with the Chinese 'tongs', within forty-five minutes I had applied five mixes of resin and fibreglass. *'Sitting by the Tamar, Nether Br. – Spiky glass fingers. Hate starting with sticky fingers. Sticking together / looks like rain. Photo from bridge – see the rapids? Fish rose – soon be away from traffic…'* To pass the time while waiting for the repair to set, I meandered a clockwise circuit of the bridges. The plaque on 'my' bridge read – 'Higher New Bridge 1504 A.D.' (The solid construction was relatively new at the time of Queen Elizabeth I.) The equivalent to today's pantechnicons would have been much lighter; even so, I doubt the replacement will last four hundred and fifty years.

'Not raining … had sandwich and banana and water – bottle broached! Repair still tacky – wonder if it matters – I'll give it till 1:45!p.m. Think I will have a Mars – brought red box this time – soon be no food left. 1:55 still tacky …' At ten past two I turned Epic over and slid her down the steep grassy bank into the river. With the painter looped over a branch I loaded the dinghy. Unhitching, I scrambled down into the cool Tamar, christening my new, sturdy looking, and hopefully kind to feet, sandals. On board, the river flowed over my feet – again I had forgotten to fit the bung. Bung screwed in, I drifted down the remaining thirty yards of the long pool to the first rapids. With rivers Carey, Kensey and Lyd and several brooks and ditches joining the Tamar in the next four miles, I was looking forward to more drifting – forever the optimist.

More or less all my items fitted into the sail-bag. On that 'bolster' I imagined reclining when Epic reached longer and more frequent 'floating' pools. In the following day or two I hoped to repeat those blissful moments enjoyed after first stepping into the little blue unnamed dinghy on the River Fowey. 'I lay on my back … and watched the mast turn lazy circles against a few cotton wool clouds.' There would be a fair amount of wading and levering, I imagined, but still relished the final confrontation. *'Drizzle! Mostly walking / dragging rap* (rapids) *every 5 mins 3.00 Drifting now for a min. absolute quiet. No – cows munching – that's all.'*

Slowly I ticked off the remaining miles. A lone stone pillar stood in the river, a reminder of a disused railway, out of place in that pastoral setting. *'3:45 sewage wks outlet looked cleanish.'* (Not so pastoral.) I stepped onto the Cornish side of a slightly downward curved concrete weir. The river flowed swiftly over the centre – to aerate the water I supposed. Epic rode down the concentrated flow. I pulled her in to the side and stepped carefully in (the dinghy). That area of riverbed was furred with a slimy brown contamination. A few hundred yards downstream, I was pleased to record, the fast flowing river was clear of all traces of Launceston's sanitary arrangement. My earlier complaining about the lack of volume of the poor old Tamar was rather unfair; I should have been praising the overall clarity.

At four o'clock I passed under a wide, shallow arched road bridge, a crow and a bit mile east of Launceston. There was a '... *lot of walking 4:15 Rain (Slight')*. A further third of a mile on and fifteen minutes later, the lofty concrete slab of the A30 hove into view. The structure was soon out of sight, but alas, not out of mind. The audio infringement was significant and prolonged. (It is perfectly okay for this hypocrite to motor up the A30 without a care.) *'Mars / water. Not quite so gloomy* (the weather). *5:45. Still hear A.30 sunny periods 6:10 R. Lyd ...*

This time, extra contributions from the Lyd and other small rivers did help matters a tiny bit. Had there been a greater flow, I now believe the gradient would be too steep for even small boat 'navigation'. Long stretches of silvery rapids were punctuated with great numbers of angular rocks, two to three feet across. Trees skirted the river along much of its length. Where few trees edged the river, extra brightness added more sparkle to the scintillating scenes. Dense woodland, on the other hand, created dark, mysterious views.

Though not that difficult or dangerous, the advancement of Epic was extremely time consuming. The changing aspects of the river as it passed through narrows, then spreading itself about, concealed the fact that it was inexorably growing. The Tamar began to show hidden depths. *'6:15* (pm) *rushed down rapid – hang on back to lift myself dry!'* To avoid soakings it was necessary to ride straight armed, gripping the tipped down transom, with legs dangling, till foot, shin or knee made contact. Had that technique been employed at half past seven, Epic would not have been holed a second time. With a bit of effort I could have got out before it gathered speed to rush through a gap at the end of a roughly dammed, long pool. (I don't blame the dammed pool; though later ...) My added weight was part of the problem. The tender dinghy hitting a submerged rock was the other. After the crunch I sat on the transom, feet inboard, drifting downstream, keeping the new piercing out of the water. At the next barrier/dam, a repair in the pre-described manner was effected. Conveniently, the second black patch neatly abutted the first.

Three more man-made weirs or dams had to be negotiated before Greystone Bridge was reached. The random structures, with central breaches, were circumvented by aiming Epic nose first into the gap while I stood on the lip holding a long painter with which to tow the dinghy back into slack water. The dam constructions were obviously man made and I should have guessed there would be a price to pay. My decision to travel down the river was made without the slightest thought that there might be a problem. At the time I was happily ignorant of my trespassing. In due course I would be informed that my presence on the river was not entirely welcome.

With Greystone Bridge in sight, I came upon a weir that led to fast tumbling water. I deemed it prudent to restrain Epic with a line from the bow and lower away slowly through the turbulence, while I stood in the river, well back from the slippery, boulder barrier. With the dam-buster safely in the side shallows, I picked my way precariously through the tugging current to the bank. The river was becoming stroppy.

With great pleasure, I wrote – *'Greystone 8:40 pm'*. All was quiet, as if I had rented the river for my sole use. It was a peaceful, wind-less evening in early August, but no one was about. Not a single dreamer peering down from the bridge, wishing vague shapes of swaying weed into wondrous trout. With leisurely strokes I rowed beneath the central arch, turned back under the bridge and glided onto a small, steep, mud and shingle Devon beach. To reduce waterlogging, I wedged my roller logs under the stern, raising Epic clear of the water. By a quarter past eight, Epic was baled out and tidied up, and I, watered and 'Marsed'.

Next on the agenda was a hearty meal. The OS revealed three options, each one more than a three-mile hike. Rejecting Launceston for pastures new, I decided on the Devonshire village of Milton Abbot in favour of the Cornish Treburley. I have no idea why, for both are blessed with a PH (pub). A few yards of wet undergrowth and muddy terrain had to be negotiated before I reached the road at the end of the bridge. After clambering over the parapet, I changed into trainers and socks,

Epic in Fast Water

10˝ x 10˝

dropping the wet sandals back into the field. With jumper and painting bag over my shoulder, I set off at a brisk pace in order to reach the PH by ten o'clock, hoping to beat the catering curfew. It was a gamble I know, the Countryman deadline being nine o'clock. The chance of a proper meal was a long shot, but I would have settled for a pie or sandwiches. Despite much exertion on the steep, winding climb (600 feet), I put on my jumper, for dusk arrived bringing a chill to the air. Well before reaching the village I was hurrying along in complete darkness. Pale legs flashed my presence to those behind blinding headlights. The motorists chased after their patch of light, leaving me to guess the way for a few seconds.

After burning up an energetic fifty-five minutes worth of calories, I entered the Edgcumbe Arms. It was barely ten o'clock. To my delight, I read from the menu board, 'Last orders 10:00'. The comprehensive list suggested pre-prepared meals. Customers more enthusiastic for food of any description than I, at that time, do not exist. I addressed the lady behind the counter who had just finished a conversation. "Hello, may I have …"

"… last orders ten."

"… just a sandwich …"

"… chef's just left." she said with some definition.

"I've walked especially from Greystone … very hungry …" She went to ask the boss. You just have to be polite, pleasant of manner and smile; it seldom fails.

"No … he said would you like a Peperami?"

'Sod me!!' I exclaimed later to my logbook.

I declined the spiced stick. Though feeling decidedly down on the sociability scale, I joined a merry throng in the bar. The company, two pints of 6X and three packets of crisps failed to restore my wellbeing. After half an hour I fumed back to Epic. In the corner of a dark damp field, an unhappy troll slipped into wet sandals before skulking under a bridge. Perhaps I should have paid the PH at Treburley a visit. A Peperami indeed.

Bolshie Fishermen
Greystone Bridge to Horsebridge

On a slight slope of lump-free ground, under the arch next to the one in which Epic was housed, I camped in a cave-like den, too dim for vegetable life, but eminently suitable for odd animals. Due to heavy dew, spasmodic drops fell from the vaulted ceiling. Following recent experience, the odd spots, far from bothering me, emphasized the near perfection of the situation. Having the 'swiss roll' and a larger piece of polythene than last time, plus the absence of driving rain, I was assured a restful night. The gentle incline and comfortable surface made me reluctant to leave the comfy grotto in the morning. *'Sat. 6th Aug. 7:45 Breakfast in Bag. 8.30 Sun   breaking through. Walk in river for photos. Not v cold. Patches on hull seem O.K. 8:45 off to first rapid 30yds away!! 9: Br. Disappears* (due to fog) *stand up and one oar laze my way down a long (300 yds) dark silent greenish pool – quiet – car noise recedes – heaven. 9:07 2nd rapids …'*

It was on that 'seven-minute' pool, or maybe the one after, that I noticed simple wooden steps leading six feet or so down the bank into the river. At the time, I thought the reflected geometry no more than an agreeable subject for painting. Little did I know then, that such details would soon strike fear into a semi-hardened troll. My heavenly drifts were due to an increasing number of man-made dams. Many were sympathetic stone constructions; others blighted by an insensitive use of concrete.

At a quarter to ten I rowed towards a low, flat-topped, stone dam that constricted the river from about fifty feet down to twelve. Within twenty yards or so of the narrows, I heard a telltale 'csssh' that rapidly turned into a rumbling, weir warning. My sedate progress was halted for a while. I stepped onto the Devon bank and walked along the top of the dam to inspect the furious churning below the three feet drop. Not wishing to risk Epic in that watery confusion, I manhandled the dinghy over the dam. Once unloaded, it was a straightforward task to lift the bow onto the ledge, drag the boat up to a balanced position, swing it round and tip it stern first down to the other side; then using the painter, gently lower to horizontal.

An hour later I approached another breached dam. Of similar construction, it differed by funnelling water through in a speeding flow without a drop (as in waterfall). Not wishing to manhandle the boat over the dam and a large area of rough shale the other side, or ride through the gap at speed, I decided to walk in the river and guide Epic from behind. All went well till the force of the river carried me into the sluice before I could adopt the 'straight arms on the stern' position. Wet through, I pulled Epic onto the shale beach. The picturesque spot was well lit, having an empty field behind. It was an ideal location in which to produce a painting. Swirling, light reflecting water slid into a dark void beneath the canopy. Seated on a rock below the level of the riverbank, with my soaked shorts lying on the sun-warmed, dry riverbed, I set out my painting equipment.

Not only did the gentle rush of water soothe and relax me, it drowned the sound of approaching antagonists. Range-Rover access, I was about to find out, was never far away in the 'occupied territory'. My river-filled water pot hung from a driftwood twig, paints were squeezed onto the palette and I sat in contemplation, brush in hand. In water-colour painting, there is more calculating than pigment application. I was unaware of the fishermen until they were nearly upon me. With the speed of Jack Flash I was inside slightly damp shorts, facing the inquisitors.

"… private property … we are about to fish …" I was being spoken at by a member of the archetypal, 'huntin-shootin-fishin' brigade.

"I did not intend to use your bank … got wet … decided to paint. Hope that's O.K?"

"No; this is private …"

"Where am I?"

"Endsleigh Fishing." A trace of confusion showed in the elderly gentleman's demeanour.

He must have found it difficult communing with one who did not know where he was. Departure seemed my best strategy. I hurriedly packed away my things and escaped onto the stretch of enclosed 'rowing water' downstream. A young man aged about sixteen stood silently by his irate senior as the farce unfolded. But for him, I may have been more vocal. The defence may have been flawed, but had my admonisher cared to hear the evidence, the engagement need not have been confrontational. When the 'gentleman' relates his version of this, 'one that got away', I am sure my trespass will be deemed flagrant – possibly dastardly.

Until that moment it had not occurred to me that the river would be out of bounds. I was not welcome. After all, it was not I who had taken liberties with concrete, driven a four-wheel drive vehicle through peaceful countryside to festoon trees with fly-fishing lines. Knowing game angling to be sacrosanct, I had not cleared away lines lest I became a suspect angler. Had I had doubts concerning boating on the river and made enquiries, my river voyage would not have been.

During the following two hours, Epic and crew passed unmolested through glorious landscape. Red stone cliffs draped with ferns and mosses rose to infiltrate dense wooded slopes. The lie of the land ensured a great deal of dinghy dragging down rapids, interspersed with very little floating. From time to time I glimpsed large headed, long necked, sleek black birds about a foot long (shags). Their harpoon bills suggested they were serious fishers, which was why, I supposed, they kept a wary distance – obviously unwelcome in the vicinity; I empathised.

A dam, funnelling fast water into a long, wide pool, came into view. A larger dinghy than Epic was held on station by an oarsman in slack water towards the Devon side of the river. A fisherman on board cast a fly across the river towards overhanging trees. The line was taken downstream by the current, then the angler recast. Each repetition took about a minute. Not wishing to interrupt proceedings, I parked Epic a little way back from the dam, against the opposite bank. I sat on a log and ate a Mars bar. During a lull in activity I made my way to the breach (once more). The floating fly-fisherman ordered me to cross the river and pass behind their craft. Unfortunately, the fast water claimed Epic, leaving me no choice but to disobey orders and shoot through the gap. Keeping close to the trees I silently drifted out of range. Though my behaviour was reverential, I still received admonishment from the enemy ship's company and small entourage of supporters on the Devon bank. From my point of view, the unintentional manoeuvre was a perfect, if accidental, non-engagement tactic – worthy of splicing the mainbrace; but as you know I run a 'dry' ship. My end of voyage experience was soured by the behaviour of those 'sportsmen'.

The next but one dam/weir took a full fifteen minutes to negotiate, even though I worked at pace. As a peaceful pirate, fearing fishermen intervention, my ears were tuned to pick up the first hint of danger. Stone steps led down to a ten feet wide, rocky beach that flanked the considerable construction. From the oars, log collection and a few large rocks, I hastily fashioned a crude ramp. I heaved the unladen dinghy over the dam, happily uninterrupted – no clink of cold cutlass steel against stone.

It was twenty past two when I hitched Epic to an overhanging branch midway along a deep pool. From that safe haven I looked back through dark greens to a slash of bright silvery rushing water that cut through distant blue-black. Without fear of impending danger, I set about reproducing the composition on rough watercolour paper. (Dragging a loaded brush over a textured surface will create a granular effect leaving specks of previous colouring – a useful technique for representing foliage.) Epic had let in a few pints and I found it most convenient painting from a 'water pot'. In little under an hour, my watery Tamar colour was complete. While the picture dried in the warm air, I lunched on diluted orange juice and a Crunchie bar.

The painting put me in good heart. Better still, when I drifted past a pair of fishermen and exchanged friendly 'good afternoons'. I rowed on, feeling more at ease. Perhaps I had been unlucky on previous encounters, meeting only bolshie factions. More dams were circumvented. When several were close together, the river's random beauty was compromised, though it made fish slaughter easier. As the general public cannot view that section of the Tamar, does it really matter? To be honest, at the time I would have welcomed a 'blighting' service station.

Wide, fast flowing stretches where I had to resist the temptation to ride with Epic became numerous. Visible, flood-resisting rocks were not the problem; the danger came from those just below the surface.

Trepidation only partly allayed, I waded down rapids towards another group of anglers. Excited animation broke out. A fishing rod curved into juddering conflict, stabbing in the direction of a hooked salmon. Bad luck for the fish, I assumed, would mean a free passage for me. I waited for a chance to slip by. After the netting, there followed a victorious clambering up the bank. Seizing the opportunity I vacated the scene as discreetly as possible towing a ten foot white dinghy.

"Where do you think you're going?"

"Morwellham Quay," I shouted back, having nothing to hide. The triumphant fisher cupped a hand to his ear. The rushing river and his congratulatory attendants must have drowned out my reply.

"Morwellham Quay" I roared. There was no easy response an elated fisherman could make without ruining his moment of glory. Interrogation ceased. The jubilant angler turned away and bashed the salmon to death with a metal bar. I got off lightly, but still communed with the log, '... *Bastard. With a fish I thought he must be friendly (4:30ish)*'.

I hoped the end of the Endsleigh zone was nigh, if not behind me, when I asked a chap not carrying a fishing rod how far it was to the Horsebridge? The river crossing, which had a PH nearby, was less than a mile away with only one weir en route. It was half past seven when I arrived at the bridge – a Greystone clone. Epic was soon perched on a broad bridge foundation towards the Devon side of the river that was partly exposed due to the low level. From the sloping stone ledge it was an easy leap to the shore. I hopped over and clambered up the steep, grassy bank on the downstream side of the bridge. To retain anonymity, not wishing to advertise the fact that I was a river dweller/traveller, with a vessel parked nearby, I nipped onto the roadway in a trice. Acting in a casual manner, feeling there might be a reward for my apprehension, I sat nonchalantly on the parapet, legs dangling roadside. It was unfortunate that the stone capping at that point was deceptively narrow (but then you would expect a little wear since 1437). Casually leaning back, my palms met thin air, my legs flew over my head and I crashed back down onto the slope. My back-flip, landing on feet then knees was extremely lucky, only losing marks for a pronounced stumble (spelt s t u m b l e, pronounced, stumble. Thank you, Spike Milligan).

The Royal Inn, combining the very small Horsebridge Brewery, is but a few steps down the road. Arriving at a respectable hour for leisurely dining, I sensed a change in fortune. Being adjacent to a small brewery, or one of any size come to that, could not be a bad thing. The evening started at the pinnacle with a pint of the pub's own brew – and excellent it was too. Hopeful of concluding the circumnavigation the next day, I felt a celebration feast was in order. A couple at the bar ordered venison in red wine, but as only one portion was available, they both opted for an alternative. It was my lucky day. I could have eaten a horse, but settled for the elk. A rapid reverse of fortune followed; that can happen when starting on a high. My descent from mount happiness was swift. The remains of the deer were few and the red wine sauce exuded a burnt, warmed-up and watered down once too often nuance. I was not expecting miracles, but changing wine into water was too much to bear. The gristly scraps were accompanied by lots of lettuce and topped with a small, sculpted vegetable. It rated poorly, even compared to the crisp fare the previous night. It had been a bad day for discourse. That final insult was so contemptuous that I did not make a scene for fear of further upsetting myself. (I have since returned to the Royal Inn, now under new management, and can thoroughly recommend it.)

An early night was not a bad idea. Cutting short my Saturday night out, I strolled back to Epic, gathered my bedding and retired under the bridge. Later, as the 'chucking out' was celebrated, faint conversation drifted my way, car engines revved for a while, then all was silent beside the still Tamar.

Dam

Horsebridge to Morwellham Quay

Sunday morning: up at five thirty. Thick silent mist confused perception. Epic glided away, leaving behind the bridge enveloped in grey. The river sounded its chuckling challenge as the first rapids appeared. The dinghy nudged a heavy stone and I tentatively dipped a dry sandaled foot into the slightly chilly Tamar.

Soon after entering the river at North Tamerton, I settled into an agreeable, river life style. Until entering fishermen territory, I seemed to be travelling through my own private world. Loneliness was never a problem – in fact I usually work alone. A few days surrounded by glorious landscape is not a bad way to pass the time. (I'll be fluttering and dancing in the breeze next.) When on the move there was little time for daydreaming, though I did tend to drift off in the latter stages. There were times when greater concentration would have saved spells of heaving back over hard won ground, retracing my course past rocks marked with Epic white.

At six forty, an anxious twenty minutes ensued. I spied tents and a Range-Rover close to the bank in a field, thirty or forty yards off the starboard bow. Epic's front protruded above the first dam of the day, in the manner of a sitting duck. Hoping the encamped complement was sleeping soundly that Sunday morning, I feverishly set about rapid relocation downstream. Water thundering through the gap in the centre of the dam drowned out the bangings and rumblings of the unladen dinghy being dragged across flattish shelves of rock. I wished to avoid confrontation, for there was obviously access to the roadway and easy banishment of Epic from the river. I rushed the dinghy to the side of the surging flow. Flinging my gear onboard I escaped under oar power, passing close to the bank, out of sight of the enemy. Relaxing after the exertion I recorded, '*I DREAD FISHERMEN*'.

A few hundreds yards downstream I photographed a splendid atmospheric scene reflected in the still water. Great trees overhung both banks and faded into misty distance. A pale round object, barely discernible, hove into view, low down above the river. I clicked again to capture the UFO. What luck to have my camera poised at that precise moment. A couple of seconds later the sphere had drifted out of sight. The (identified FO) hot air balloon, caught in the centre of the small target area, would be a prize-winning sensation – 'Misty Dawn Balloon'. I imagined a grainy blown-up reproduction with a trace of washed-out, subtle colour pinpointing the FO. Disappointment developed later – nothing but pure nature in both shots. Only the higher numbered negative indicates the picture 'without' the balloon. My camera never leaks, but sometimes lies.

For two hours I passed weirs and shallows, but no fishermen. Perhaps Sundays are truce days. Fortune favoured me at the next dam. A low, planked footbridge linking Devon to the dam was just high enough for Epic to be squeezed beneath. The narrow channel had sufficient flow for me to ease the dinghy back into the main river. '*... this is the most difficult yet 9:40 4th weir must unload and drop Epic over the wall!!*' As I tried to lower the bow into shallow water from the four-foot high wall, my foot slipped into a crevice, trapping my knee for a while. I was fortunate to emerge, leg undamaged. A squashed middle finger on my left hand was a reminder, for a day or two, of my goodish fortune.

'10:45 Just over another dam then weir then rapids … Now big rocks – fast water!! 1 pint or so leak every 5 – 10 minutes or so!' A greater flow was outside the boat, seemingly running over steeper ground. There were wide stretches where it was difficult to stand. The powerful weight of water pressing against my legs caused difficulty, particularly when restraining Epic as we threaded our way between slippery rocks. Occasionally the current would force the boat to pivot against a boulder. If I could not tip the balance in my favour, Epic would take a route of its own, heading off to further rocky traps. Extrication using the oar-ramp method could be employed on occasions, avoiding straining back against the flow. Despite severe treatment, my 'cheapo' sandals stood up to the test with distinction.

'… slipped over again … 11:30 end of 1ˢᵗ Big Rock Rapids?' Two hundred yards downstream there was more of the same – *'12:20 Through next Boulder Run (600 yds long) 200 yds downstream.'* Just a couple of minutes later I faced a further half hour negotiating large rounded rocks. Those smooth, water-worn specimens, like giant grey dumplings, rose up to five feet above river-level. *'1' water in bottom. 1:04 Row – last of the boulders? … shorts wet – long pool I hope. Nearly there!'* The notes suggest I was pretty tired.

Rowing. No problems; just rowing. I had waited a long time. *'1:25 Under the ____ Bridge can't believe it. I thought it was hours away.'* (I left the space to insert the name later. It is another 'New Bridge' – as imaginative as the 'Gull Rocks'.) That last bridge, the first above the tidal Tamar, was a dead ringer for the previous two. Perhaps a fifteenth century McAlpine had won a package deal. The OS indicated I had a mile to go before reaching the final weir. *'River became v. still. Lots of leaves turning yellow floating – stalks up – like little boats. Wind blowing me back upstream …'* (I had stopped to make notes.) The last page of my logbook shows a drawing of a couple of leaf 'boats' along with a floating lager can. Such shorthand sketch-notes recorded information rapidly – perhaps not painting a thousand words, but a glance takes me back instantly to time and place. Were my scribbles symbolic? – The autumn of the voyage, time to celebrate with a pint. I must not be flippant. It was an emotional time. Those few hundred yards, thinking all surprises were behind me were rowed at a leisurely pace. In contemplative mood, I realized my journey was all but over (over being the operative word). In peaceful privacy I savoured those moments.

'1:42 do I hear the weir – or wind in the trees?' (I was being serious.) A little later, *'It is the weir – bloody hell'*.

As if I had arrived in Rhineland, tree-cover on the Devon side gave way to a red, stone bluff, topped with a few conifers. A structure on the Cornwall side did not possess schloss grandeur, being a simple concrete and steel affair for counting fish. The device to hurry unsuspecting salmon to a possible encounter with an iron bar stood beside a construction much larger than the regular weirs and dams. I was heading towards the top of a really big dam. If you 'dahhhh, dah dah' to the Dambuster's theme, it will help set the scene.

A few yards from the lip, I held station for a while. Shell-shocked, pondering, so near yet so far. From my vantage point I looked across at a particular group of trees that shielded Lock Cottage. After my ride up from Morwellham three years before, I had taken a photograph of the cottage. Also in the picture was a strip of white water – a regular weir that would not cause a problem when descending into tidal waters. Unfortunately, that weir was two hundred yards downstream from the monster I floated above. If only I had wandered up to inspect that 'strip of white water', I would have heard, if not seen, the cause of my present alarm.

The tremendous roaring as the river crashed over the dam partly prepared me for the alarming sight, though I did not expect anything of that magnitude. At first there seemed no way to get Epic and myself safely down the fall. Victoria, Niagara and splintered barrels came to mind. The drop to the pool below may 'only' have been eight to nine feet, but it suggested a dead end.

Towards the Devon side of the dam, a substantial fish ladder had been constructed to enable athletic salmon to return to their spawning grounds. That was before the sissy bypass had been installed. Two parallel walls, one foot wide and four feet apart, ran out twenty-five feet or so beyond the roughest water at the base of the dam. The walls, topped with thick spongy weed, sloped down about a one in five gradient ending four or so feet above the lower river level. Four churning pools lay between the walls. They were fed in some cunning way, for although little water seemed to enter, each chamber boiled as though giant mixers were set at whisking speed.

Epic remained afloat at the dam rim, resting against the end of the right hand fish ladder wall that stood a couple of inches proud of the water. I stepped gingerly onto the small flat area of weedy concrete. With due care, I managed to balance my gear there on top of the red box. My mind was running on single track – I was not in the mood to be sidelined. Though controlled progress would be precarious, retreat was not an option. With the end in sight, literally, I had no wish to row back up beyond the bridge seeking an alternative route. Doubtless there would be more prolonged portage, with much Epic heaving. With a 'what the hell' cavalier approach, I dragged the dinghy up onto the Devon-side 'slide', balanced it there for a few moments, then boldly went. Half expecting Epic to take a nosedive, I edged the dinghy down the incline. My treaded sandals, together with the hull's scarred bottom, had purchase enough for a controlled descent. I use the word 'controlled' in the loosest sense. At the end of the slope I pivoted the dinghy, re-launching stern first. After tethering to a handy fixing on the wall, I made a few trips up the slope to collect the gear, finally lowering myself into Epic. Around twenty past two, I rowed the two hundred yards down past the Cornwall side of a wooded island to the final weir.

The upstream pointing, V-shaped obstacle that my earlier photograph inaccurately suggested was Gunnislake Dam (I can't believe I've just blamed my camera) I negotiated with practised aplomb. Transition to what would have been tidal waters, if it had been high tide, was undertaken at warp speed. Feeling like a fugitive, I desired to exit the dam area without delay. Thinking I should not be using the river authority's fixture for recreational purposes, I was spurred on. Had I felt able to relax I would have waited for the flood-tide and then taken a leisurely two-mile, carefree drift down to Morwellham.

A stiff breeze blew upriver making it difficult to row. I arrived at the spot reached three years earlier on my first day on the Tamar. From there I had enjoyed relaxing guitar music – '… the river on which Epic slowly revolved was brimful and coffee coloured …' From where Epic previously floated in deep water, I took another photograph – three years on. The water-resistant camera, that makes small frogs look smaller, was purchased originally to capture the Tamar, and in a roundabout way it eventually did that. The grounded dinghy showing her grubby underside was hardly a pinup, but dear Epic, with a little help from her friend, had circumnavigated Cornwall.

Postamble

I headed down towards Morwellham, two crow miles away. The swishing sound of fine gravel on the hull foretold grounding. I decided it was easier to walk, so I nipped over the side and continued on foot for a while, till the river got deeper – I always knew it would. At ease, walking, pushing, rowing, drifting, I returned to the old copper port. In its own time the Tamar rose, allowing me to row back onto the slip from where I set off, and where the hulk of the old Tamar barge had rested. I added my log collection to offcuts of shipbuilding timbers at the side of the slip. The Lynher had been moved some twenty yards away. Charlie, who had reclaimed the old boat from the mud, was assisting Ralph to plank the hull.

Before taking little Epic to the Tamar, I hastily applied white paint to the topsides, leaving rough sky-blue capitals, E P I C, on the transom. The Mirror did more than transport me to painting locations – she took me on exciting adventures. Though named in jest, a silly way of ensuring an epic voyage, it now seems rather fitting.

The Bosun retired after the Bude beaching. The Red Admiral lives on, threaded into the groove of the extended gaff that has replaced the heavy mast. Admirably, the red sail has since assisted on a journey from the Atlantic to the North Sea, via the Cotswolds – but that's another story. Shamefully, after that big adventure, I had left poor Epic out in the cold, half hidden in long grass, taking on a greeny tinge in the back garden. Now she stands on her transom, leaning against a wall down in the studio, acting as shelving – just like the Gremlin. I have a feeling that one fine day soon she will be dusted down and we will set off again.

Raising the glass, gleaned from the Tamar mud,
I wish fair-weather to shoestring wanderers.
Think small: cheers.

David Weston
Mevagissey

Sparkling Tamar

6" x 7"